Logical Chess: Move by Move

Irving Chernev

BATSFORD

First published by Faber & Faber

First algebraic edition published in the United Kingdom in 1998 by
Batsford
43 Great Ormond Street
London WC1N 3HZ

www.batsford.com

An imprint of Pavilion Books Company Ltd

ISBN: 9780713484649

A CIP catalogue record for this book is available from the British Library.

34 33 32

Printed and bound by Imak Ofset, Turkey

This book can be ordered direct from the publisher at the website:
www.pavilionbooks.com, or try your local bookshop

Distributed in the United States and Canada by Sterling Publishing Co., Inc.
1166 Avenue of the Americas, 17th floor, New York, NY 10036, USA

Contents

Introduction

Did you ever see a chess master play twenty games at once? Have you wondered at (and perhaps envied) his confidence and ease as he stops for a few seconds at each board, gives the position on it a moment's consideration, and then casually makes a move?

Does he move quickly because he knows dozens of openings with hundreds of variations by heart? Hardly, because most of the games in such exhibitions take original turns which are not to be found in the books. Does he analyse every conceivable combination of moves at lightning speed? Or does he count on some infallible instinct to guide him through the strangest positions? If so, he would have to analyse faster than a computer or rely on being inspired a thousand times in an evening.

How does he do it? If we could follow his thought processes, if we could persuade him to tell us the meaning of each move as he makes it, we might learn the answer.

In this book we persuade him. We find out from the master the purpose of every single move he makes in the course of a game. We follow the ideas, the methods, the very thoughts of a master as he outlines them in simple detail. We learn the inner workings of his mind, and thus acquire the knowledge – yes, the instinct – for recognizing good moves and rejecting inferior ones.

To acquire this instinct it is not necessary to memorize countless opening variations, or to burden your brain with lists of formulae and principles. True, there are principles that govern proper procedure, and applying them will help you build up strong, sound, winning positions. But you will familiarize yourself with them painlessly – not by rote but by seeing their effect in the progress of a game.

Added to the pleasure of understanding every bit of play as it unfolds – and chess is the most exciting game in the world – is the fascination of watching the mental workings of a master as he reveals the wealth of ideas that occur to him in every new situation. We will learn from him the great advantages to be derived from a knowledge of *positional play*. It is an understanding of positional play that restrains the master from embarking on premature, foolish attacks and that checks the natural impulse to hunt for combinations at every turn. It counsels him in the placing of his pieces where they have the greatest potential for attack and tells him how to seize the vital central squares, to occupy the most territory and to cramp and weaken the enemy. And it is positional play that assures him that definite winning opportunities will then disclose themselves, and *decisive combinations will appear on the board*.

The master does not search for combinations. He creates the conditions that make it possible for them to appear!

Every single move of every game will be commented on, in simple, every-day language, and whatever analysis is needed to detail the full effects of a move or clarify a motive will be clear-cut and to the point. Frequent repetitions of the purpose of each move will impress upon you the importance of certain basic concepts. After you have been told again and again that in the opening White's king's knight works best at f3, and that rooks should control the open files, you will know that such strategy, such development of these pieces, is *generally* good. You will understand as well as any master does *what moves to look at first* when you select a good spot for a knight or a rook.

This does not mean that you will accustom yourself to play thoughtless, superficial chess. You will learn when and how to apply helpful principles, and when and how to defy convention. You will acquire the habit of making good moves as easily as a child absorbs a language – by hearing and speaking it, and not by studying its rules of grammar.

Each game that you play through will be an exciting adventure in chess in which courage, wit, imagination, and ingenuity reap their just reward. It is by appreciating and absorbing what they teach so pleasurably that we can best learn to play *Logical Chess, Move by Move.*

Irving Chernev
May 1, 1957

Chess Notation and Symbols

This book uses the universally accepted *algebraic notation*, in which each chess move is written using a simple system of coordinates similar to map references.

Thus the square on which the knight stands is referred to as *d5*.

In a similar way, the rook stands on *a3*, the bishop on *d6*, the pawn on *e4*, the queen on *h5*, the white king on *e1* and the black king on *b8*.

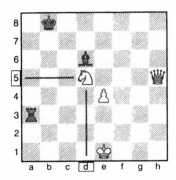

By a generally accepted convention, chess diagrams such as the above are always presented from White's point of view; i.e. White started the game at the bottom of the board. Indeed, his king stands on its original square.

The vertical rows of squares, called *files*, are lettered a to h from left to right. The horizontal rows, called *ranks*, are numbered from 1 to 8, beginning at the bottom of the diagram, i.e. from White's side. Each square lies on the intersection of a file and a rank, for example the lines in the above diagram show that the white knight stands on the intersection of the d-file and the fifth rank.

The above diagram shows how the men are set up at the start of the game, with a player's eight pieces placed on the row nearest him and the eight pawns directly in front of the pieces.

When recording the moves of a game, first the piece is given and then the square to which the piece moves. For example, if White plays the move indicated by the arrow, moving his knight from g1 to f3, then we write the move ♘f3. As is usual in books, we use figurines to denote the piece in chess notation: ♔ for king, ♕ for queen, ♖ for rook, ♗ for bishop and ♘ for knight. No figurine is used in the case of a pawn move. When writing moves down by hand (for example when keeping the record of a game played in a tournament), it is usual to use the first letter of its name instead of a figurine – K for king, Q for queen, R for rook, and B for bishop. As the letter K has already been used for the king, the knight is normally denoted by N.

There are a few other symbols that are important in chess notation:

x	captures
0-0	castles on the kingside
0-0-0	castles on the queenside
+	check
++	double check
#	checkmate
!	a good move
!!	an excellent or brilliant move
?	a mistake
??	a serious mistake or blunder

Finally, in this book the symbol *(D)* indicates a point in the game at which a chess diagram appears.

As practice in the use of chess notation, try playing over the moves of the following game, starting from the initial position:

Réti – Tartakower
Offhand game, Vienna 1910
Caro-Kann Defence

1 e4 c6 2 d4 d5 3 ♘c3 dxe4 4 ♘xe4 ♘f6 5 ♕d3 e5 6 dxe5 ♕a5+ 7 ♗d2 ♕xe5 8 0-0-0 ♘xe4 9 ♕d8+!! ♔xd8 10 ♗g5++ ♔c7 11 ♗d8# (1-0)

You should have the following final position set up on your board:

If two pieces of the same type can move to the same square, then the possible ambiguity in the notation requires extra information.

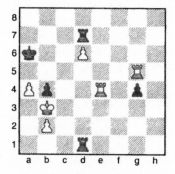

If it is White to play here then either rook can take the pawn on g4. In order to distinguish between the two captures we write ♖exg4 or ♖gxg4 according to whether it is the e4-rook or the g5-rook that takes the pawn. If Black is to play, we distinguish between the two captures on d6 by adding the rank of the capturing rook i.e., either ...♖7xd6 or ...♖1xd6. Here we cannot use the file as both rooks stand on the d-file.

The Kingside Attack

It is not the purpose of this book to bewilder you with magical effects; it is to show you how they are produced.

Take the popular kingside attack: it is attractive because it features combinative play with its brilliant sacrifices and surprise moves. It is appealing because it aims for quick checkmate and lets you play startling moves to bring it about.

But when and how do you start a kingside attack? Must you wait for an inspiration?

The answer is simple and may be surprising, so let us look behind the scenes:

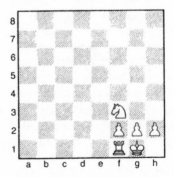

The diagram shows a castled position. The king is protected by a knight at f3 and the three pawns in front of him. While these protectors stay where they are, the king is highly resistant to attack. The moment the formation is changed, the structure is loosened and weakened. *It is then vulnerable to attack.*

The position may change when a player advances h2-h3 voluntarily to prevent a pin, or when he plays g3 to dislodge an enemy piece, but where this does not happen, the master (and here is the secret) *induces or compels by various threats the advance of the h-pawn or the g-pawn*. Once either pawn makes a move, it creates a weakness in the defensive structure which can be exploited. It is then that the master embarks on a kingside attack and achieves his brilliant – yes, magical – effects.

The game von Scheve-Teichmann (No. 1) shows what happens when White plays h3 instinctively to prevent a pin. Teichmann fixes on the pawn that stepped out of line and makes it the object of his attack. Eventually he sacrifices a bishop for the h-pawn in order to break into the position with his other pieces.

Liubarski-Soultanbéieff (No. 2) also has White playing h3 in fear of a pin, and Black punishes him by a pawn attack beginning with ...h6! (Why this move of the h-pawn is good, and White's is bad, is explained in the game.)

In Colle-Delvaux (No. 3) Colle forces ...h6 and then cleverly induces ...g6. After this, a knight sacrifice demolishes the weakened position.

Black plays ...h6 of his own free will to stave off an unlikely attack in Blackburne-Blanchard (No. 4). Blackburne sacrifices a bishop to remove Black's indiscreet h-pawn and forces an entrance into the enemy camp.

Ruger-Gebhard (No. 5) illustrates the danger of castling prematurely, coupled with neglect of the centre. When Black adds an attack on a piece with ...h6 to his other sins, he is punished by a sacrifice that rips open a file against his king.

Zeissl-Walthoffen (No. 6) is another instance of untimely castling coupled with disregard for the importance of the centre. White is compelled to play g3, weakening the light squares no longer guarded by the pawn. Walthoffen's pieces utilize these squares to work their way into the position and get at the king.

In the game Spielmann-Wahle (No. 7), Black advances his g-pawn to prevent a knight settling too close to his king. This deprives his own knight on f6 of the pawn's stout support and creates weaknesses on the squares no longer under the pawn's surveillance. Spielmann's pieces invade, fasten themselves on the weak squares and deliver mate.

Przepiorka-Prokeš (No. 8) is an illustration of ...g6 being forced, with a resultant weakening of the dark squares. Przepiorka takes the precaution of destroying the bishop that travels on the dark squares (to accentuate the weakness) before launching the decisive attack.

The game between Znosko-Borovsky and Mackenzie (No. 9) shows Black trying to keep an enemy knight out of his territory by playing ...g6. He succeeds, but at the cost of weakening the dark squares near his king. White finds them convenient for his own pieces, which take turns in occupying the critical squares.

Tarrasch-Eckart (No. 10) is an interesting example of the danger incurred in playing mechanical chess. Black is compelled to play ...f5 and then ...g6, after which he succumbs to a bishop sacrifice which removes all the pawns guarding his king.

The next two games are delightful miniatures with a lot of meat in them. Flohr-Pitschak (No. 11) is a fascinating illustration of the process of chipping away at the king's guards to impel them to move. Pitschak forces the g-pawn to advance, then the h-pawn, after which he crashes through the barriers with a queen sacrifice.

Pitschak-Flohr (No. 12), in which Flohr gets his revenge, has White playing h3 to evict a bishop. It leads to the loss of the pawn and the entrance of Flohr's queen uncomfortably close to White's king. The concentration of attack that follows leaves White with one solitary pawn to defend his king.

In Dobias-Podgorny (No. 13), Dobias compels the advance of the g-pawn, then the h-pawn. Then he subtly undermines the weakened position and causes it to collapse.

Tarrasch-Mieses (No. 14) shows Tarrasch destroying the f6-knight, Black's best defender of a castled position, and uprooting the g-pawn in the process. The disruption of the pawn formation makes things easy for Tarrasch, who caps the victory with a quiet little pawn move.

The next two games do not belong, strictly speaking, in the category of kingside attacks. I include them to show the consequences of failure to provide for the safety of the king.

Alekhine-Poindle (No. 15) has some delightfully unconventional moves by Alekhine to punish time-wasting play. Black is hindered from castling, and his king kept in the centre, where it is exposed to a fatal attack.

Tarrasch-Kurschner (No. 16) is a short story depicting harsh treatment of plausible but perfunctory chess. Tarrasch punishes his opponent's infractions of principle by driving his pieces back where they interfere with each other, prevents Black's king from castling and then assails him with every piece available.

Game 1
von Scheve – Teichmann
Berlin 1907
Giuoco Piano

The chief object of all opening strategy is to get the pieces out quickly – off the back rank and into active play.

You cannot attack (let alone try to checkmate) with one or two pieces.

You must develop all of them, as each one has a job to do.

A good way to begin is to release two pieces at one stroke, and this can be done by advancing one of the centre pawns.

1 e4

This is an excellent opening move. White anchors a pawn in the centre of the board and opens lines for his queen and a bishop. His next move, if he is allowed, will be 2 d4. The two pawns will then control four squares on the fifth rank, c5, d5, e5 and f5, and prevent Black from placing any of his pieces on those important squares.

How shall Black reply to White's first move? He must not waste time considering meaningless moves, such as 1...h6 or 1...a6. These and other aimless moves do nothing toward developing the pieces, nor do they interfere with White's threat to monopolize the centre.

Black must fight for an equal share of the good squares. Black must dispute possession of the centre.

Why all this stress on the centre? Why is it so important?

Pieces placed in the centre enjoy the greatest freedom of action and have the widest scope for their attacking powers. A knight, for example, posted in the centre, reaches out in eight directions and attacks eight squares. Standing at the side of the board, its range of attack is limited to four squares. It is only half a knight!

Occupation of the centre means control of the most valuable territory. It leaves less room for the enemy's pieces, and makes defence difficult, as his pieces tend to get in each other's way.

Occupation of the centre, or control of it from a distance, sets up a barrier that divides the opponent's forces and prevents them from cooperating harmoniously. Resistance by an army thus disunited is usually not very effective.

1 ...   e5

Very good! Black insists on a fair share of the centre. He fixes a pawn firmly there and liberates two of his pieces.

2 ♘f3! (D)

Absolutely the best move on the board!

The knight develops with a threat – attack on a pawn. This gains time as Black is not free to develop as he pleases. *He must save the pawn before he does anything else,* and this cuts down his choice of reply.

The knight develops *towards the centre,* which increases the scope of his attack.

The knight exerts pressure on two of the strategically important squares in the centre, e5 and d4.

The knight comes into play early in the game, in compliance with the precept: *develop knights before bishops!*

One reason for the cogency of this principle is that the knight takes shorter steps than the bishop. It takes longer for him to get to the fighting area. The bishop can sweep the length of the chessboard in one move (notice how the f1-bishop can reach all the way to a6). Where the knight takes a hop, skip and jump to get to b5, the bishop makes it in one leap.

Another purpose in developing the knights first is that we are fairly sure where they belong in the opening. We know that they are most effective on certain squares. We are not always certain of the right spot for the bishop. We may want the bishop to command a long diagonal, or we may prefer to have it pin an enemy piece. So: *bring out your knights before developing the bishops!*

At this point you will note that Black must defend his e-pawn before going about his business.

There are several ways to protect the pawn. He must evaluate and choose from these possibilities: 2...f6; 2...♕f6; 2...♕e7; 2...♗d6; 2...d6; and 2...♘c6. How does Black decide on the right move? Must he analyse countless combinations and try to visualize every sort of attack and defence for the next ten or fifteen moves?

Let me hasten to assure you that a master does not waste valuable time on futile speculation. Instead, he makes use of a potent secret weapon

– positional judgement. Applying it enables him to eliminate from consideration inferior moves, to which the average player devotes much thought. He hardly glances at moves that are obviously violations of principle!

Here is what might go through his mind as he selects the right move:

2...f6: "Terrible! My f-pawn occupies a square that should be reserved for the knight and it also blocks the queen's path along the diagonal. And I've moved a pawn when I should be developing pieces."

2...♕f6: "Bad, since my knight belongs at f6, not the queen. Also, I'm wasting the power of my strongest piece to defend a pawn."

2...♕e7: "This shuts the f8-bishop in, while my queen is doing a job which a lesser piece could handle."

2...♗d6: "I've developed a piece, but the d-pawn is obstructed, and my c8-bishop may be buried alive."

2...d6: "Not bad, since it gives the c8-bishop an outlet. But wait – it limits the range of the f8-bishop, and again I've moved a pawn when I should be putting pieces to work."

2...♘c6: "Eureka! This *must* be best, as I have developed a piece to its most suitable square and protected the e-pawn at the same time."

2 ... ♘c6!

Without going into tedious analysis, Black picks out the best possible move. He follows the advice of the Frenchman who said, *"Sortez les pièces!"*. He brings a piece out and saves the e-pawn *without any loss of time*.

I would caution you that this and other maxims are not to be blindly followed. In chess, as in life, rules must often be swept aside. In general, though, the principles governing sound chess play do make wonderful guideposts, especially in the opening, the middlegame and the ending!

3 ♗c4 (D)

"The best attacking piece is the king's bishop," says Tarrasch, so White puts this piece to work and clears the way for early castling.

The bishop seizes a valuable diagonal in the centre and attacks Black's f7-pawn. This pawn is particularly vulnerable as it is guarded by one piece only – the king. It is not unusual, even early in the game, to sacrifice a piece for this pawn, so that the king in capturing it is uprooted, driven into the open and exposed to a violent attack.

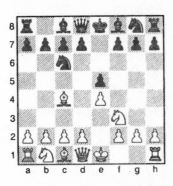

3 ... ♗c5

Is this the most suitable square for the bishop? Let us look at the alternatives:

3...♗b4: Inferior, because Black's bishop takes no part in the struggle for control of the centre and has little scope here.

3...♗d6: Poor, since the d-pawn is blocked, and the other bishop may have trouble coming out.

3...♗e7: Not too bad, because the bishop looks out on two diagonals and is well placed for defence. At e7 the bishop has made only one step forward, *but it has been developed once it has left the back rank.* The important thing to remember is that *every* piece must be put in motion.

The strongest developing move is 3...♗c5. On this excellent square the bishop commands an important diagonal, exerts pressure on the centre and attacks a weak pawn. This deployment conforms to two golden rules for opening play:

Place each piece as quickly as possible on the square where it is most effective.

Move each piece only once in the opening.

4 c3 (D)

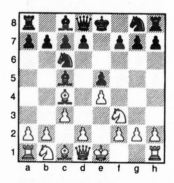

White's primary object is to establish two pawns in the centre and with this move he intends to support an advance of the d-pawn. After 5

d4, attacking bishop and pawn, Black must reply 5...exd4. The recapture by 6 cxd4 leaves White with two pawns in control of the centre.

His secondary aim is to bring the queen to b3, intensifying the pressure on the f7-pawn.

These are its virtues, but there are drawbacks to 4 c3:

In the opening, pieces not pawns should be moved.

In advancing to c3, the pawn occupies a square that should be reserved for the b1-knight.

4 ... ♛e7

Very good! Black develops a piece while parrying the threat. If White persists in playing 5 d4, the continuation 5...exd4 6 cxd4 ♛xe4+ wins a pawn. The capture *with check* gives White no time to recover the pawn, and an extra pawn, everything else being equal, is enough to win the game.

5 0-0

White postpones the advance of the d-pawn and moves his king to a safer place.

Castle early in the game, preferably on the kingside.

5 ... d6

Strengthens the centre and supports the e-pawn and bishop. Now the c8-bishop can get into the game.

6 d4

With the hope that Black will exchange pawns. This would leave White with an impressive line-up in the centre, while the c3-square is then available for his knight. If now 6...exd4 7 cxd4 ♛xe4, White punishes the pawn-snatching by 8 ♖e1 pinning the queen.

6 ... ♗b6

But Black need not capture! Now that his e-pawn is secure, the bishop simply retreats, still bearing down on the white centre from its new position.

Despite its formidable appearance, White's pawn-centre is shaky. The d-pawn is attacked three times, and White must keep a triple guard on it while trying to complete his development. On 7 ♕b3, which he contemplated earlier, the queen's protection is removed, while on 7 ♘bd2 it is cut off. Meanwhile White is faced with the threat of 7...♗g4 pinning and thereby rendering useless one of the pawn's supports.

Before committing himself to a definite course of action, White sets a little trap:

7 a4 (D)

A tricky move, but an illogical one. White threatens an attack on the bishop by 8 a5. If then 8...♗xa5, 9 d5 strikes at the knight protecting the bishop. After the reply 9...♘d8, White captures by 10 ♖xa5, winning a piece. Should Black, after 8 a5, play 8...♘xa5, the continuation 9

♖xa5 ♗xa5 10 ♕a4+ nets White two pieces for a rook.

But what right has White to play combinations when his development is so backward? An attack such as he initiates here is premature and should not succeed.

Develop all your pieces before starting any combinations!

7 ... a6

Black prepares a retreat for his bishop. This does not violate the precept about making unnecessary pawn moves in the opening. Development is not meant to be routine or automatic; threats must always be countered first. If more justification is needed, consider that Black's loss of time is compensated for by White's fruitless 7 a4 move.

8 a5

There is just a wee chance that Black will be tempted to take the pawn.

8 ... ♗a7

But Black does not bite!

9 h3 (D)

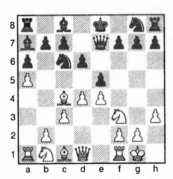

A coffee-house move! Weak players make this move instinctively in dire dread of having a piece pinned.

It is better to submit to the pin – a temporary inconvenience – than to prevent it by a move that loosens the position of the pawns defending the king and weakens the structure permanently. Playing h3 or g3 after castling creates an organic weakness that can never be remedied, as a pawn once advanced cannot retreat, and the position, once altered, cannot be restored. The pawn that has moved forward itself becomes a target for direct attack, while the square it guarded earlier (here it is g3) becomes a landing field for the enemy's troops.

"You should never, unless of necessity or to gain an advantage, move the pawns in front of the castled king," says Tarrasch, "for each pawn move loosens the position."

Alekhine expresses it even more strongly:

"Always try to keep the three pawns in front of your castled king on their original squares as long as possible."

Black can now speculate on breaking up White's kingside by removing the h3-pawn, even at the cost of a piece. The recapture tears open the g-file and exposes White's king to attack. This plan is of course not to be put into action until more pieces are brought into play.

9   ...   ♘f6

The knight swings into the fray with an attack on the e-pawn.

The move is excellent and conforms with a useful general principle:

Develop with a threat whenever possible!

Remember that to meet the threat the opponent must drop whatever else he is doing.

10   dxe5

White exchanges, and opens up lines for his pieces. Unfortunately this reacts in Black's favour, in accordance with the rule in these cases:

Open lines are to the advantage of the player whose development is superior.

10   ...   ♘xe5 (D)

Much stronger than taking with the pawn. The knight on e5, beautifully centralized, radiates power in every direction (something a pawn cannot do).

The disappearance of White's d-pawn has benefited Black's bishop, hidden away at a7. Its range has been extended, so that it now controls the whole of the long diagonal leading to White's f2-pawn – and the king is just behind the pawn!

What shall White do now? He has done nothing to relieve the plight of his e-pawn – it is still attacked by one of Black's knights, while his bishop is threatened by the other.

11 ♘xe5

This looks plausible, as White gets rid of a powerfully placed piece, but in making this exchange, White's own f3-knight, *the best defender of the castled position*, also comes off the board. The importance of holding on to the knight in such situations was pointed out by Steinitz more than seventy years ago, when he said, "Three unmoved pawns on the kingside in conjunction with a minor piece form a strong bulwark against an attack on that wing." Tarrasch attests to the valuable properties of the f3-knight with a simple emphatic statement: "A knight at f3 [f6 for Black] is the best defence of a castled position on the kingside."

11 ... ♕xe5 (D)

Observe that White's knight has disappeared completely from the board, but *Black's knight has been replaced by another piece*.

This new piece, the queen, is magnificently posted at e5. She dominates the centre, bears down on the hapless e-pawn, and is poised for quick action on any part of the board.

How does White solve the problems posed by the position of the menacing queen and the attacks on his e-pawn? He would love to dislodge the queen by 12 f4, but unfortunately the move is illegal. Can he save the pawn?

12 ♘d2

Desperately hoping that Black will snatch up the pawn by 12...♘xe4, when there would follow 13 ♘xe4 ♕xe4 14 ♖e1, and the pin wins the queen.

But Black is not interested in grabbing pawns. His positional superiority is great enough to justify looking for a combination that will conclusively force a win. His bishops exert terrific pressure on their respective diagonals (even though one bishop is still undeveloped!). Each of them attacks a pawn shielding the king. Black's queen is ready to swing over to the kingside, while the knight can leap in if more help is needed. Black controls the centre, a condition that, Capablanca says, is essential for a successful attack against the king. In short, Black is entitled to a winning combination as reward for his methodical positional play.

The question is: is there a target available for the explosion of this pent-up power?

12 ... ♗xh3!

Yes, indeed! The h-pawn, which innocently moved to h3 to prevent a pin!

Black removes the offending pawn – fit punishment for the crime of weakening White's position and betraying his king.

13   gxh3

White must capture the bishop or be a pawn down with nothing to show for it.

13   ...   ♛g3+!

A crashing entrance! Notice how Black has exploited the two main defects of 9 h3. *He captured the h-pawn itself and utilized the g3-square, weakened by its advance, as a point of invasion.*

14   ♔h1

White may not take the queen, as his f-pawn is pinned.

14   ...   ♛xh3+

Black destroys another defending pawn, further exposing the king.

15   ♔g1

White's only move. In return for the sacrificed bishop, Black has two pawns and the attack.

15   ...   ♞g4 (D)

Threatens mate on the move. White must guard against the threat at h2 or give his king a flight-square. If he tries to give his king room by 16 ♖e1, he falls into 16...♗xf2#. Hence...

16   ♞f3

To guard h2 and stop mate by the queen.

How does Black conclude the attack? He reasons it out this way: I have captured two of the pawns near the king. If I can remove the third pawn it will deprive the king of the last shred of protection, and he will be helpless. This last defender, the f-pawn, is attacked by my knight and bishop, and protected by his rook and king. I must either drive off one of the defenders or attack the pawn a third time. Perhaps I can do both!

16   ...   ♛g3+

Again exploiting the circumstance that the f-pawn is pinned, Black attacks it with a third piece, the queen.

17   ♔h1 (D)

The king must move to the corner and desert the pawn. Only the rook defends it now, against an attack by queen, knight and bishop. The pawn must fall, and with it the game.

17   ...   ♗xf2

Covers the king's flight-square, g1, and prevents him from returning there in answer to a check.

0-1

Black's threat was 18...♛h3+ 19 ♞h2 ♛xh2#. As 18 ♖xf2 runs into 18...♞xf2#, there was no escape.

Game 2
Liubarski – Soultanbéieff
Liège 1928
Giuoco Piano

1 e4

One of the best moves on the board! A pawn occupies the centre, and two pieces are freed for action.

One hundred and fifty years ago the great Philidor said, "The game cannot better be opened than by advancing the e-pawn two squares." This advice is still good today.

Only one other white first move, 1 d4, releases two pieces at the same time.

1 ... e5

"Probably the best reply," says Capablanca.

Black equalizes the pressure in the centre and frees his queen and a bishop.

2 ♘f3

This is superior to such developing moves as 2 ♘c3 or 2 ♗c4, which are less energetic. The g1-knight comes into play *with attack*, which cuts down the choice of reply.

Black must defend his pawn with 2...♘c6 or 2...d6 or he may decide to counterattack by 2...♘f6.

Whatever his answer, he cannot dawdle. *He must do something to meet White's threat.*

2 ... ♘c6

Undoubtedly the logical move. The pawn is protected without loss of time and the b8-knight is developed to its best post in the opening in one move.

3 ♗c4

Excellent, since the bishop seizes an important diagonal. The bishop strikes at f7, *Black's weakest point.*

A bishop is utilized to greatest effect either in controlling an important diagonal or in pinning (and rendering useless) an enemy piece.

3 ... ♗c5

3...♘f6 is a good alternative. Either move is in accord with the maxims of the masters, which they advocate *and put to use*:

- Get your pieces out fast!
- Move each piece only once in the opening.
- Develop with a view to control of the centre.
- Move only those pawns that facilitate the development of pieces.
- Move pieces, not pawns!

4 c3 *(D)*

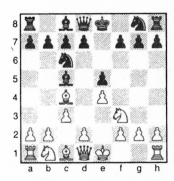

White's intentions are clear: he wants to support a pawn advance in the centre. His next move, 5 d4, will attack pawn and bishop. To save his e-pawn, Black will be forced to play 5...exd4. The recapture by 6 cxd4 will give White a strong formation of pawns in the centre.

White's idea has some point if it can be enforced. If the plan fails, his pawn standing at c3 deprives the b1-knight of its most useful square.

4 ...   &b6!

Chess is not a game to be played mechanically. Usually, moving a piece twice in the opening is a waste of time, but *threats must be parried before continuing development*.

The bishop retreats in order to pre-empt White's contemplated 5 d4, which attacks pawn and bishop.

5 d4 *(D)*

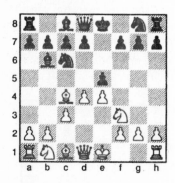

Hoping to induce Black to exchange pawns. Note that Black's e-pawn is attacked, *but not his bishop*.

5 ...   &e7

Instead of exchanging pawns (as he would have been compelled to do if his bishop were also under attack) Black defends his e-pawn while bringing another piece into play. His queen has advanced only one square, but even so the move is laudable:

The act of leaving the back rank constitutes a developing move.

In addition to developing a piece and defending a pawn, Black's last move threatens to continue 6...exd4 7 cxd4 &xe4+, winning a pawn.

6 0-0

Besides the usual benefits derived from castling (safeguarding the king and mobilizing the rook) White's move indirectly protects his e-pawn. If Black tries 6...exd4 7 cxd4 &xe4, then 8 &e1 pins and wins the queen.

6 ...   &f6! *(D)*

The knight develops with a threat – attack on the e4-pawn.

7 d5

Tempting, as it will dislodge the c6-knight from its strong post.

The move is natural, but to be censured on several counts:

1) The d-pawn blocks the path of White's own c4-bishop, greatly limiting its action.

2) The range of Black's b6-bishop has been increased; now its attack leads straight to White's king.

3) White has moved a pawn while his queenside pieces are crying to be released.

In the opening, move only those pawns that help develop the pieces.

7 ... ♘b8 *(D)*

Retreat is safer than moving the knight to the side of the board. After 7...♘a5 White's response is 8 ♗d3 after which he threatens to win the awkwardly placed knight by 9 b4.

8 ♗d3

Defends the e-pawn, but the development of another piece is more consistent with opening strategy. Either 8 ♘bd2 or 8 ♕e2 protects the pawn while bringing one more piece into play.

Do not move the same piece twice in the opening.

It is interesting to see how Black punishes these infractions of principle. On the chessboard, if nowhere else, justice does triumph.

8 ... d6

No exception can be taken to this pawn move: it strengthens the centre, opens a path for the c8-bishop and relieves the queen of the burden of watching over the e-pawn.

9 h3 *(D)*

To prevent Black from pinning his knight by 9...♗g4, but as Publius

Syrus observed some considerable time ago, "There are some remedies worse than the disease."

In disturbing the position of the pawns shielding his king, White weakens *organically* the structure of the kingside castled position *and sets up the unfortunate h-pawn itself as a convenient target for direct attack.*

All chess theorists affirm the validity of the concept of leaving the kingside pawns unmoved, from Staunton, who said more than a hundred and forty years ago, "It is seldom prudent in an inexperienced player to advance the pawns on the side on which his king has castled," to Reuben Fine, who said a century later, "The most essential consideration is that the king must not be subject to attack. He is safest when the three pawns are on their original squares."

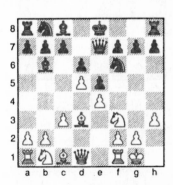

How does Black take advantage of White's last move? What is the best way to expose its imperfections?

9 ... h6!

By playing a move similar to the one I have severely censured!

What is the justification for Black's advance of the h-pawn?

Black has not weakened his defensive position, since his king is not castled on the kingside. *His advance of the h-pawn is a gesture of attack,* not a timid attempt to ward off a pin. The h-pawn will constitute a base for the g-pawn, which will march up to g5 and then g4. From there it will strike in two directions, at White's knight and his h3-pawn. White will be compelled either to capture this pawn or let it capture his own h3-pawn. No matter which exchange occurs, it results in an opening up of the g-file, along which Black can align his pieces for an attack on the king.

10   ♕e2

A developing move, but it may be too late.

10   ...   g5!

A bayonet thrust! The next step is to g4, where the pawn will break up White's position.

11   ♘h2

To prevent the intended advance. If the pawn moves on, it will be attacked three times and defended only twice.

Has Black's plan miscarried?

11   ...   g4!

Not at all! If necessary, Black will sacrifice a pawn for the sake of ripping away the defensive screen around White's king.

12   hxg4 *(D)*

Practically forced, as Black was threatening 12...gxh3, as well as 12...g3.

White has managed to close the file, for the time being.

12   ...   ♖g8

Now it is Black who attacks the g-pawn three times, while only two pieces defend it!

Obviously, White may not give his pawn more support by 13 f3, as it's against the law. It exposes his king to check.

13   ♗xh6

Desperately snatching at a loose pawn. In view of his retarded development and the plight of his king, such a capture is risky policy. If any hope remains it lies in some such move as 13 ♗e3. Not only does this bring another piece into play, but also in opposing one force with another of equal strength, it neutralizes the pressure of Black's bishop. The text-move disregards the admonition:

Do not grab pawns at the expense of development or position.

13   ...   ♘xg4

Gaining time by threatening the bishop – among other things.

Can White save the game?

If he tries 14 ♘xg4, Black forces the win by 14...♗xg4 (attacking the queen) 15 ♕c2 ♗f3 (threatening

16...♖xg2+ 17 ♔h1 ♕h4#) 16 g3 ♕h4! and mate will come at h1.

In this line of play, Black skilfully exploits the helplessness of White's pinned pawns.

14 ♗e3

The bishop flees and attempts to repel one of the assailants.

14 ... ♘xh2

This capture greatly limits White's choice of reply. The knight has taken a piece and now threatens the rook.

15 ♔xh2

On the alternative 15 ♗xb6 Black wins by 15...axb6 16 ♔xh2 ♕h4+ 17 ♔g1 ♖xg2+! (the fastest) 18 ♔xg2 ♗h3+! and White must either walk into mate by 19 ♔g1 ♕g5+ 20 ♔h2 ♕g2#, or into a discovered check by 19 ♔h2 ♗xf1+ 20 ♔g1 ♗xe2, when the loss of material is ruinous.

15 ... ♕h4+

Black has two major pieces operating with full force on the two open files near the enemy king. The attack plays itself.

16 ♔g1 (D)

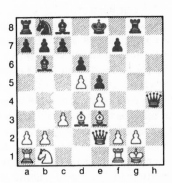

White's only move.

16 ... ♕h3

Threatening mate on the move.

0-1

There is no defence that will postpone the mate for long:

If 17 g3, then Black continues 17...♖h8 18 f3 ♗xe3+ 19 ♕xe3 (or 19 ♖f2 ♕h1#) 19...♕xg3#.

Or if 17 f3, guarding the g-pawn with his queen, then 17...♗xe3+ 18 ♖f2 ♕xg2# is mate. Strange that White, who feared the pin so much, should perish by the pin!

Game 3
Colle – Delvaux
Gand-Terneuzen 1929
Colle System

1 d4

Modern players consider this to be one of the best opening moves. It is equal in value to 1 e4 in that two pieces are freed for action, while a pawn seizes a central square. The difference is that the d-pawn stands protected whereas the e-pawn would be vulnerable to an early attack.

1 ... d5

This move and 1...♘f6 are by far the most common replies to 1 d4. White must not be allowed to play 2 e4 and dominate the vital central squares with his pawns.

2 ♘f3

So great an authority as Emanuel Lasker, World Champion for 27 years, says of this move, "In my practice I have usually found it strongest to post the knights at B3, where they have a magnificent sway." Here 'B3' refers to the squares c3 and f3 for White, or c6 and f6 for Black.

2 ... ♘f6

Black follows suit in trumps, developing his king's knight to its most useful square.

3 e3

Generally, it is dubious strategy to release one bishop while shutting in the other. In this game, White is adopting a system that calls for a storing up of dynamic energy behind the lines, which is released at the right time by an explosion at the key e4-square.

To this end, White develops so that his pieces exert their maximum pressure at e4. His bishop will therefore occupy d3, and his b1-knight will move to d2. If more concentration of force is needed, his queen will supply it by developing at e2, or he may play 0-0 followed by ♖e1. Then, with all this potential energy ready to let loose, the e-pawn advances to e4, to rip the position apart and open fire on Black's kingside.

Development in the Colle System is on positional lines, but the objective is a kingside attack!

3 ... e6 (D)

This is a routine developing move which serves to maintain the symmetry but has the defect of not crossing White's plans. Clearly, it was better strategy either to attack White's pawn-centre by 3...c5 or to counter by 3...♗f5. Not only is this latter a simple, sound developing move, but

also it prepares to oppose White's bishop, which is headed for d3, with an equal force. The exchange of bishops, which follows sooner or later, will deprive White of a most valuable weapon in kingside attacks.

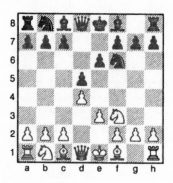

4 ♗d3

Notice the difference! White's bishop commands a beautiful (and undisputed) diagonal, while Black's c8-bishop, covering squares of the same colour, is hemmed in by the e-pawn.

4 ... c5!

Very good! Black strikes at the pawn formation in the centre and gives his queen access to the queenside.

This freeing move of the c-pawn is of the greatest importance in queen's pawn openings.

5 c3

"Move only one or two pawns in the opening!" say all the authorities, but no principle must be followed uncompromisingly.

This move permits White to meet the advance ...c4 by ♗c2, keeping the bishop lined up against Black's kingside. In the event that pawns are exchanged on d4, White can recapture with the e-pawn and free his c1-bishop.

5 ... ♞c6

Another good move. The knight comes into play toward the centre, increasing the pressure on the d-pawn.

6 ♞bd2 (D)

An odd-looking sortie. Not only does this knight block the paths of the queen and a bishop, but also the piece itself seems to be doing little good. Yet, an expert would make this move without a moment's hesitation! For one thing, the knight adds its weight to the pressure on the strategically important e4-square, the springboard of the coming attack. For another, *it is mobilized once it gets off the back rank.* Finally, it can hop out of the way of the queen and the bishop when it is expedient for it to do so.

6 ... ♝e7

Black brings another piece into play (remember that the bishop is doing a job once it leaves the back rank) and prepares to get his king into safety by castling.

7 0-0

The king flees to a less exposed sector, while the rook comes out of hiding.

7 ... c4

This is the sort of move instinctively made by a beginner. Its purpose is to chase off an annoying piece from its favourable post. The move is weak because it releases the pressure on White's centre. Tension must be maintained if Black is to have something to say about affairs in this vital area.

Counterplay in the centre is the best means of opposing a kingside attack and to secure counterplay, the pawn position must be kept fluid.

8 ♝c2

Naturally the bishop retreats, but stays on the diagonal leading to the e4-square, where the break will come.

8 ... b5 (D)

Primarily to make room at b7 for his light-squared bishop, but also with an eye to making trouble with a possible advance of his queenside pawns.

9 e4!

The key move in this opening! It will open up lines for an attack by White's pent-up pieces.

9 ...   dxe4

Not an attractive choice for Black, but he cannot have the threat of the e5 advance (displacing his knight and severely cramping his movements) perpetually hanging over his head.

10 ♘xe4 (D)

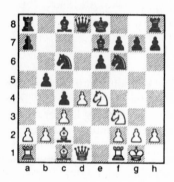

With this recapture, White's pieces that were crouched in the background spring into play.

White has the initiative and a commanding position in which to exercise it. If no immediate attacking opportunities present themselves, he can quietly put on more pressure by ♕e2, ♖e1, ♗f4 (or ♗g5) and ♖ad1, and wait for Black's game to crack.

10 ...   0-0

It might have been wiser to postpone castling (contrary to usual principles) as White is poised for an attack in that direction. This is another case where the value of a precept is conditioned by circumstances.

Black would do better to try for counterplay by 10...♕c7 followed by 11...♗b7 and 12...♖d8.

11 ♕e2

This developing move also threatens to win a piece. The idea is 12 ♘xf6+ ♗xf6 13 ♕e4, and the threat of mate on the kingside wins the exposed knight on the queenside.

11 ...   ♗b7

Black guards his knight while developing another piece.

12 ♘fg5!

Threatening the deadly 13 ♘xf6+ ♗xf6 14 ♗xh7+ ♔h8 15 ♕h5.

Why an exclamation mark for a simple threat which is so easily countered? Why glorify this move when Black can not only save the pawn but also cause White to lose time? Black simply moves the h-pawn one square, rescues the pawn, and forces White's knight to retreat.

The answer to these questions is that White's purpose with his brilliant knight move *is to compel one of the pawns defending the king to step forward.*

The secret of conducting a successful kingside attack is to create a breach in the cordon of pawns surrounding the enemy king; to induce or force one of the pawns to move. The change in the line-up of pawns fixes the defence with *a permanent weakness.*

12 ...   h6

"Touch the pawns before your king with only infinite delicacy," says Santasiere. But, alas, it's too late – Black must disturb the pawn position.

Had he tried 12...♘xe4, the recapture by 13 ♕xe4 threatens mate, and compels 13...g6 – and the pawns are disarranged!

13 ♘xf6+

Destroying the f6-knight, the best defender of a castled position.

13 ... ♗xf6

The alternative 13...gxf6 loses quickly. White could win either by gobbling up pawns with 14 ♘xe6 fxe6 15 ♕g4+ ♔h8 (15...♔f7 16 ♕g6#) 16 ♕g6 f5 17 ♕xh6+ ♔g8 18 ♕xe6+ and the f-pawn falls next, or with 14 ♘h3 (threatening 15 ♗xh6) 14...♔g7 15 ♗xh6+ ♔xh6 16 ♕e3+ ♔g7 17 ♕g3+ ♔h8 18 ♕h4+ followed by 19 ♕h7#.

14 ♕e4

Threatening instant mate.

14 ... g6 *(D)*

Making room for the king's escape by 14...♖e8 does not look inviting, as after 15 ♕h7+ ♔f8 16 ♘e4 White's attack appears dangerous. However, it is preferable to Black's actual move, which stops the queen coming any closer, but alters the pawn configuration. This change in the pawn formation saddles Black with a weakness that is *organic*, and one that can turn out to be fatal.

All this is encouraging to White, but how does he proceed? How does he exploit the weaknesses in Black's position? Above all, what does he do about his knight which is still under attack? Shall it retreat abjectly?

Before moving the knight back to f3 mechanically and unthinkingly, White looks carefully at the situation. The opportunity to strike a decisive blow may be here at this very moment, but one hasty 'obvious move' may give Black just enough breathing time to reorganize his defences.

This is the position, and here is how White reasons out his attack:

The key point must be Black's g-pawn, which guards his king from invasion. If anything happens to this pawn – if it is captured – the defence crumbles, and I can break into the fortress. How do I go about removing it from the board?

The g-pawn is protected by the f-pawn; suppose I destroy its support by sacrificing my knight for the f-pawn? After 15 ♘xf7 ♔xf7 (or 15...♖xf7) 16 ♕xg6+, and I have two pawns for my knight, with a third one in sight, as the h-pawn must fall. Material is then approximately even, but his position is completely broken up, and clinching the win should be easy.

This might be the general plan, but before putting it in motion, White analyses the combination for possible flaws and comes up with this: after 15 ♘xf7 ♖xf7 (bringing another piece to the defence) 16 ♕xg6+ ♖g7 17 ♕xh6 ♘xd4!, suddenly Black is the aggressor! He threatens mate in two by 18...♘e2+ 19 ♔h1 ♗xg2#, as well as outright ruin by 18...♖xg2+, followed by a deadly discovered check.

Clearly this line of play is too dangerous. Is there another way to break through, without letting Black's rook come into the game? Can I get rid of the f-pawn without disturbing the rook? It is important that I remove this pawn, as it supports the g-pawn and the e-pawn. Wait a minute! *There is a clue in the last sentence.* The f-pawn, guarding two other pawns, is serving two masters. Obviously it is overworked! I must add to its burden by luring it away from its present important post!

Therefore:

15 ♘xe6!

The knight captures a pawn and attacks queen and rook.

15 ...   fxe6

Black must accept the sacrifice or lose rook and pawn for the knight.

16 ♕xg6+ *(D)*

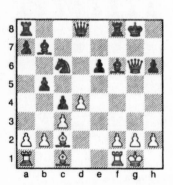

Stronger than taking the e-pawn, after which Black has four ways to get out of check. Each of these replies might lose, but it is more practical to attack the enemy with blows that leave him little choice of reply.

16 ...   ♗g7

The only move, since 16...♔h8 walks right into mate.

17 ♕h7+

White has other attractive continuations in 17 ♗xh6 or 17 ♕xe6+, but this forces the king out into the open where White's other pieces can get at him.

17 ...   ♔f7

The only move.

18 ♗g6+

Stronger than 18 ♗xh6, to which Black retorts 18...♕f6 followed by 19...♖h8. The text-move keeps him on the run.

18 ...   ♔f6

Certainly not 18...♔e7, when 19 ♕xg7+ lets White pick up a couple of bishops.

19 ♗h5 *(D)*

White is still angling for 20 ♕g6+ ♔e7 21 ♕xg7+, when both black bishops come off the board.

19 ...   ♘e7

The only way to prevent the queen check.

20 ♗xh6

White is not playing to pick up stray pawns, but to bring another piece into the attack. The pawn that is added to the collection is incidental to the general scheme of things.

> **20 ... ⌶g8**

To parry the threat of 21 ♕xg7+ ♔f5 22 ♕e5#.

On 20...♗xh6 White intended 21 ♕xh6+ ♔f5 22 ⌶ae1, when the threat of mate either by the rook or the g-pawn is decisive.

> **21 h4**

The new threat is 22 ♗g5#.

> **21 ... ♗xh6**

Loses on the spot, but there was no defence for Black: if 21...e5, then 22 ♗xg7+ ⌶xg7 23 dxe5+ and the king must abandon the rook.

> **22 ♕f7# (1-0)**

Game 4
Blackburne – Blanchard
London 1891
King's Gambit Declined

> **1 e4**

Values were constant in many fields of endeavour at the time this game was played:

Stories began, "Once upon a time,"

Tic-tac-toe players put a cross in the central square,

Checker masters started with 11-15,

Chess masters opened with 1 e4.

Despite the researches of the scientists, these remain good beginnings.

> **1 ... e5**

Black opens lines for two of his pieces and establishes equilibrium in the centre.

> **2 f4**

An offer of a pawn to induce Black to surrender his share of the centre.

Accepting the gift enables White to continue with 3 ♘f3, followed by 4 d4, and dominate the centre with his pawns. In addition, the opening of the f-file will offer White the opportunity of directing his attack at the vulnerable point f7. This is a tender spot whether Black's king stays at home or castles.

> **2 ... ♗c5 (D)**

Probably the safest way to decline the gambit:

1) The bishop bears down on the centre and controls an excellent diagonal.

2) The bishop supplements the pawn's attack on d4 and prevents White from moving his d-pawn to d4.

3) The bishop's presence at c5, overlooking g1, forbids White from castling in a hurry.

3 ♘c3

White avoids 3 fxe5 because the reply (coming like a shot, probably) 3...♕h4+ 4 g3 (even worse is 4 ♔e2 ♕xe4#) 4...♕xe4+ wins a rook for Black.

White's actual move is not as energetic as 3 ♘f3, but in playing 3 ♘c3 Blackburne was trying to lure his opponent into playing 3...♗xg1 4 ♖xg1 ♕h4+ 5 g3 ♕xh2, when 6 ♖g2 followed by 7 fxe5 gives White a fine game.

3 ...   ♘c6

A simple retort to the dubious invitation.

Black continues mustering his forces on the field of action. In the fight for control of the centre, his knight does its share by exerting pressure on the squares e5 and d4.

4 ♘f3

Did White miss a chance to win material by 4 fxe5 ♘xe5 5 d4? No, because 4 fxe5 is met by 4...d6, whereby Black offers a pawn for the sake of securing a free, easy development.

The text-move puts an end to the possibility of being bothered by a queen check and revives the threat of winning the e-pawn.

4 ...   exf4 (D)

This is a poor move on at least four counts:

1) In moving a pawn instead of a piece, Black loses sight of the chief objective in all opening strategy: Move the pieces! Get them off the back rank and on the job!

2) He surrenders his hold on the centre and the privileges it confers.

3) He wastes time capturing a pawn which he cannot retain.

4) He permits White to seize the centre next move, which forces a retreat by his bishop and a consequent loss of time.

Tarrasch considered a move such as the one just made by Black a worse offence than an outright blunder, such as leaving a piece *en prise*.

Instead of this, Black might better have played 4...d6, which holds everything and lets the c8-bishop see daylight.

5 d4!

Of course! No player should take more than half a second to see the power of this pawn push! The pawn seizes control of a good bit of the centre (occupying d4 and attacking two other important squares), dislodges the bishop from its strong position, and uncovers an attack by his own c1-bishop on the f4-pawn.

5 ...   ♗b4

It would have been sounder strategy to retreat to e7 instead, where the bishop is invaluable for defence.

6 &xf4

White gains a tempo with this capture, as he recovers the lost pawn and develops a piece at the same time.

6 ... d5

Black attacks the white e-pawn, disputing possession of the centre. Meanwhile, Black gives his queenside pieces more air.

7 e5

All pawn moves have positive and negative aspects. (Tarrasch used to say, "Every pawn move loosens the position.")

One drawback for White in the advance of his e-pawn is that the occupation of e5 by a pawn deprives his pieces of a useful square. The knight especially operates to great advantage when posted at e5.

In compensation, the pawn exercises a cramping effect on Black's entire position and imposes particular restraint on Black's king's knight, which cannot develop naturally at f6.

7 ... &xc3+

Black is intrigued by the prospect of saddling Blackburne with a doubled pawn, but why capture a piece that is pinned and can do no harm? Why relax the pressure at all?

A more commendable procedure was to bring up the reserves, starting with 7...&f5.

8 bxc3

In return for the handicap of the doubled pawns (little enough, since the advance c4 forces an exchange and undoubles the pawns) White enjoys advantages in his two bishops and in the open b-file which his rook will put to good use.

8 ... &e6 (D)

A superficial move, as the bishop could develop to greater effect at f5. There it would hinder White from freely posting his bishop at d3, except at the cost of permitting the bishops to be exchanged.

Developing the pieces to squares where they are most effective assures an advantage; preventing the opponent from doing likewise increases it.

It is important to fight for control of the vital squares.

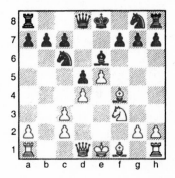

9 &d3

Clearly an excellent deployment: the bishop reaches out in two directions, ready to take a hand on either side of the board.

9 ... h6

Apparently to prevent 10 &g5 or 10 &g5.

White, who is interested only in completing his development, has not the slightest intention of making either of these moves.

The move ...h6 by Black (or h3 by White) should be played only if the h-pawn is to form a base for an attack by pawns, i.e. if it supports an advance by the g-pawn. Defensively, the move does more harm than good, as it loosens the pawn structure and weakens its resistance to attack. It is especially dangerous if the king has castled on the kingside, as the pawn itself, standing out from the ranks, provides a convenient target. Also (as if the foregoing were not enough) it does nothing to further the cause of development and wastes time which should be devoted to the liberation of pieces which are still shut in.

10   0-0

At one stroke White secures the safety of his king and brings his rook on to an open file. It is true that the file is cluttered up by a knight and bishop, which interfere with the rook's influence, but they are pieces, not pawns, and can move quickly out of the way.

10   ...   ♘ge7 (D)

Not the happiest spot for the knight, but how else can it get into the game? Poor as this development is, it is by far preferable to letting the knight stay uselessly at home.

11 ♖b1!

The master makes this move in a flash, while the run-of-the-mill player never even looks at it!

What is the rook's future on this file? It attacks a pawn, but the pawn is easily protected. Why not try for a kingside attack, instead of this futile demonstration?

The answer lies in this: the master's instinct (or perhaps his knowledge or experience) tells him that he must seize any files that are open – control them at once with his rooks or his queen. "Make the moves," it says, "that conform with the requirements of the position, and you will be suitably rewarded. Play the moves necessary to establish a superior position! Develop your pieces so that they enjoy maximum mobility, and control most of the territory. Direct your efforts to weakening the enemy position, cramping the movements of his pieces, and reducing the capacity of his resistance before you make the first move of a combination. When the time is ripe, the attack will play itself. The decisive combination will stare you in the face."

11   ...   b6

This too is a move that distinguishes the master from the amateur!

How easy it is to advance the pawn, safeguard it from attack, and let the rook bite on granite! Obvious as this defence is, no top-ranking player would rush to adopt it! He would try to avoid disturbing the pawn formation and consider instead such alternatives as 11...♖b8 or 11...♕c8.

After the actual move, the light squares on Black's queenside have been weakened. More to the point, the advance of the pawn deprives the c6-knight of solid support – a circumstance that White will exploit in his forthcoming attack on the king, *away over at the other side of the board.*

12   ♛d2

The queen leaves the first rank to enable the rooks to get in touch with each other. They may wish to increase the pressure on an open file by doubling on it, or otherwise work in concert.

The full meaning of White's queen move might easily be overlooked by an opponent who makes plausible but superficial replies.

Chess must not be played mechanically, even in the simplest, most placid positions.

12   ...   0-0 (D)

Walking right into the teeth of the storm!

Before making a move that suggests itself so readily, Black might have asked himself, "How can I exploit White's one weakness, the doubled pawns on the c-file?"

He might then have hit upon 12...♘a5, with the object of swinging the knight to c4. There it blockades the doubled pawn, interferes with the free movement of White's pieces, and in general sticks like a bone in the throat. White could capture the knight, but then he parts with one of his valuable bishops, and as a result of the exchange his pawn position would be inferior to Black's. Finally, Black could then anchor one

of his pieces to great effect on d5, a square from which it could never be evicted by pawns.

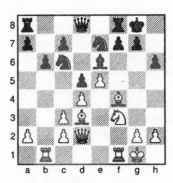

13   ♗xh6

Blackburne must have snatched this pawn up at lightning speed!

At the price of a bishop, he immediately gets two pawns as material return, demolishes the barricade of pawns near the king – and more, as we shall see.

13   ...   gxh6

Black must capture the bishop, or be a pawn down without any positional compensation.

14   ♛xh6

Let us see what White's return is for the piece that he sacrificed:

1) He has two pawns in tangible assets.

2) His queen is powerfully placed in enemy territory – threatening mate on the move, in fact!

3) He has ripped away the screen of pawns that sheltered Black's king.

4) He has a strong attack in prospect, starting with 15 ♘g5.

5) If more help is needed, he can call up the reserves (after 15 ♘g5) by 16 ♖f3, followed by 17 ♖g3.

14   ...   ♘g6 *(D)*
Was there any other defence?

1) 14...♘f5 (to interfere with the action of the bishop), then 15 ♗xf5 ♗xf5 16 ♕xc6 picks up the unprotected knight on the queenside, a consequence of Black's instinctive advance of his b-pawn at his eleventh move.

2) 14...♗f5 15 ♗xf5 ♘xf5 16 ♕xc6, and again White scoops up the unfortunate knight.

3) 14...f5 leaves Black's bishop *en prise*. White would capture it following Tartakower's excellent advice: "Take it first and philosophize afterward!"

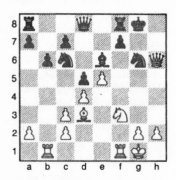

15   ♘g5
Again threatening mate at h7. This is speedier than the brutal alternative 15 ♗xg6 fxg6 16 ♕xg6+ followed by 17 ♕xe6, which wins material, and eventually the game.

Blackburne heeds the injunction laid down by Baron von Heydebrand und der Lasa, who flourished in the nineteenth century: "The simplest and the shortest way of winning is the best way."

15   ...   ♖e8 *(D)*

The rook provides the king with a flight square.

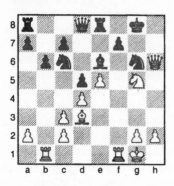

16   ♖xf7
Again there is a pleasant choice of winning methods: two others are 16 ♗xg6 and if 16...fxg6, then 17 ♕h7#; and 16 ♘h7, followed by 17 ♘f6+ and a quick mate.

The move actually made nails down the king and renews the threat of mate on the move.

16   ...   ♗xf7
Forced, if Black wants to avoid resigning.

17   ♕h7+
Nudging the king into a fatal situation.

17   ...   ♔f8
The only move.

18   ♕xf7# (1-0)

The danger in playing plausible but perfunctory chess is finely illustrated in this game. Blackburne, who played this and seven other games simultaneously while blindfolded, relied on order and method to achieve victory. It proved easily superior to the move-to-move groping of his sighted opponent.

Game 5
Ruger – Gebhard
Dresden 1915
Giuoco Piano

1 e4

The most important target in the opening is to develop the pieces as fast as possible in order to occupy and control the centre.

White's first move fixes a pawn in the centre and, as the first step in getting his pieces off the back rank, opens avenues for his queen and bishop.

1 ... e5

Black equalizes the pressure in the centre and releases two pieces for action. He must be content with this, as he cannot hope at this early stage to wrest the initiative away from White by force.

2 ♘f3

It is good strategy to make developing moves that embody threats, as it cuts down the choice of reply. Against the passive 2 ♘c3, which develops a piece but attacks nothing, Black can choose from among such good responses as 2...♘f6, 2...♘c6 and 2...♗c5. Likewise, if White's second move is the quiet 2 ♗c4, Black has three good options in 2...♘f6, 2...♗c5 and 2...c6 (with a view to an early ...d5).

2 ... ♘c6

Black saves his e-pawn and develops a piece. The knight comes into play efficiently: its action is directed toward influencing the centre. It defends the e5-pawn and attacks d4.

3 ♗c4 *(D)*

The bishop comes out, taking up a post where it commands a diagonal leading towards Black's king. It attacks a pawn which is peculiarly vulnerable as it is defended only by the king.

This does not mean that White will capture the pawn in the next few moves, *but the threat is always there*. Many a short brilliancy owes its life to similar captures in which the bishop is sacrificed simply to draw the king out into the open where White's other pieces can get at him.

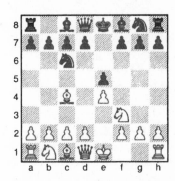

3 ... ♗c5 *(D)*

Black follows suit, bringing his bishop out to the most suitable square.

In the opening, a bishop is best placed for attack when it controls a diagonal passing through the centre or when it pins a hostile knight and renders it immobile. Defensively, the bishop would do a fine job at e7, where it radiates power in several directions, making an intrusion by an enemy piece difficult.

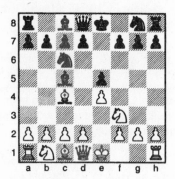

4 c3

Supporting an advance of the d-pawn with a view to controlling the centre. White postpones castling as his king is in no danger.

4 ... ♘f6

A powerful counter to the threat: Black develops a piece and attacks a pawn.

5 d4

White meets this by attacking a piece.

5 ... exd4

Practically forced, since 5...♗d6 guarding the e-pawn is clumsy, since it blocks the d-pawn, while 5...♗b6 permits 6 dxe5 ♘xe4 7 ♗xf7+ ♔xf7 8 ♕d5+ and White regains his piece, remaining a pawn ahead. White could also play 7 ♕d5, attacking the knight while threatening mate, instead of 7 ♗xf7+.

6 cxd4

White's array of pawns looks impressive, but can the centre be maintained?

6 ... ♗b4+

Far superior to the timid 6...♗b6 after which Black is crushed somewhat like this: 7 d5 ♘b8 8 e5 ♘g8 (both knights return home ingloriously) 9 0-0 ♘e7 10 d6 ♘g6 11 ♘g5 0-0 (Black's king is protected by three pawns and the knight; in four moves the knight and one pawn disappear, while the remaining two pawns are pinned and helpless) 12 ♕h5 (threatening 13 ♕xh7#) 12...h6 13 ♕xg6 (again threatening mate – the white queen is of course taboo) 13...hxg5 14 ♗xg5 ♕e8 15 ♗f6 *(D)* and White, exploiting two pins, forces mate within two moves. This is the final position of this line:

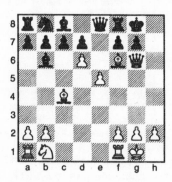

After the actual move, White must get his king out of check, and if possible save the threatened pawn.

7 ♘c3

White prefers this, which offers a pawn, to 7 ♗d2 ♗xd2+ 8 ♘bxd2, when the e-pawn is protected.

7 ... 0-0

"Chess is not for timid souls," wrote Steinitz in a letter to Bachmann. Castling early in the game is *generally* sound strategy. In this case it is inappropriate, as White's centre is formidable and must be destroyed. Black must play 7...♘xe4, accepting the offer of a pawn, and take his chances of surviving whatever attack might follow. It cannot be worse than this passive castling, which results in both his knights being evicted from their fine posts. Pillsbury gave as his rule, which he said was absolute and vital: "Castle because you want to or because you must, but not because you can."

8 d5 *(D)*

Ordinarily, such moves are suspect, as d5 should be occupied by a piece, but here the pawn dislodges the knight and prevents Black forever from freeing his game by ...d5.

8 ... ♘e7

As good as there is. The shift to a5 is countered by 9 ♗d3, and the knight is stranded at the side of the board.

9 e5

Now a shot at the other knight!

9 ... ♘e4

Retreating to e8 does not look attractive, so Black plays to exchange knights.

10 ♕c2

Protects his own knight, which was twice attacked, and threatens the enemy's.

10 ... ♘xc3

Practically forced, as defending the knight by 10...f5 allows 11 d6+ and the other knight falls.

11 bxc3

This recapture gains a tempo: Black's bishop must lose a move retreating, while White's advantages multiply. Now he enjoys an open b-file for his rook and an extra diagonal for his dark-squared bishop.

11 ... ♗c5 *(D)*

Naturally, this offers better chances than moving to a5, the only other flight square.

A comparison of the two sides' positions shows that White's is decidedly superior. He has more pieces in play, and they have far more mobility than Black's. He also has better prospects of bringing more pieces into the battle.

The recommended recipe now is to occupy Black with threats – keep him on the run and give him no time to put up effective resistance.

12 ♘g5!

Ostensibly to scare Black by the threat of mate; actually, the purpose is to induce a weakening advance of one of the king's retinue of pawns.

If one of these pawns does move, Black is done for! For example, 12...f5 13 d6+ wins a piece, or if 12...g6, then 13 ♘e4 forces 13...♗b6, when 14 ♗h6 drives the rook to e8, and 15 ♘f6+ wins the exchange.

12 ...   ♘g6 (D)

The only defence! The kingside pawns remain intact, but Black has been compelled to place his pieces where White wants them. Under such circumstances the chances of Black putting up a good fight are not too bright.

White must avoid Black's error of castling as a matter of routine development. Such a quiet course would give Black time to play 13...d6 or 13...h6, beating the knight back. White must not give his opponent a moment to catch his breath. He must attack, attack, attack!

13 h4

Threatening to move on to h5, dislodging the knight, and then mate with the queen.

13 ...   h6

What else is there? Black tries to drive off the menacing knight. He cannot do this by 13...f6 as 14 d6+ ♔h8 15 ♘f7+ wins the exchange.

14 d6!

A powerful stroke! Black's bishop is cut off from the defence, while a line is opened for White's bishop. White now threatens 15 ♕xg6, as the pinned f-pawn could not capture the queen.

14 ...   hxg5

Black might as well take whatever material he can.

15 hxg5!

The knight will not run away (the penalty being 16 ♕h7#). Meanwhile, the rook has a lovely open file, and the queen still threatens to capture the knight.

15 ...   ♖e8

The king needs more room!

16 ♕xg6

Regaining the piece without relaxing the pressure. White threatens one mate in one, and two mates in two.

16 ...   ♖xe5+

Black consoles himself by equalizing the material and gives one despairing check before he yields.

17 ♔f1

Simplest, as the mate threats are still on tap. There was little chance that White would blunder by 17 ♔d2 ♕xg5+ 18 ♕xg5 ♖xg5, when all the good work has gone for naught.

1-0

Black can avoid mate on the move by 17...♕e8 (incidentally threatening mate himself!), only to fall into 18 ♕h7+ ♔f8 19 ♕h8#.

Game 6
Zeissl – Walthoffen
Vienna 1899
Ruy Lopez

1 e4

"Always deploy," says Franklin K. Young, "so that the right oblique may be readily established in case the objective plane remains open or becomes permanently located on the centre or on the king's wing, or that the crochet aligned may readily be established if the objective plane becomes permanently located otherwise than at the extremity of the strategic front."

If this is somewhat obscure (and I see no reason to believe otherwise) the conclusion it reaches is stated in limpid prose by the same writer: "The best initial move for White is 1 e4".

1 ... e5

Black's best chance to equalize is to get a fair share of the most important squares – those in the centre.

With 1...e5 he stakes out his claim, meanwhile freeing two of his pieces.

2 ♘f3

You may play this confidently, secure in the knowledge that no master alive can make a better move.

- The knight develops in one move to its most suitable square in the opening.
- It exerts pressure on two of the four squares in the vital central area.
- It comes in toward the centre so that it enjoys maximum mobility.

- It helps clear the kingside, enabling early castling of the king on that side.
- It is posted ideally for the defence of the king after he castles.
- It comes into play with a gain of time – an attack on a pawn!

In short, it's a very good move!

2 ... ♘c6

A commendable reply: Black develops a piece, protecting his pawn at the same time.

3 ♗b5 *(D)*

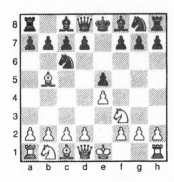

Probably the strongest move on the board. The bishop puts a restraining hand on the pawn's defender. There is no immediate threat of winning the pawn as after 4 ♗xc6 dxc6 5 ♘xe5, the reply 5...♕d4 regains the pawn. But there is pressure on the knight, and this pressure becomes intensified when Black sooner or later advances his d-pawn since the knight is then pinned.

3 ...   f5

A bold attempt to seize the initiative. The idea is to lure White into surrendering the centre by taking the f-pawn.

4 d4

An aggressive player would like White's counterattack on the e-pawn. Another dynamic line is 4 ♘c3, aiming for piece-play, while a conservative player might be content with 4 d3, supporting the e-pawn so that in the event of an exchange on e4 he would retain a pawn in the centre.

4 ...   fxe4 *(D)*

Black's capture is intended mainly to evict the knight from its strong post.

5 ♘xe5

Apparently a strong move. White gets his pawn back and prevents 5...d6 or 5...d5. After either of these moves, the continuation 6 ♘xc6 bxc6 7 ♗xc6+ wins the exchange.

White also has a powerful threat in 6 ♗xc6 dxc6 7 ♕h5+ ♔e7 8 ♕f7+ ♔d6 9 ♘c4#.

This is all very tempting, since the possibility of mating so early in the game is attractive to the young player, but such ambition should be suppressed. Premature mating attacks are usually repulsed with loss of time or material to the aggressor.

A safer continuation is 5 ♗xc6 dxc6 6 ♘xe5.

5 ...   ♘xe5

Black removes the best defender of White's kingside position and puts an end to any combinative notions White might have entertained.

6 dxe5

White has nothing to show for the over-energetic move 4 d4. The simple and natural development of the b1-knight by 4 ♘c3 would have been preferable.

6 ...   c6! *(D)*

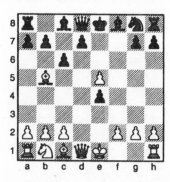

A pawn move when pieces should be brought into play? Yes, if the move is justified by the particular position. Black has four good arguments for the pawn push:

1) He must drive off the bishop before he can advance his d-pawn (otherwise the king is in check).

2) The time lost in moving the pawn is compensated for by the fact that the bishop must also lose a move in retreating.

3) He opens a fine diagonal for his queen.

4) The attack on the bishop will win a pawn, and "A pawn is worth a little trouble," according to Steinitz.

7 ♗c4

Ordinarily, this is an excellent place for the bishop, but e2 is more consistent with the requirements of the position. White has lost the services of his king's knight, and the bishop might help the defence of the kingside.

7 ... ♛a5+

Double attack on king and e5-pawn.

8 ♘c3

The best way to get out of check. White places the b1-knight where it belongs in the opening.

8 ... ♛xe5 (D)

Black has won a pawn, which is a good start toward winning the game. His aim now is to get an attack rolling in the direction of White's denuded kingside.

9 0-0

Plausible – and bad! It was more discreet to conceal his intentions, develop the queenside pieces, and castle later, perhaps on the queenside.

9 ... d5!

Of course! Black seizes the centre, chases off the enemy bishop, and enables his own c8-bishop to make an appearance. All this in one move!

10 ♗b3

Here too the defensive move 10 ♗e2, placing the bishop where he overlooks two diagonals, is preferable.

10 ... ♘f6

Organizing a kingside attack by a simple process – developing his pieces!

11 ♗e3 (D)

Partly to prevent Black from playing 11...♗c5, partly to dislodge the centralized queen by 12 ♗d4 or 12 ♛d4.

11 ... ♗d6!

This fine move has more significance than the mere development of a piece combined with a mating threat. The ulterior object is to create a *permanent irremediable weakness* in White's kingside position by forcing one of the defending pawns to make a move.

12 g3

The only possible defence. If instead 12 f4, then 12...exf3 13 ♕xf3 ♕xh2+ 14 ♔f2 ♗g4 and Black wins.

After the text move, Black starts an attack, but using his pieces rather than trying to break into the position by the pawn assault 12...h5 followed by ...h4.

12 ...   ♗g4! *(D)*

Black bases his attack on the theme of *penetration*. White has weakened the f3- and h3-squares by 12 g3, as these squares are no longer guarded by the g-pawn. These squares are now 'holes', as Steinitz first named them. Enemy pieces that settle themselves on these squares stand firm, as *no pawns can ever drive them away*.

The bishop attacks the queen, with the object of insinuating itself into f3 without loss of time.

13 ♕d2

As good as there is. If White interposes the knight at e2 instead, then 13...♕h5, attacking the knight once more, forces 14 ♖e1, whereupon 14...♕h3 plants a piece in one hole. Black's following move is

15...♗f3, occupying the other hole, and the stage is set for mate at g2.

13 ...   ♗f3

The second step in the process of penetration.

14 ♗f4 *(D)*

Hoping for a line such as 14...♕e7 15 ♗xd6 ♕xd6 16 ♕f4, when an exchange or two might ease his difficulties.

After White's fourteenth move, Black has a forced mate in a few moves.

14 ...   ♕f5!

Deserts the bishop, but Black is interested only in getting the queen to h3, with a death grip on the light squares.

15 ♘d1

The only possible chance to defend. The knight is to be brought to e3 to guard the g2-square, where mate impends.

15 ...   ♕h3

Threatening instant mate.

16 ♘e3

Defending the critical square.

16 ...   ♘g4

The new threat is mate at h2. Notice the clever use of the weakened light squares on the kingside as the black pieces infiltrate the enemy position.

17 ⃞fc1

Room for the king!

17 ... ♛xh2+

And mate comes next move.

0-1

Game 7
Spielmann – Wahle
Vienna 1926
French Defence

1 e4

This move accomplishes a great deal:

• A pawn is fixed in the centre of the board.

• The pawn exerts a grip on d5 and f5, and keeps Black's pieces from settling on those squares.

• White's queen and bishop immediately have breathing space.

1 ... e6

With several objects in view:

One, to prevent White from dictating the opening. After the conventional reply 1...e5 White can play the Ruy Lopez, the Giuoco Piano, the Scotch, the Vienna Game or a dangerous gambit of some sort.

Another is that Black's cramped position may tempt White into a disastrous premature attack.

A third is that the pawn at e6 supports an advance by 2...d5, an attack on the e-pawn which might wrest the initiative.

The French Defence is not to be underestimated. It conceals a great deal of dynamic energy behind a modest facade.

2 d4

If it's worthwhile to establish one pawn in the centre, then keeping two

pawns there should double the benefits.

2 ... d5

Black gives his queen more scope and challenges the centre.

3 ♘c3

Clearly an excellent response, as the knight develops to its proper square, protects the e-pawn, and bears down on d5.

3 ... ♘f6 *(D)*

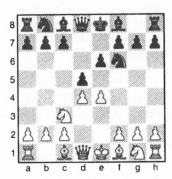

Black in turn brings his own knight to its strongest position with gain of time – a further attack on the e4-pawn.

4 exd5

Many players prefer to add to the pressure by 4 ♗g5 (which develops a piece and renders one of the enemy's impotent) rather than exchange pawns, which relaxes the tension.

Spielmann, who likes wide-open positions, clears away a couple of pawns to give his pieces more room for their activities.

Which move is better? Which should you play? The answer is: play the move that you like, the one that best suits your style and temperament. If you are a careful, cautious player who knows the full value of a pawn – that each one is a potential queen, and that the loss of a pawn may be the loss of the game – stick to 4 ♗g5 and the openings of positional chess, the Ruy Lopez, the Queen's Pawn openings, the Réti and the English. On the other hand, if you prefer daring, adventurous chess, and a pawn is simply a barrier to the sweeping onrush of an attack by your pieces, play openings which allow scope for your imagination, the Evans, Danish, King's and other gambits.

The best openings to play are the ones you are most at home in.

4 ...   exd5

Better than taking with the knight. Black keeps a pawn in the centre and frees his c8-bishop.

5 ♗g5

White pins the knight and threatens to break up Black's game by 6 ♗xf6 gxf6 (6...♕xf6 loses the d5-pawn), when Black is left with a weak doubled pawn.

5 ...   ♗e7

The simplest way of unpinning the knight. Moving the bishop only one square may not seem much of a move, but it complies with the first

law of rapid development: *Get your pieces off the back rank!*

6 ♗d3

This bishop's stand is aggressive, especially against kingside castling.

6 ...   ♘c6 (D)

This knight's debut is even more menacing, as it threatens to take the d-pawn.

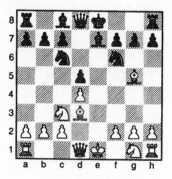

7 ♘ge2!

After the customary development 7 ♘f3, Black pins the knight by 7...♗g4 and again threatens the d-pawn. White could save the pawn, for instance by 8 ♗e2, but would lose the initiative.

After the text-move, if Black pins the knight by 7...♗g4, 8 f3 repels the bishop and causes it to lose time retreating.

7 ...   ♘b4

Intending to get rid of a dangerous enemy piece and also to assure himself of a little advantage in keeping both his bishops.

8 ♘g3

Now we see another reason for developing the knight to e2. White wants to anchor a piece at f5, a dominating position for a knight or a bishop. A piece need do no more than just stand there and look menacing to rattle the opponent.

> **8 ...**   ♘xd3+

Mission accomplished. Black has a slight technical superiority in retaining two long-range bishops against White's knight and bishop, but...

> **9 ♕xd3**

...at the cost of a loss of time. Black has made three moves with the knight to exchange it for a bishop that moved only once. More than that, his knight came off the board completely, while the bishop left a piece in its place. The result is that White has four active pieces in play against two of Black's. White is also prepared to castle on either side and mobilize both rooks quickly. Whatever advantage exists is therefore White's.

> **9 ...**   **g6** *(D)*

This pawn move prevents White from placing his knight at f5, but it creates an organic weakness in Black's position, *one that is irremediable*. The squares f6 and h6, no longer guarded by the pawn, are weak *and remain so permanently*.

Notice that the pawn was induced but not forced to move forward. The mere threat of an inroad by the knight was enough to influence Black to make a natural preventive move. It is the sort of move nine out of ten players make automatically in similar situations, which is why it is important to know how to exploit its defects, for no move is weak unless proper advantage is taken of its flaws.

> **10 0-0**

No violence, please, until the reserves have been brought up. Blackburne used to say, "Never start an attack until your queen's rook is developed."

White secures the safety of his king and gets one rook out of hiding.

> **10 ...**   **c6**

Strengthens Black's pawn-centre and opens another avenue for his queen.

> **11 ♖ae1**

White seizes the only open file (since rooks belong on open files or on files likely to be opened) and pins the bishop.

It is worth noting that a pinned piece not only is unable to move but is also powerless to capture. *It does not protect any other pieces, since it is completely paralysed*. Hence it follows that not only is the bishop immobilized and in danger of its life (as it may be attacked again and again) but the knight that depends on it for protection is no longer secure. Briefly, Black is now threatened with loss of a piece by 12 ♗xf6.

> **11 ...**   **0-0** *(D)*

The king takes refuge in flight, incidentally unpinning the bishop and preserving his knight.

Spielmann's strategy to this point and the decisive combination that follows would have pleased Lasker, who once said, "In the beginning of the game ignore the search for combinations, abstain from violent moves. Aim for small advantages, accumulate them, and only after having attained these ends search for the combination – and then with all the power of will and intellect, because then the combination must exist, however deeply hidden."

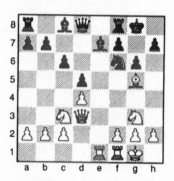

A glance shows that White has achieved the requisite positional superiority. If there is a combination to be evolved, it must be now, before Black has time to reorganize his pieces for defence. Now, while he has five pieces actively in play against two of Black's. Now, while he has an open file – enough! enough! The combination *must* be there!

Here is White's line of reasoning:

Black's advance of the g-pawn has deprived the knight of stable support. It is still guarded by two pieces, but *if the bishop were not there* it would be defended only once. In fact, *if the bishop were not there*, the knight would be pinned and subject to an enduring attack. *The bishop appears in both equations.* Obviously the bishop is the culprit, and it must be destroyed! And at once, before Black has time for 12...♗e6!

12 ♖xe7!!

"When we know about the inspiring ideas, how simple the sacrifices appear!" says Znosko-Borovsky.

12 ...   ♕xe7 (D)

Black must recapture, leaving the knight pinned and a fine target for further attack.

13 ♕f3

Putting pressure on the pinned piece, and threatening to take the knight.

13 ...   ♔g7 (D)

The king comes to the rescue of the knight. Against the alternative defence 13...♗f5 Spielmann had this pretty continuation: 14 ♘xf5 gxf5 15 ♕g3 (threatening mate on the move by 16 ♗xf6#) 15...♔g7 (or

15...♔h8 16 ♕h4 ♔g7 17 ♕h6+
♔g8 18 ♗xf6 and White wins) 16
♗xf6++ ♔xf6 17 ♕h4+ ♔e6 18
♖e1+ ♔d7 19 ♕xe7+ and all Black's
pieces come off.

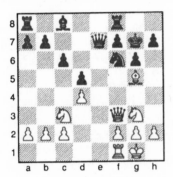

14   ♘ce4!
White must keep hammering at
the pinned knight, no matter how
many brilliant moves he has to find!
Again, White's immediate threat is
simple: 15 ♗xf6+, winning instantaneously.

14   ...   dxe4
Black must take this knight or
lose his own.

15   ♘xe4
Three pieces now attack the helpless knight. "Chess is not for the
kind-hearted," says the French prov-
erb.

White now threatens 16 ♗xf6+
followed by 17 ♗xe7.

15   ...   ♕e6
On 15...♕xe4 White has the pleasant choice of winning the queen by
16 ♗xf6+ (removing the protector
of the queen), followed by 17 ♕xe4,
or forcing mate by 16 ♕xf6+ ♔g8
17 ♗h6 followed by 18 ♕g7#.

In the last line of play, notice
how White screws his pieces firmly
into the two holes in Black's position, f6 and h6, the squares no longer
guarded by the g-pawn after its advance.

With his last move, Black saves
the queen. He is still ahead in material but has a lost game, as White's
pieces will insinuate themselves along
the dark squares to get at the king.

16   ♗xf6+
White regains a piece and limits
Black's king to two moves.

16   ...   ♔g8
If 16...♔h6, then 17 ♕f4+ and
mate next move.

17   ♕f4
Threatening a final invasion at h6
followed by mate at g7 – triumph on
the dark squares.

1-0
Black, powerless to prevent mate,
resigned.

Game 8
Przepiorka – Prokeš
Budapest 1929
Colle System

1   d4
One reason for the popularity of
queen's pawn openings is that from

the very first move they present
problems for the defender. There is
no method by which Black can seize

the initiative or even equalize in a hurry.

Despite its inherently positional nature, the queen's pawn appeals tremendously to attacking players and has always been a favourite weapon of such aggressive spirits as Alekhine, Keres, Pillsbury, Bogoljubow, Spielmann and Colle.

1   ...   ♘f6

Brings a piece into play where it has an influence on the centre. The knight move prevents White from continuing with 2 e4.

A master moves his knight to f6 as instinctively as he breathes.

2   ♘f3

The knight develops toward the centre, where he has the greatest freedom of action and the widest scope for his activities.

The knight possesses the peculiar property of being able to attack any other piece (except another knight) without being under attack in return. This attribute makes it a fascinating piece to manoeuvre about the board. Combinations involving play with the knights often have a ballet-like quality to them.

2   ...   e6

Black can avoid the general attack of the Colle by playing 2...d5, ready to reply to 3 e3 with 3...♗f5. Then 4 ♗d3 ♗xd3 exchanges bishops and Black rids himself of White's most dangerous attacking piece (in this form of the opening).

With his actual move, Black releases his f8-bishop and does not commit himself to any specific line of defence.

3   e3

Indicating his design: obviously White is preparing the typical Colle formation of bishop at d3 and knight at d2, to control the key e4-square, a jumping-off point for the pieces in this attack.

3   ...   d5

Black plants a pawn firmly in the centre but this move, in combination with 2...e6, does block in the c8-bishop.

4   ♗d3 (D)

White begins the concentration of pressure on e4, essential in the Colle. Generally speaking, it is a good plan to mobilize the pieces on the kingside first, to enable early castling on that side.

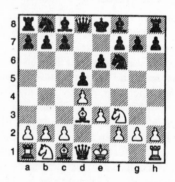

4   ...   c5

This move is almost indispensable in queen's pawn openings. It is important not to play ...♘c6 first, as Black's c-pawn must not be obstructed.

Black's move strikes at the centre and establishes a state of tension in that area.

5   c3

White reinforces the d-pawn. In the event of 5...cxd4, White can recapture with the e-pawn and open the diagonal for the c1-bishop.

It may seem that White's last move denies the b1-knight his best square, but in this form of attack the knight belongs at d2.

5 ...   ♘bd7 *(D)*

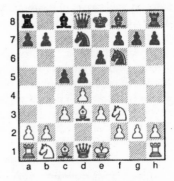

This is probably superior to placing the knight at c6. At d7, the knights are in touch with each other, so that if the f6-knight is exchanged the other can get to f6, an ideal square for attack or defence. At d7, the knight keeps clear of the c-file. The more open the file is, the more useful will it be for the queen or rook that occupies it. Finally, should White play 6 dxc5, the knight can recapture and come strongly into the game.

In queen's pawn openings, Black's queen's knight often does a better job at d7 than at c6.

6 ♘bd2

Intensifying the pressure on e4. To the uninitiated, White's development has an awkward look. The pieces seem to be in each other's way, but as will be seen they can spring into action smoothly and easily.

6 ...   ♗d6

More energetic than 6...♗e7, when the bishop is limited to defensive duties.

7 0-0

White secures the safety of his king before starting any decisive action. It is dangerous to open up the position and leave the king in the centre where it is exposed to a possible counterattack.

White's castling is aggressive in character as the king's rook plays an important role in the coming attack.

7 ...   0-0 *(D)*

Black's castling is a defensive measure. But why give the king's permanent address when White has revealed that he is preparing an assault on the kingside? It would be better strategy to keep the opponent in the dark – delay castling for a while and continue developing the pieces (which surely can do no harm). Black might bring his queen to c7, with a view to an early ...e5, and then fianchetto his c8-bishop (...b6, followed by ...♗b7).

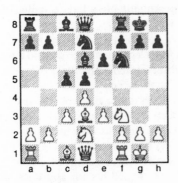

8 ♖e1

Still more pressure on e4! The rook gets a grip on the e-file; it is closed now but will be opened after White plays e4 and pawns are exchanged.

8 ...   ♛c7 (D)

An ideal location for the queen. From c7 the queen bears down on the centre, especially e5, and exerts great pressure on the c-file.

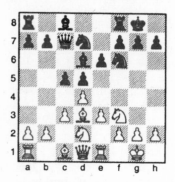

9 e4!

The key move in the Colle! With this move White intends to blast the position wide open and release all the stored-up energy of his pieces in a searing attack.

The immediate threat is 10 e5, a simple, brutal attack on two pieces.

9 ...   cxd4

As compensation for being on the defensive, Black controls the open c-file – temporarily.

10 cxd4

Better than taking with the knight, which lets Black place pieces on e5 and c5.

White meanwhile renews the threat of winning a piece by 11 e5.

10 ...   dxe4

Black parries the threat and saddles White with an isolated d-pawn. Such a pawn is especially vulnerable

to attack as it cannot be protected by another pawn, the nearest one being a couple of files away.

11 ♘xe4

Certainly not 11 ♗xe4 because 11...♘xe4 would be the response, and White loses the services of his valuable light-squared bishop. "As Rousseau could not compose without his cat beside him, so I without my king's bishop cannot play chess," says Tarrasch. "In its absence the game to me is lifeless and cold. The vitalizing factor is missing, and I can devise no plan of attack."

11 ...   b6

Intending to mobilize his c8-bishop. Somewhat more to the point was 11...♗f4 restraining one of White's menacing bishops.

12 ♗g5

The bishop joins the attack, and vacates the c1-square. The a1-rook will swing there, drive the queen off and assume complete control of a beautiful open file.

12 ...   ♘xe4

Apparently Black was afraid to play 12...♗b7 as the continuation 13 ♘xf6+ ♘xf6 14 ♗xf6 gxf6 breaks up his kingside pawn position.

13 ♖xe4!

Superior to the natural 13 ♗xe4, when Black might reply 13...♗b7 forcing 14 ♗d3 (to avoid exchanging bishops). Then he could continue 14...♗xf3 15 ♛xf3 ♗xh2+ consoling himself with a pawn for his troubles.

13 ...   ♗b7 (D)

There is hardly anything better than this, which offers the bishop a long diagonal. If, for example, Black plays 13...♘f6, then 14 ♖h4 is hard to meet. Then the threat of winning a pawn by 15 ♗xf6 gxf6 16 ♗xh7+ could not be parried by 14...h6 as 15 ♗xf6 gxf6 16 ♖xh6 still wins a pawn.

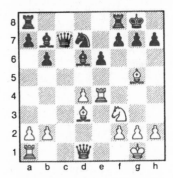

14 ♖c1!

A fine 'in-between' move! The rook is developed effectively on the open file, while the queen is banished to the first rank. There she interferes with the a8-rook, preventing its development for a long time – forever, as it turns out!

14 ...   **♕b8**

There is nothing else as 14...♗xe4 15 ♖xc7 ♗xf3 16 ♕xf3 ♗xc7 17 ♕c6 wins a piece for White.

15 ♖h4!

The point! White's threat of 16 ♗xh7+ forces one of the pawns in front of the king to move forward. White gets an advantage, no matter which pawn advances, as:

Every pawn move loosens the defending structure.

Every undefended square (occasioned by such an advance) creates a weakness in the position.

15 ...   **g6 (D)**

If Black tries defending the h-pawn by 15...♘f6, then 16 ♗xf6 gxf6 17 ♗xh7+ wins the pawn just the same. Or if Black advances the h-pawn by 15...h6, then 16 ♗xh6 gxh6 17 ♖xh6 is an obvious sacrificial combination which shatters the cordon of pawns and exposes the king to a mating attack.

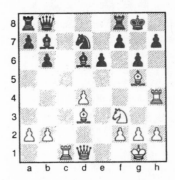

After the text-move, White has accomplished what he set out to do: he has forced the advance of the g-pawn. But how does he exploit the resulting weakness? Is there an attack against the pawn? Apparently there isn't, as in order to strike at it with the h-pawn, he must move the rook out of the way, and then play h4 and h5, a process which takes time and achieves little.

What other line is there? Sacrifice a piece for the g-pawn? Obviously this is useless, as White still does not break through.

But the pawn did advance, and *there is a weakness somewhere.* We know this fact to be true, and *in this fact there must be the clue to the winning combination.*

The pawn's advance weakened the squares h6 and f6, as they are no longer guarded by the pawn. This means that White must try to get control of these squares, either seize and occupy them with his pieces, or use them as a means of penetrating into the enemy camp.

But wait! Doesn't Black's knight still guard the f6-square? Indeed it does, and this knowledge provides us with the information we need. The knight is the guardian of the dark squares, and the knight must be destroyed!

16 ♗b5!

Attacks the knight, which strangely enough has no place to escape to!

16 ...   ♛e8

What other way is there to protect the knight?

If 16...♗c8, then 17 ♗c6 wins the exchange.

If 16...♗xf3 17 ♛xf3 ♛e8, then 18 ♛b7 wins a piece.

After the actual move, the knight is pinned and a good target for further attack.

17 ♘e5

In chess you may hit a man when he's down.

17 ...   ♗c8

No better is 17...♗xe5 18 dxe5 (uncovering the queen's attack on the knight) 18...♗c8 (or 18...♗d5) 19 ♖c7, when the miserable creature must perish.

18 ♖xc8!

Taking the props out from under the knight! The technique is simple: if you cannot increase the pressure on a piece, see if you can dispose of one of its defenders.

18 ...   ♛xc8

Certainly not 18...♖xc8, when 19 ♗xd7 wins two pieces for a rook, and then corners the queen!

19 ♗xd7

White has two pieces for the rook – and the attack!

19 ...   ♛c7

Not 19...♛b7 or 19...♛b8, as 20 ♗c6 wins the exchange. The alternative was 19...♛a6, but Black hopes for some counterplay on the c-file.

20 ♘g4!

The first step toward exploiting the weak dark squares brings with it a threat of mate by 21 ♘f6+ ♚h8 (21...♚g7 is the same) 22 ♖xh7#.

20 ...   h5 *(D)*

The king needs lots of room. The freeing attempt by 20...f5 loses to 21 ♗xe6+ ♚h8 (21...♚g7 22 ♗h6+ wins the exchange) 22 ♘f6 and resistance is hopeless.

21 ♘f6+

The knight comes in on one of the critical dark squares to strike the first blow.

21 ...   ♚g7

If 21...♚h8, then 22 ♖xh5+ forces a quick mate.

22 ᐤxh5+

Sacrificing the knight to sweep away the pawns shielding the enemy king.

22 ... gxh5

Black must take the knight, because White mates after 22...♔g8 (or 22...♔h7) 23 ᐤf6+ ♔g7 24 ♖h7#.

23 ♕xh5

The queen's first move threatens two immediate mates on the h-file.

23 ... ♖h8

The only move to stop mate – temporarily.

24 ♗h6+ 1-0

Appropriately enough, White administers the *coup de grâce* on the second critical dark square.

Mate follows in two moves.

Game 9
Znosko-Borovsky – Mackenzie
Weston-super-Mare 1924
Ruy Lopez

1 e4

This first move occupies the centre with a pawn and frees four squares for the queen and five for the f1-bishop. One of the reasons many players prefer 1 e4 to any other opening move is that it gets the kingside pieces rolling quickly, enabling early castling on that side.

1 ... e5

In the old days this was almost compulsory. It indicated that you were willing to stand toe-to-toe and slug it out. Only a coward would avoid 1...e5 and a possible gambit by White.

Objectively considered, the text-move is perhaps Black's strongest response. It challenges possession of the centre and prevents White from monopolizing it by continuing 2 d4.

2 ᐤf3

What happens if White persists and plays 2 d4? The reply 2...exd4 leads to 3 ♕xd4 ᐤc6 4 ♕e3 ᐤf6, when Black has two pieces in play to

one of White's. This amounts to taking the initiative away from White early in the game.

The text-move is far more effective than random development of the knight, for instance at h3, where it is out of touch with affairs in the centre, or at e2, where it blocks all traffic.

2 ... ᐤc6

The logical way to meet the attack on the pawn; a minor piece develops toward the centre and defends the pawn.

The general plan of mobilization is to establish a pawn in the centre, develop the minor pieces (the knights before bishops, whenever feasible), then castle to get the rooks to the centre files, and finally bring the queen out – but not too far from home. Premature development of the queen is dangerous, as it is subject to annoying attacks by pawns and minor pieces.

3 ♗b5 *(D)*

The most natural move on the board: White strikes at the defender of the pawn he attacks. It is true that he cannot win the pawn at once, as after 4 ♗xc6 dxc6 5 ♘xe5 ♕d4 Black regains the pawn, but the pressure on Black is constant, and the threat is always in the air.

The Ruy Lopez is probably the strongest of all kingside openings. White has more to say in the centre, since he will be able to play d4 without much trouble, while Black will find it difficult to achieve ...d5.

White's pieces have more room to move around in, while Black's game is considerably cramped in many variations.

3   ...   a6

This can become like the story *The House that Jack Built*: the pawn attacks the bishop that attacks the knight that defends the pawn that the knight attacks.

Black's purpose is to dislodge the bishop from its favourable position. The loss of time involved in moving a pawn is compensated for by the fact that the threatened bishop must also lose a move in retreating.

4   ♗a4

This is in the spirit of the opening as it maintains pressure on the knight. The alternative withdrawal to c4 is inferior, as the same position could have arisen after the move 3 ♗c4, except that here Black has the additional move ...a6, which can only be to his benefit.

4   ...   ♘f6

Black develops a piece, attacks a pawn and prepares early kingside castling. More could hardly be expected of one move.

5   0-0 (D)

White brings his king to safety and swings the rook over toward the centre files.

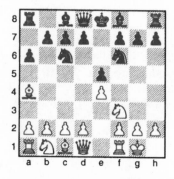

5   ...   ♗e7

A favourite continuation with many players is 5...♘xe4, not with the idea of winning a pawn, as White regains it easily, but in order to obtain a free, open game. The danger in this line is that it leaves Black's position in the centre somewhat insecure.

The text leads to a more blocked position, difficult to break through, but requires patience on Black's part.

The bishop's development at e7 is satisfactory even though it has moved only one square away from home. The important thing is that it has left the back rank and facilitated castling.

6 ♖e1

White brings his rook toward the centre. In lieu of an open file, the rook prepares to take command of a file liable to be opened. In guarding his own e-pawn, White renews the threat of 7 ♗xc6 dxc6 8 ♘xe5 winning a pawn.

The rook's move is preferable to developing the b1-knight to c3. White may want to provide a retreat for his bishop by c3, guarding it against an exchange.

6 ... b5

White meets the threat by forcing the bishop back.

7 ♗b3

Obviously the only move.

7 ... d6 *(D)*

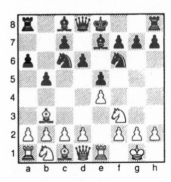

Black protects the e-pawn, releases the c8-bishop and prepares 8...♘a5 to remove the troublesome enemy bishop.

At first glance it seems illogical to give one bishop freedom while hemming in the other, but since the dark-squared bishop does a good job at e7, it remains for the light-squared bishop to go out into the world.

8 c3

With two objects:
- To provide refuge for the bishop against an attempt to remove it by 8...♘a5.
- To support an advance of the d-pawn, establishing a strong pawn-centre.

8 ... ♘a5

Not so much to strike at the bishop as to make way for 9...c5 to dispute control of the central squares. In this line of the Lopez, Black's best counter-chances lie in action on the queenside.

9 ♗c2

Naturally, White wants to keep both bishops. He loses a tempo, but it is offset by Black's posting of a knight at the side of the board.

9 ... c5 *(D)*

Black intensifies his pressure on the central square d4 and provides an egress (as the old books used to say) for the queen.

10 d4

One of the chief objectives in king's pawn openings is to advance *the d-pawn* to the centre as soon as circumstances permit, just as in queen's pawn openings it is desirable to get *the e-pawn* to e4 when there is an opportunity to do so.

White again threatens to win the e-pawn by the double attack on it.

10 ... ♛c7

Black gives his pawn further support and develops his queen at the same time. It would not do to exchange by 10...exd4 11 cxd4 cxd4 12 ♘xd4 as it surrenders the centre and leaves Black with an isolated centre pawn. "An isolated pawn," says Tartakower, "casts gloom over the entire chessboard." White would benefit too in that his knight, standing firmly in the centre of the board, could not be dislodged by unfriendly pawns.

11 h3 *(D)*

To prevent the pin ...♝g4, which might embarrass the knight and the piece it shields, the queen. Both pieces are needed for the protection of the d-pawn and the maintenance of the pawn formation in the centre.

An exchange of the white knight by ...♝xf3, and the recapture by the queen, removes at one stroke two supports of the d-pawn.

Is White violating principle in moving one of the pawns near his king? Maybe, but one must know when to slight conventions as well as observe them. In this particular situation it is important to prevent an attack on the knight, its subsequent exchange and the break-up of White's pawns in the centre. The move of the h-pawn is weakening, but a lesser evil than would result from permitting the pin. But wait a moment! Is it a weakening move if Black is unable to benefit by it? Is it detrimental to the position if Black cannot exploit it by a kingside attack?

The answer is no! A move is weak only if the opponent can turn its imperfections to his advantage. The entire position is strong or weak *only in relation to the position of the opponent*. In this case, the move of the h-pawn is expedient as it conforms to the requirements of the specific position.

11 ... ♘c6

The knight returns and adds weight to the pressure on the d-pawn.

Black threatens a series of exchanges by 12...exd4 13 cxd4 cxd4, resulting in the gain of a pawn, as the further sequence 14 ♘xd4? ♘xd4 15 ♛xd4 ♛xc2 would cost White a piece. Black hopes to tempt White into playing 12 d5 to meet this threat. This looks good, as it would evict the c6-knight from a good post, but it has the drawback (for White) of releasing the tension in the centre, as well as making d5 unavailable for the use of his pieces.

12 ♗e3

White is in no hurry. He brings aid to the d-pawn by developing another piece.

12 ...   0-0 *(D)*

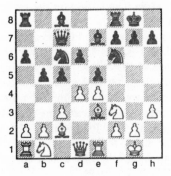

Removing the king to safer quarters and pressing the rook into active service.

13 ♘bd2

This knight has been developed where he has little mobility and seems to have no future to speak of, but *it is the first step that counts*. Little as this is, its consequence is worth emphasizing:

The knight's move clears the first rank and enables the major pieces (the queen and the rooks) to get in touch with each other.

Get your pieces off the back rank and into active play!

13 ...   ♗d7

Black does likewise: his bishop vacates the back row to let the rooks come to the centre files.

The rooks are powerful pieces and must not be shut in.

14 ♖c1

In the early stages of the game, the rooks may not do much but they must be ready for action when it comes. This they best do by placing themselves at the head of open files. If none are available, then they should work on partly open files. If none of those exist, the rooks should still be brought toward the centre, as those files are most likely to be opened. But in any case, *get the rooks out of the corners!*

14 ...   ♘e8 *(D)*

Planning to advance the f-pawn. This pawn will dispute the centre with White's e-pawn while opening the f-file for the rook.

15 ♘f1

The knight retreats to gain momentum for a leap to g3 and then f5, a beautiful outpost.

15 ...   g6

Not only to keep the knight out but also to support 16...f5, a thrust at the centre.

The advance of the g-pawn weakens the squares f6 and h6, as they are no longer guarded by the pawn. This may strike the average player as an interesting but perhaps insignificant point, but recognizing a weakness and knowing how to take advantage of it marks the master player. Good players do not win games by waiting for you to make monumental mistakes. They don't expect you to leave pieces *en prise*.

16 ♗h6

White immediately anchors a piece on one of the vulnerable kingside squares.

16 ... ♘g7

The only move to prevent loss of the exchange by 17 ♗xf8.

17 ♘e3 (D)

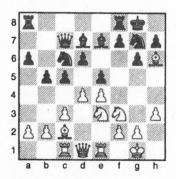

The knight comes back into the game by a slightly different route than was planned earlier. Not only does it add to the pressure on d5 but it also threatens to settle down powerfully on that square.

17 ... ♖ae8

Black could not stop the knight coming in by 17...♗e6, as 18 d5 in reply wins a piece.

He also abandons the contemplated break by 17...f5, as it opens the position, and open lines favour the player whose development is

superior and who is better equipped to use these lines in an attack.

With his actual move, Black tries to keep a tightly knit defensive position, one that is difficult to break through.

18 ♘d5!

A very fine move whose object is more profound than the obvious one of fixing a piece on a strong central square.

18 ... ♕b7

The queen must flee from the knight's attack.

19 ♘xe7+!

This is the point! The knight gives up his good position for a worthy cause. It is important, in order to capitalize on the weakness of the dark square f6, to remove the guardian of this square, the dark-squared bishop on e7. With this bishop out of the way the weakness is accentuated and White can then consider some means of invading, and then fastening a piece, on the critical square.

19 ... ♖xe7

This is forced, as 19...♘xe7 20 dxe5 dxe5 21 ♘xe5 costs a pawn.

20 dxc5

The purpose of this exchange is to open a nice long file for the queen.

20 ... dxc5

Black must recapture or lose a pawn.

21 ♕d6

Beautiful exploitation of the open d-file! The attack on the c-pawn gains a tempo toward the queen's entry at f6.

21 ... c4

Black must lose a move in saving this pawn.

22 ♕f6! *(D)*

With this move, which incidentally threatens instant mate, White fastens another piece in the holes in Black's position created by the move ...g6. White's advantage is decisive and the winning procedure should be what the books call 'a matter of technique'. The process of realizing his advantage is an interesting one.

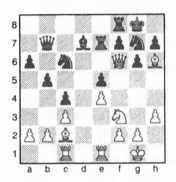

22 ... ♞h5

Black stops the mate and attempts to drive the queen away.

23 ♕h4

It would be a mistake to play 23 ♕g5 as Black, instead of moving his threatened rook on f8, would first play 23...f6, banishing the queen completely from his premises.

23 ... ♞g7

The knight blocks the bishop's attack on the rook and is prepared to counter 24 ♕f6 by 24...♞h5, repeating the device of harassing the enemy queen.

How does White continue, to force a win?

24 ♗e3! *(D)*

By rearranging his pieces and bringing up the reserves!

This first move in the new formation gains time by the threat of 25 ♗c5 winning the exchange.

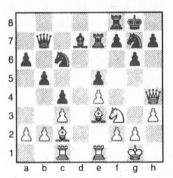

24 ... ♞e6

The only way to prevent 25 ♗c5, after which White completely dominates the dark squares.

25 ♕f6

Once more into the breach! Black cannot save the game by repeating moves, since after 25...♞g7 26 ♗c5 ♖e6 (or 26...♞h5 27 ♕h4, and White wins the exchange) 27 ♕h4 ♖fe8 28 ♞g5 the threat of mate will win the rook at e6.

25 ... ♕c7

Black must hang on to the valuable e-pawn.

26 ♗h6

Once again White has his ideal position, with pieces firmly planted in the holes near Black's king. It will be hard for Black to chase them off as he does not have the earlier resource of ...♞h5.

26 ... ♖c8

The rook must flee the bishop's attack. Interposing the knight instead is of course a blunder as mate follows instantaneously.

27 Rcd1 *(D)*

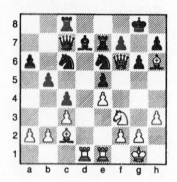

Before proceeding to the final attack, White gets a stronger grip on the position by seizing the open d-file. The next step (since Black must wait helplessly) is 28 Rd5, attacking the e-pawn a third time and threatening to double rooks on the file. This ought to be enough to beat down resistance if no quicker win is available.

Note that White has not embarked on dubious long-range combinations. His plan, in most cases aimed at increasing his positional superiority, is made *for a few moves only.* Don't believe all those stories you hear of chess masters analysing intricate combinations with dozens of variations for thirty moves ahead. They don't do this because they don't have to! It is far easier and more to the point to look only a few moves ahead and try to maintain at least an equal game at every stage. Winning by accumulating small advantages is more consistent with a common-sense approach than to seek to overwhelm the opponent with bewildering combinations and venturesome sacrificial

attacks. Strengthening one's own position gradually while undermining that of the opponent is more important than indulging in fruitless speculative fancies.

27 ... Ree8

Black's idea is to reduce the pressure by offering an exchange of queens. White will then either have to acquiesce to the exchange, or withdraw his queen.

28 Nh2!

A very fine move! The knight, which seemed well posted at f3, is re-routed to augment the pressure on the dark squares.

28 ... Qd8

Continuing the plan of evicting White's queen from his camp.

29 Ng4!

White supports his queen and is ready, in the event of an exchange of queens, to maintain a tight grip on the dark squares. If Black plays 29...Qxf6, then 30 Nxf6+ Kh8 31 Rxd7 wins a piece for White.

29 ... Qe7

This does not help, but there is no way to save the game: if 29...Re7, then 30 Be3 (threatening 31 Nh6+ Kf8 32 Qh8#) 30...Ree8 31 Nh6+ Kf8 32 Qxf7#.

30 Qxe7

The simplest. If no mate is in sight, the modern master dispenses with the fireworks. Dawdling is for dilettantes, so he simplifies and cuts down any chance of resistance. After 30...Rxe7 31 Nf6+ Kh8 32 Rxd7 White wins a piece, giving Black no opportunity to complicate the ending.

1-0

Game 10
Tarrasch – Eckart
Nuremberg 1889
French Defence

1 e4

This opening move makes an outlet for two pieces, the queen and light-squared bishop. It does more than that.

It frees a square for the king and gives an extra one to the g1-knight. It is true that the knight is best developed at f3, but there are times when it is expedient to bring it to e2 – perhaps to reach f5 by way of g3. It is just as well to add to the knight's freedom of movement, if no time is lost thereby. As to the king, there's no harm in letting him have a bit more breathing space too. Many a king has been smothered by a lack of consideration, or by carelessness.

Consider this case history, from a minor tournament: **McGrouther-McCann**, *Dundee 1893*: **1 e4 c5 2 ♘f3 ♘c6 3 d4 cxd4 4 ♘xd4 e5 5 ♘f5 ♘ge7 6 ♘d6#** (1-0).

And if this seems farfetched, here is another specimen, again in a minor tournament: **Arnold-Böhm**, *Munich 1932*: **1 e4 c6 2 d4 d5 3 ♘c3 dxe4 4 ♘xe4 ♘d7 5 ♕e2 ♘gf6 6 ♘d6#** (1-0).

1 ... e6

Though less aggressive than 1...e5, this move does release two pieces and has the advantage of restricting White's choice of attack. White no longer has the whole range of Open Games at his disposal, and he is less able to steer the game into highly

tactical channels by adopting an opening such as the King's Gambit.

The French Defence conceals a great deal of potential dynamic energy and is a fine weapon against an over-enthusiastic attacking player. Black's position is not easily assaulted despite its cramped appearance.

2 d4

As strong as it is natural. Of this pawn formation, Staunton, in the nineteenth century, said, "It is generally advantageous for your pawns to occupy the middle of the board, because when there they greatly retard the movements of the opposing forces. The e-pawn and the d-pawn at their fourth squares are well posted, but it is not easy to maintain them in that position, and if you are driven to advance one of them, the power of both is much diminished."

2 ... d5

Black attacks the e-pawn while giving his queen more mobility.

It is important to dispute control of the centre.

3 ♘d2

White has two reasons for developing the knight at d2:
• He wants to avoid the knight being pinned, as might occur after 3 ♘c3.
• He is prepared, in the event of an attack on his d-pawn by ...c5, to reply c3, supporting the centre.

Should pawns be exchanged on d4, he recaptures with the c-pawn and keeps a pawn in the centre.

It is true that his c1-bishop is blocked, but this condition is only temporary. *Pieces can get out of each other's way.*

3 ...   ♘f6 (D)

If followed up correctly, there is nothing wrong with this move. The idea is that by attacking the e4-pawn, Black aims to force this pawn forward to e5. As Staunton explained above, once White's two central pawns do not stand abreast, his whole central structure is weakened.

An alternative and equally good plan was to fight for control of the centre by 3...c5, incidentally permitting his queen the use of another diagonal and access to the queenside.

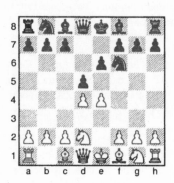

4 e5

Why does White disregard Staunton's advice about keeping two pawns on the fourth rank? He knows that the pawn may be weaker at e5, but he weighs strengths and weaknesses. At e5 the pawn drives the knight away from its most useful post and sends it off to another

square where it interferes with the free movements of Black's other pieces.

Clearly, the value of this or any other move is arrived at by balancing the benefits it confers against any disadvantages that might accrue.

4 ...   ♘fd7

Just about the only move left. On 4...♘e4, White plays 5 ♘xe4 dxe4 and then has the pleasant choice between 6 ♗c4 and 6 ♗e3. In both cases White controls more space and has free development for his pieces. Black, on the other hand, has to worry about his pawn on e4, which is disconnected from the rest of his forces and extremely vulnerable to attack.

5 ♗d3 (D)

White gets his kingside pieces rolling to facilitate early castling on that side.

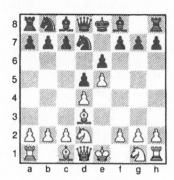

5 ...   c5

Very good, as Black must not delay in trying to free his constricted position. The pawn move strikes at the centre and opens another path for Black's queen.

6 c3

Ready to reply to 6...cxd4 with 7 cxd4, and preserve the pawn-chain, which so cramps the enemy.

    6   ...   ♘**c6** *(D)*

The knight develops with tempo, as the d-pawn is now twice attacked.

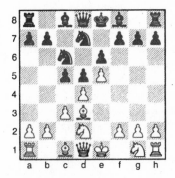

    7 ♘e2!

One of those rare times when the knight belongs here instead of at f3. It is true that f3 should be occupied by a knight, and White will arrange to have one there. His plan is to swing the knight from d2 to f3, meanwhile freeing his c1-bishop.

    7 ...   ♕**b6**

Black puts more pressure on the white d-pawn, threatening to win it by 8...cxd4 9 cxd4 ♘xd4 10 ♘xd4 ♕xd4.

    8 ♘f3

A clever knight shift protects the pawn and clears the decks for the dark-squared bishop's appearance.

    8 ...   ♗**e7**

Another plausible move, but far too passive. Black's position is cramped by the chain of enemy pawns on d4 and e5, and he should not allow this situation to persist. He must try to break White's grip on the centre to

obtain more space for his pieces. The correct continuation was 8...cxd4 9 cxd4 f6, virtually forcing 10 exf6 ♘xf6. Then the problem with the d7-knight blocking in the c8-bishop has been resolved, and the disappearance of the e5-pawn means that Black has gained the d6-square for the development of his dark-squared bishop. If Black does not take the necessary liberating action, then he is likely to be gradually squeezed to death. Such a fate befell even so great a player as Capablanca in his game with Alekhine at AVRO 1938. As a consequence of his inferior opening play, Capablanca was tied up so badly that he could not stir and that he resigned with nearly all his pieces still on the board.

    9 0-0

The king must be spirited off to a safer spot before any violent action is undertaken.

    9 ...   **0-0** *(D)*

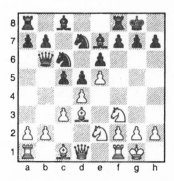

Black is still playing mechanical chess, unconscious of possible danger. With this move he misses the last chance of striking at the pawn chain by 9...f6.

10   ♘f4!

Definitely putting an end to any possibility of disturbing the line-up of pawns, as 10...f6 is refuted by 11 ♘xe6, while 10...cxd4 11 cxd4 ♘xd4 12 ♘xd4 ♕xd4 13 ♗xh7+, uncovering an attack on the queen, is unthinkable.

10   ...   ♘d8

Black recognizes at last that his pieces will remain impotent until he rids the board of White's annoying e-pawn. He therefore protects his own e-pawn so that he can enforce 11...f6 and break up White's pawn formation.

11   ♕c2

Creating an obvious threat to the black h-pawn. The profound purpose of the move is to compel one of the pawns near the king to move forward.

The advance of any pawn around the king loosens the defensive structure and results in a permanent weakening which can be exploited, while the pawn that made the forward step itself often becomes a target for direct attack.

11   ...   f5

What choice is there? If Black plays 11...h6 or 11...g6, he can never afterward play ...f6 without making the g6-square vulnerable to invasion by White's pieces or the focal point of a sacrificial attack that would demolish his kingside.

12   exf6

This relaxes the bind on Black, but it opens up lines for an attack. Open lines favour the player whose development is superior and whose pieces enjoy greater mobility.

12   ...   ♘xf6

Not only to get the knight back into the game but also to defend his h-pawn, which again was threatened.

13   ♘g5

Once more attacking the pawn, this time including a threat of 14 ♗xh7+ ♚h8 (14...♘xh7 15 ♕xh7#) 15 ♘g6#.

13   ...   g6 (D)

Forced, as 13...h6 saves the pawn but allows the mate.

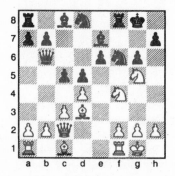

With the advance of the g-pawn, a target comes into view at which White can direct his attack. He can visualize a decisive blow, one that will wreck Black's entire defensive structure!

14   ♗xg6!

This sacrifice must be accepted, as otherwise Black will be a pawn down with nothing to show for it but a shattered position. If he tries 14...h6, then 15 ♗h7+ ♚g7 16 ♕g6+ ♚h8 17 ♕xh6, and the threat of mate by the knight as well as the danger of discovered check is too much to withstand.

14   ...   hxg6

One lone pawn remains of the three which surrounded the king, and even that one is not long for this world.

15 ♕xg6+

With this dramatic entrance on the scene, the queen, attended by her two knights, will quickly force submission.

15 ...   ♔h8

The only move.

16 ♕h6+

Clearing the g6-square for the knight.

16 ...   ♔g8

Interposing the knight instead allows mate on the move.

17 ♘g6   1-0

The threats of mate by 18 ♕h8# or 18 ♘xe7# cannot both be parried.

Game 11
Flohr – Pitschak
Bilin 1930
Colle System

1 d4

In chess, unlike tennis, you cannot win by serving an ace. There is no trick move in the opening that will catch even a fair-to-middling player off-balance.

What you can do is apply order and method in your conduct of this phase, so as to increase your chances of getting a favourable position. All you need do is follow a few simple rules for sound development:

- Begin with 1 e4 or 1 d4, either of which moves releases two pieces.
- Anchor at least one pawn in the centre and give it solid support. Pawns in the centre keep enemy pieces from settling themselves on the best squares.
- Wherever feasible, bring out your knights before the bishops. Broadly speaking, the knights do their best work at f3 and c3 (f6 and c6 when Black), where their power is tremendous for defence as well as offence.

- Of two developing moves, select the more aggressive one. Develop with a threat if you can.
- Move each piece only once in the opening. Place it at once on a square where it has some bearing on the centre and where it has the greatest scope for attack.
- Move at most two pawns in the early stages of the game. *Play with the pieces*.
- Develop the pieces with a view to controlling the centre, either by occupying it or bearing down on it from a distance, as fianchettoed bishops do.
- Develop the queen, but close to home to avoid her being harassed by pawns and minor pieces.
- Do not chase after pawns at the expense of development.
- Secure the safety of the king by early castling, preferably on the kingside.

Capablanca summed all this up when he said, "The main thing is to develop the pieces quickly: get them into play as fast as you can."

Now back to Flohr and Pitschak:

White's first move fixes a pawn in the centre and liberates two pieces.

1   ...   ♘f6

Black brings his king's knight out to its most favourable post and hinders White from continuing with 2 e4.

2   ♘f3

Napier recalls that in the first of several lessons he took from Steinitz, the World Champion said, "No doubt you move your knight out on each side before the bishop? And do you know why?" Napier says he was stuck for an intelligent answer. Steinitz went on to explain: "One good reason is that you know where the knight belongs before you know that much of your bishop; certainty is a far better friend than doubt."

2   ...   e6

Black postpones the straightforward reply 2...d5, which lets him in for the regular lines of the Queen's Gambit. Meanwhile he opens a line for the f8-bishop.

3   ♘bd2

A typical knight manoeuvre in the Colle Attack: the knight puts pressure on the critical e4-square without blocking the c-file.

3   ...   c5

Black strikes a blow at the d-pawn in an attempt to secure control of the centre. This flank thrust is almost compulsory in queen's pawn openings because Black must try to disturb White's central formation.

The immediate threat is 4...cxd4, so that the recapture by 5 ♘xd4

leaves no white pawn remaining in the centre.

4   e3

White shores up the d-pawn and provides an outlet for the f1-bishop.

4   ...   b6 (D)

Black too props up his advanced pawn and prepares to fianchetto the c8-bishop.

5   ♗d3

Customary practice in this system of attack: the bishop adds his strength to the pressure exerted on e4 in preparation for an advance by the e-pawn, which will open up lines of attack for the pieces in the background. The bishop also aims at Black's h-pawn, a fine target after the enemy king castles on that side.

5   ...   ♗b7

This solves one of Black's chief problems in queen's pawn openings – an effective disposition of the light-squared bishop. By means of this fianchetto arrangement, the bishop commands the longest diagonal on the board and participates in the fight for domination of e4, the strategic square in the Colle System.

6   0-0

As part of the process of development, White shields his king from danger and brings his rook closer to the centre files.

6 ...　　　　　♗e7

Despite its modest appearance, there is a great deal of latent energy in the placement of this bishop at e7. It is close enough to home to help defend the king, yet easily manoeuvrable to a more aggressive post if occasion requires.

7 c4 (D)

More in the spirit of the Colle formation is the quiet 7 c3 to supply a support for the d4-pawn. The e-pawn is then free to advance, and if Black at any time plays ...cxd4, White recaptures with the c-pawn and maintains a strong pawn in the centre.

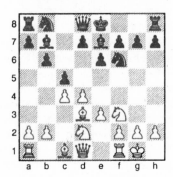

The idea of the text-move apparently is to prevent Black's pieces from using d5 as a pivot for their movements about the board.

7 ...　　　　　0-0

Black goes quietly about the business of mustering out all the troops. At one stroke his rook appears on the scene while the king is whisked away.

8 b3

Clearly in order to develop the bishop at b2. This fianchettoing of the bishop is not conventional procedure in the Colle, but Flohr may have wanted to test some ideas of his own.

8 ...　　　　　d5

Black seizes the opportunity to dispute possession of the centre. He also puts an end to White's contemplated advance of the e-pawn, as he bears down on the critical e4-square with knight, pawn and bishop, while White has only two pieces trained on it.

It is true that the b7-bishop's diagonal is blocked, but this condition is only temporary.

9 ♕c2 (D)

Considerably better was the simple development of the dark-squared bishop at b2, which he prepared with his previous move.

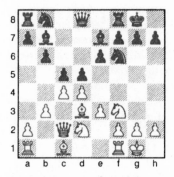

The purpose of 9 ♕c2 is to secure control of e4 and to prevent Black from establishing an outpost on that square by 9...♘e4. The trouble with the move is that it permits Black to seize the initiative and thereafter direct the course of events.

9 ...   ♘c6

A powerful move which combines development, aggressive intent and prophylaxis!

Development, in that the knight is placed at once on its most suitable square.

Aggression, in the knight's threat to advance to b4, attacking queen and bishop and forcing an exchange which rids the board of White's dangerous light-squared bishop.

Prophylaxis, in the prevention of 10 e4, the continuation after which would be 10...♘b4 11 ♕c3 ♘xd3 12 ♕xd3 dxe4, and Black wins a piece.

10 a3

White must preserve his valuable light-squared bishop.

Unfortunately, the time lost in being forced to make a pawn move is costly, as we shall see.

10 ...   cxd4 (D)

Black exchanges to clarify the position in the centre and to open the c-file for the convenience of his a8-rook.

11 cxd5

The alternative capture 11 exd4 was unpleasant as the reply 11...dxc4

forces 12 ♕xc4 (otherwise White's d-pawn is lost), when 12...♖c8 exercises uncomfortable pressure on White's centre. Another possibility instead of the text-move is 11 ♘xd4 ♘xd4 12 exd4 dxc4 13 ♕xc4 (to save the d-pawn) 13...♖c8 14 ♕a4 ♗c6 15 ♕xa7 (or 15 ♕c4 ♗xg2 and Black wins easily) 15...♖a8 and Black wins the queen.

11 ...   ♕xd5

Black nets a pawn with this and (as if it were not enough) takes over the attack.

The queen is in no danger, as White's pieces are not sufficiently well developed to cause her any inconvenience.

12 exd4

White opens the position to get some counterplay; he hopes to utilize the e-file for his rook and the e4-square as a pivot for his pieces.

Instead the superficially attractive 12 e4 does not accomplish much, as after 12...♕h5 the vital e4-square is occupied by a pawn, making it unavailable for the manoeuvring of pieces, while Black benefits in having an extra passed pawn on the d-file.

12 ...   ♘xd4

This attack on the queen gains time as White must lose a move with his queen.

13 ♕b1

Obviously 13 ♘xd4 would not do, as Black's queen pounces down with instantaneous mate, while 13 ♕b2 ♘xf3+ 14 ♘xf3 ♕xd3 costs a piece. On 13 ♕c3, Black continues 13...♖fd8 followed by 14...♖ac8, and again the queen must flee.

White's actual move is probably the least of the evils.

13 ...   Ïfd8

Intensifying the pressure along the d-file and particularly on the bishop, whose life is threatened by 14...Øxf3+ 15 Øxf3 Ôxd3 16 Ôxd3 Ïxd3.

14 Øe1 (D)

White protects his bishop as well as the vulnerable g-pawn.

Against 14 Ôc2 Black can choose from these themes:

1) Simplification (being a pawn ahead), by 14...Øxc2.

2) Stepping up the pressure by 14...Ïac8, banishing the c2-bishop to the first rank.

3) Combination, by 14...Øe2+ 15 êh1 Ôa6 (threatening to win the exchange by 16...Øc3) 16 Ïe1 Øg4 17 Øe4 Ôxe4! 18 Ôxe4 Øxf2#.

14 ...   Ôh5!

There is no direct threat in this queen move, but Black threatens to threaten! He intends to storm White's citadel of pawns with his queen supported by a minor piece, for instance by 15...Ôd6 or 15...Øg4. This would compel one of the pawns to leave its base and create weaknesses that Black could exploit. The advanced pawn itself might be susceptible to attack, or avenues might be opened leading to the king.

This chipping away at the foundation is an interesting process for rendering an apparently strongly fortified position vulnerable to assault.

15 Ôb2

White has no dependable defence (especially against nebulous threats) so continues to develop his pieces. The more he has in play, the better his chances of surviving the coming storm.

15 ...   Ôd6

With a simple but unmistakable threat: mate on the move!

How does White defend?

1) 16 Øef3 Øxf3+ 17 Øxf3 Ôxf3 18 gxf3 Ôxh2#.

2) 16 f4 Ôc5 (threatening the deadly 17...Øe2++ 18 êh1 Øg3#) 17 êh1 Øg4 18 h3 Ôxh3+ and mate next move.

3) 16 h3 Ôe5 (again aiming for mate at h2) 17 g3 Ôd5 (now trying for 18...Ôh1#) 18 f3 Ôg5, and White's game falls to pieces.

16 g3

By a process of elimination, the only defence, if one still exists.

16 ...   Øg4

White's g-pawn has been compelled to step forward; now the threat of 17...Ôxh2# forces the h-pawn's advance.

17 h4 (D)

White has no other move than this, which keeps the queen out – or does it?

17 ...   ♕xh4!

This is brilliant! Not because of the fact that the queen is offered, but because it brings to an appropriate climax the systematic exploitation of pawn weaknesses cleverly brought into being.

Black introduces two threats of mate in one, at h1 and h2.

0-1

After 18 gxh4 the reply 18...♗h2# would come quick as a flash.

Game 12
Pitschak – Flohr
Liebwerda 1934
English Opening

1   c4

Despite the fact that only one piece is freed by this move, against the two that are released by 1 e4 or 1 d4, the English is one of the strongest opening weapons in White's arsenal. It appeals to those who like originality right from the start, as it allows manoeuvring of the pieces without coming to grips too early with the enemy. In many forms of this opening, White does not even try to occupy the centre. He lets Black mass pieces and pawns there, and then attacks them from the sides. He might fianchetto his bishops, for example, and strike at the centre from a distance, in order to undermine it.

Should White decide to temper his originality with caution, he can transpose from the English to some form of queen's pawn opening and still retain a fine game.

1   ...   e5

Black develops in the good old-fashioned way: he plants a pawn in the centre and frees two pieces for action.

2   ♘c3

White brings a piece out in preference to advancing a centre pawn.

In fact, on 2 d4 exd4 3 ♕xd4 ♘c6 the queen must retreat and lose a move. Or if 2 e4, White remains with a backward d-pawn, while the f1-bishop cannot get to c4.

2   ...   ♘f6

Black watches the order of his moves. The knight move is not merely routine development of a piece. Its purpose is to offset the pressure of White's knight and pawn on the d5-square.

3   g3

Clearly with the intention of making room for the bishop at g2, where it will operate on a long diagonal and also contribute to the pressure on d5.

3 ... d5!

Black frees his game by opening new paths for the queenside pieces. Simultaneously, he puts the question to White's c-pawn.

4 cxd5

White is happy to exchange a flank pawn for a centre pawn. At the same time, his c-file, now clear of pawns, offers good prospects for his queen's rook when it gets to c1.

4 ... ♘xd5

Such recaptures are practically compulsory. A delay might give White time to protect and hold on to the extra pawn.

5 ♗g2 *(D)*

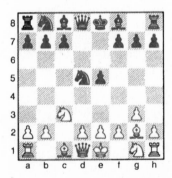

White develops a piece with gain of tempo – an attack on the d5-knight.

In the old days, Black would probably have met this by 5...♗e6, protecting the knight while developing another piece. Today's players regard with suspicion even the most natural moves, in their search for truth (and new ways to win).

5 ... ♘b6!

The bishop can wait! The advantage of this move is that Black is able to retain control of the d4-square, and so prevent White from opening up the centre by advancing his d-pawn to d4. After 5...♗e6, on the other hand, play might continue 6 ♘f3 ♘c6 7 0-0 ♗e7 8 d4, when Black is in trouble, since the position is becoming open while his king is still in the centre.

6 ♘f3

Again one of White's pieces develops with a threat – this time against the e-pawn.

6 ... ♘c6

Black defends in the simplest, most natural, way by posting the b8-knight on its most effective station.

Despite the fact that Black has fewer pieces in play than White, his game is not inferior. He does have a pawn in the centre, and his bishops, undeveloped as yet, have great potential, as their cruising range is more extensive than White's.

7 0-0 *(D)*

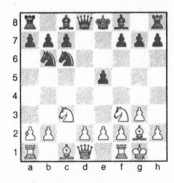

White does not commit himself, but spirits away the king and mobilizes one of his rooks.

7 ...   ♗e7

As in the previous game, the bishop's unobtrusive position at e7 is deceptive: it is prepared to keep out invaders and is also on the alert to switch to the attack.

8 d3

White makes room for the c1-bishop to take a hand in the game.

8 ...   0-0

Removes the king from the danger area and gets the rook up on deck.

9 ♗e3

With the bishop on this square, White may be able to get in 10 d4 and rid himself of Black's cramping centre pawn.

9 ...   ♗g4! *(D)*

An excellent deployment, as the bishop has a powerful restraining effect on White's kingside, as well as on the contemplated advance of his d-pawn.

If White does try 10 d4, the response 10...♘c4 is hard to meet. If White replies 11 ♘xe5, then after 11...♘6xe5 12 dxe5 ♘xe3 13 fxe3 he is left with a rickety column of pawns on the e-file. Or if White plays 11 ♕c1 to save his b-pawn and

to recapture at e3 with the queen, then 11...♘xe3 12 ♕xe3 exd4 13 ♕e4 ♗xf3, followed by 14...dxc3, wins a piece for Black.

White's best line is probably 10 ♘a4, in order to swing the knight to c5, a square which White must try to control in this type of English Opening. Otherwise he might continue developing by 10 ♖c1 and only then consider the knight manoeuvre.

10 h3

A move which is impelled by a desire to make the annoying bishop declare his intentions – either take the knight or vacate the premises! Unfortunately, moves such as this, dictated more by instinct than reason, have an injurious effect on the castled position, as the structure is loosened. Once the pawns near the king make a move, they themselves become more susceptible to attack, in spite of the cluster of pieces ranged around them for protection.

10 ...   ♗h5

The bishop retreats one square but maintains the pressure. Despite the bishop's restricted mobility, its continued influence is more troublesome to White's position (and his frame of mind) than would be its return to e6, where it enjoys more freedom but does nothing to disturb the opponent.

11 ♖c1

Evidently in order to control the c-file and perhaps work up an attack on the queenside.

A good alternative is 11 ♕b3 followed, when feasible, by ♖ad1 and d4, to open the d-file for White's rooks and get some counterplay in the centre. *Action in the centre is the best remedy against a kingside attack.*

11 ...   ♛**d7** *(D)*

All the pieces must do their bit! The queen moves only one step forward and dominates an important diagonal!

Development of the queen serves another purpose in that the first rank is cleared for the rooks. They can now switch over toward the centre and get control of the most important files.

12 ♘a4

White's idea is to create a diversion by taking command of c5 with his knight and keeping Black occupied with threats on the queenside.

Against routine defensive moves, for instance 12 ♔h2, Black gets an attack rolling by 12...f5 and 13...f4, and the pawn will demolish White's kingside pawn formation.

12 ...   ♗**xf3**

Presenting White with an unhappy choice of recaptures: if he takes with the pawn, his d-pawn becomes isolated and weak; if he takes with the bishop, he loses a pawn immediately.

13 ♗xf3

White gives up the h-pawn, trusting that he will regain a pawn quickly by his next exchange of pieces.

13 ...   ♛**xh3**

After this capture, Black's attacking prospects are very bright. Without bothering to analyse the petty details, he can visualize winning lines of play beginning with 14...f5 followed either by 15...f4, to destroy White's g-pawn (the key to the defensive structure), or by 15...♖f6, and then swinging the rook over to g6 or h6.

14 ♗xc6

Better than this, which regains the pawn, is 14 ♗g2 banishing the queen from the neighbourhood of his king.

14 ...   **bxc6**

Forced, but an agreeable obligation. Black is quite pleased to see the last of this long-range bishop.

15 ♖xc6 *(D)*

Material is now equal, but the white king is in danger, with the enemy queen breathing on his neck.

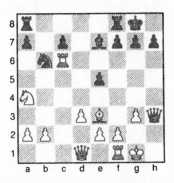

15 ...   ♘**d5!**

A tremendous move! One threat from this beautifully centralized knight is 16...♘xe3 17 fxe3 ♕xg3+ 18 ♔h1 ♕h3+ 19 ♔g1 ♗g5, and White's game is in ruins, while another threat is 16...♘f6, followed by 17...♘g4 and 18...♕h2#.

16 ♕e1

This awkward move is absolutely necessary to save the g-pawn from 16...♘xe3 17 fxe3 ♕xg3+. Should this pawn fall, his king could not withstand the attack.

White may have intended to play 16 ♗c5, when after 16...♘f6 he could have put up a fight by 17 ♖xf6 ♗xf6 18 ♗xf8, but at the last moment saw the refutation: 16...♗xc5 17 ♘xc5 ♘f6, and in order to stop 18...♘g4 and 19...♕h2#, he must give up his rook for the knight, a course which means an eventual loss.

16 ... f5! (D)

Not at once 16...♘f6 as 17 f3 keeps the knight out (note how essential it is to have the g-pawn protected).

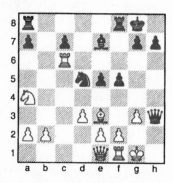

With his last move Black prepares to play 17...f4. If 18 gxf4 then 18...♖xf4 19 ♗xf4 ♘xf4, and Black

mates at g2. If White does not take the pawn but plays 18 ♗c5, Black wins cleverly by 18...f3 (threatening 19...♕g2#) 19 exf3 ♘f4 (again aiming at the mate) 20 gxf4 ♖f5, and White can only stop 21...♖h5, followed by mate, by giving up his queen with 21 ♕xe5.

17 ♗c5

If White tries to rid himself of Black's troublesome knight by 17 ♘c3 Black pursues the attack by 17...♘f6 18 f3 ♘h5 (concentrating on the vital g-pawn) 19 ♗f2 ♗h4 (still hammering at the pawn) 20 gxh4 ♘f4 and forces mate at g2.

The text-move gives White a faint chance of holding out after 17...♗xc5 18 ♘xc5 ♘f6 19 f3, or if 17...♘f6 then 18 ♖xf6.

17 ... f4!

Not only to strike at the g-pawn but also to clear a path for the rook's passage to f5 and h5 to assist the queen in a mating operation.

18 ♗xe7

If instead 18 g4 to keep the rook out, Black has three or four easy wins on tap:

1) 18...f3 19 exf3 ♘f4, followed by mate at g2.

2) 18...♕xg4+ 19 ♔h2 and then:

2a) 19...♖f5, and the rook mates.

2b) 19...f3 20 ♖g1 ♕h4#.

The move played exchanges to reduce the number of pieces besetting his king. He hopes for the simple recapture by 18...♘xe7, when the knight, no longer centralized, is less of a menace.

18 ... fxg3

With the simple, brutal threat of 19...♕h2#.

19 fxg3 *(D)*
The only reply.

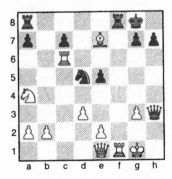

19 ... ♘e3!
Threatening 20...♕g2#.

0-1

There is no defence: 20 ♖f2 ♕xg3+ 21 ♔h1 ♖xf2 wins easily, or 20 ♖xf8+ ♖xf8 21 ♕f2 ♖xf2 22 ♔xf2 ♕g2+ 23 ♔xe3 ♕xc6 and the rest is elementary.

In this game Flohr gained revenge for his loss to Pitschak in the previous game by adopting the technique with which he was defeated. He weakened the pawns around the castled king and then ripped open the defences with a devastating attack.

Game 13
Dobias – Podgorny
Prague 1952
French Defence

1 e4

This is one of the best ways to begin what is a race and a struggle: a race to get the pieces out rapidly and onto squares where they can operate most efficiently; a struggle to gain control of the centre.

At one stroke the e-pawn takes up an important square in the centre and attacks two others, while the queen and bishop control eight more squares.

1 ... e6

This quietly aggressive move prepares to dispute White's centre by 2...d5.

This defence has the merit of avoiding the many strong openings White can play after the customary 1...e5 reply.

2 d4

Of a similar move, Philidor in his *Chess Analysed* (1791) says, "This Pawn is played two Moves for two very important Reafons: the firft is, to hinder your Adverfary's King's Bifhop to play upon your King's Bifhop's Pawn; and the fecond, to put the Strength of your Pawns in the Middle of the Exchequer, which is of great Confequence to attain the making of a Queen."

We may ftill follow the advice if not the fpelling.

2 ... d5

An attack on the e-pawn which immediately challenges the centre.

3 ♘c3

Of the various courses open to White (advancing the e-pawn to e5, exchanging pawns, sacrificing his centre pawn or protecting it) he takes that which enables him to develop a piece and maintain the pressure.

3 ...   dxe4

Temporarily allowing White more freedom of action, but Black hopes to play ...c5 later and destroy the troublesome d-pawn.

4 ♘xe4

The recapture leaves White with a slight edge in his centralized knight and pawn position.

4 ...   ♘d7 (D)

Preparing a support for the g8-knight's development at f6. If White then exchanges knights, Black can recapture with the d7-knight.

If he played instead 4...♘f6 then comes 5 ♘xf6+ and Black must either break up his kingside pawns by 5...gxf6 or capture with the queen and risk its being bothered by the minor pieces. A sample of what could happen (after 4...♘f6 5 ♘xf6+ ♛xf6) is this little trap: 6 ♘f3 ♗d7 (to seize the long diagonal) 7 ♗d3 ♗c6 8 ♗g5 ♗xf3 9 ♛d2! ♛xd4 10 ♗b5+ and White wins the enemy queen.

5 ♘f3

The best possible way to put the king's knight to work – by developing it at f3 where it has enormous influence on the centre, and where it stands peerless in defence of the castled king.

5 ...   ♗e7

A noncommittal developing move (it brings a piece off the back rank and helps the king castle quickly) but not so good as the conventional 5...♘gf6.

If Black tries instead the fianchetto development of his c8-bishop (tempting in view of White's exposed knight), there is a pretty trap he can stumble into: 5...b6 6 ♗b5 ♗b7 7 ♘e5! ♗xe4 (or 7...♗c8 8 ♗g5 ♘f6 9 ♘c6, winning the queen) 8 ♗xd7+ ♚e7 9 ♗c6! and Black must lose some material.

6 ♗d3

This is probably sharper than 6 ♗c4 but either move places the bishop in a good spot and clears the first rank for kingside castling.

6 ...   ♘gf6

Black too prepares to get his king into safety by developing (at long last) his g8-knight.

7 ♛e2

White develops a piece and supports his central knight strongly with queen and bishop.

This is more restraining on Black's cramped position than 7 ♘xf6+ ♗xf6, when Black can initiate an attack on White's centre with ...c5.

7 ...   0-0

The king seeks security in the corner. There was no easy freeing manoeuvre in 7...♘xe4 8 ♗xe4 ♘f6 since 9 ♗xb7 ♗xb7 10 ♛b5+

followed by 11 ♕xb7 wins a pawn for White.

8 0-0

White's castling is less to escape danger than to let the h1-rook take an active part in the game.

White's position is so promising as to offer him a good attacking line in 8 ♗g5 ♘xe4 9 ♕xe4 g6 (certainly not 9...♘f6 to prevent mate, as 10 ♗xf6 wins on the spot) 10 h4, when White can castle on the queenside and storm the enemy bastions with his kingside pawns.

8 ...   ♘xe4 (D)

Black exchanges to get some elbow-room.

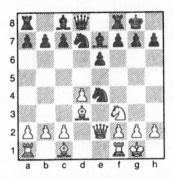

9 ♕xe4!

Takes command of the board with a threat of mate! Offhand it looks risky to make this capture and leave the queen exposed to harassment by the minor pieces, but Black is in no position (in either sense of the word) to make trouble. He has all he can do to stay alive!

9 ...   ♘f6

Naturally, Black does not wish to advance one of the kingside pawns, for instance 9...g6, unless compelled

to, but what's wrong with the move he plays, 9...♘f6? Does it not bring the knight to its best square, guard against mate, beat off the queen, and free his own queenside?

Indeed it does all these things, and under the circumstances it is probably Black's best move. It is strange that a move made under duress often does not have the same positive effect as a move made of one's own volition.

10 ♕h4

After this, Black's knight, which to be sure stands on a good square, *must remain on that square to guard against mate.*

10 ...   b6 (D)

The c8-bishop, barred by Black's very first move from coming out to the kingside, seeks other means to take part in the battle. Development at b7 looks attractive, as from there it commands the long diagonal.

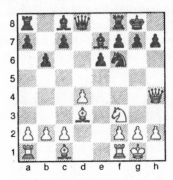

11 ♗g5!

Excellent strategy! White attacks the most important defensive piece, the knight that guards against mate. The specific threat is 12 ♗xf6 ♗xf6 13 ♕xh7#.

A simple threat and easy to meet – all Black has to do is play 11...g6 or 11...h6.

What then is White aiming at?

The hidden purpose is to *force Black to move one of the kingside pawns*, to avoid being mated. A move by either of these pawns creates a looseness in the defensive structure that can never be repaired. It weakens the position organically as it makes a breach that can never be closed. The pawn that advances can never go back to its former position in the line of defensive pawns.

11   ...   g6

On the alternative 11...h6 White wins by 12 ♗xf6 ♗xf6 13 ♕e4, when the threat of mate wins the rook on a8, an innocent bystander.

12   c4

A very good move! To begin with, it prevents Black playing 12...♘d5, to remove by exchange White's attacking pieces. Offensively, it prepares an advance of the d4-pawn, which will break up Black's pawn structure at e6. Once this is done, White's rook will have a point of entry on the e-file.

12   ...   ♗b7

Black has no effective counterattack. The best he can do is to keep on developing pieces on the most favourable squares to make a hard fight of it.

13   d5

Threatening, after the preparatory 14 ♖ad1, to take the e6-pawn so that the forced recapture by 15...fxe6 deprives Black's g-pawn of one of its props.

13   ...   exd5 (D)

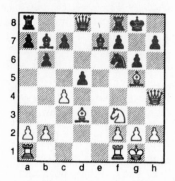

This seems to win a pawn, as should White recapture by 14 cxd5 the reply 14...♘xd5 not only holds on to the pawn but compels an exchange of bishops, taking the edge off White's attack.

14   ♖fe1!

This unexpected *zwischenzug* (in-between move) threatens immediate victory by 15 ♖xe7 ♕xe7 16 ♗xf6 ♕d6 17 ♘g5 h5 18 ♕xh5! gxh5 19 ♗h7#!

14   ...   h6

Black offers a pawn to deflect one of the pieces bearing down so heavily on his f6-knight and e7-bishop.

There was no relief in 14...♔g7 to support the knight, as White responds with the brutal 15 ♗h6+ winning the exchange.

15   ♕xh6

But not 15 ♗xh6, which permits 15...♘e4 driving off White's queen.

White now plans 16 ♗xg6 fxg6 17 ♕xg6+ ♔h8 18 ♘d4 (threatening to win by 19 ♘e6, 19 ♘f5 or 19 ♖e3 followed by 20 ♖h3+) 18...♕e8 19 ♕h6+ ♔g8 20 ♘f5 ♖f7 21 ♗xf6 winning easily.

15   ...   ♘g4

White has a neat win against the defence by 15...♘e4. He plays 16 ♗xe7 ♕xe7 17 cxd5 (threatening to capture the pinned e4-knight next) 17...♗xd5 18 ♗xe4 ♗xe4 19 ♖xe4! ♕xe4 20 ♘g5, when Black must lose his queen or be mated.

The text-move is of course an attempt to chase the queen away.

16 ♕h4

White supports the bishop, attacks the knight and threatens to win by 17 ♗xe7. What more can be achieved by one move?

16 ... ♗xg5

Returning the knight to f6 leads to catastrophe, viz.: 16...♘f6 17 ♖xe7 ♕xe7 18 ♗xf6 and White attacks Black's queen while threatening 19 ♕h8#.

17 ♘xg5 *(D)*

Once again the theme song – mate at h7.

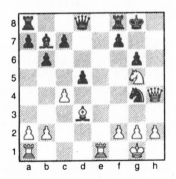

17 ... ♘f6

And Black must dance to the tune, by bringing the knight back to f6.

Here too Black posts the knight on a good square, but not of his own free will.

18 ♕h6

This restricts Black more than would manoeuvring the rook over to h3 by way of e3. For example, after 18 ♖e3 ♖e8 19 ♖h3 ♔f8 the king escapes immediate disaster.

After White's actual move, if Black tries 18...♖e8 he falls into 19 ♗xg6 ♖xe1+ 20 ♖xe1 fxg6 21 ♕xg6+ ♔h8 22 ♘f7#.

18 ... d4

To prevent 19 ♖e3, and to give the bishop more play on the long diagonal.

How does White continue the attack? Can he bring up the reserves without losing too much time? Or can he weaken the defensive formation and make it vulnerable to immediate assault?

Is there a hint in the last question? Yes, indeed!

Black's chief defence lies in his knight, which guards against the mate at h7, and the f-pawn supporting the all-important g-pawn. If only White could strike at these two defenders – threaten them, remove them, get them out of the way somehow...

There is a move, the kind that looks absurd at first glance!

Hint No. 2: A master player looks at every move he would *like* to make, *especially the impossible ones*.

19 ♖e6!!

Threatening to capture the knight, and then mate with the queen.

19 ... ♖e8 *(D)*

Had Black played 19...fxe6, there would have followed 20 ♕xg6+ ♔h8 21 ♕h6+ ♔g8 22 ♗h7+ ♔h8 23 ♗f5+ ♔g8 24 ♗xe6+ ♖f7 25 ♗xf7#.

It is interesting to note how the startling 19 ♖e6 move not only threatens to take the knight but also exploits the fact that the f-pawn dare

not capture the rook and abandon the defence of the g-pawn.

Black's last move is intended to clear the f8-square for the king, if White should take the knight and then check at h7 with his queen.

20   ♗xg6

Breaking through the pawn barrier! White's threat is 21 ♗xf7#.

1-0

There is no defence:

1) 20...fxe6 21 ♗f7#.

2) 20...fxg6 21 ♕xg6+ ♔h8 22 ♘f7#.

3) 20...♕d7 21 ♗h7+ ♘xh7 (or 21...♔h8 22 ♕xf6#) 22 ♕xh7+ ♔f8 23 ♕h8#.

Game 14
Tarrasch – Mieses
Berlin 1916
French Defence

1   e4

This is an excellent start toward developing the pieces, as lines are immediately opened for the queen and a bishop. The e-pawn itself helps in the battle for the centre by occupying a key square and attacking two others, d5 and f5.

1   ...   e6

In spite of its modest appearance, this move is just as good as the straightforward 1...e5. Black's idea is to follow up with 2...d5, attacking White's centre. He is then prepared to meet 3 exd5 by recapturing with the e-pawn, thus maintaining a pawn in the centre.

2   d4

Naturally! White puts another pawn in the centre, now making e5 and c5 forbidden territory for Black's pieces. Meanwhile, his own queen and dark-squared bishop have more freedom of movement.

2   ...   d5

Putting the question to the e-pawn!

White has a choice of various replies:

1) 3 exd5, in order to simplify.

2) 3 e5, to cramp Black with the pawn chain.

3) 3 ♘c3 (also 3 ♘d2 or, less effectively, 3 ♗d3), to protect the pawn and develop a piece at the same time.

The first method was favoured by Morphy, who liked open positions that gave his pieces wide scope for attack. Nowadays it is rarely adopted, as after the exchange of pawns the positions are equal and symmetrical and an attack is difficult to whip up, unless you are a Morphy.

The cramping move 3 e5 has a great many advocates, but the argument against this system is that White's pawn chain is rigid and susceptible to undermining tactics. Black initiates a strong counterattack on the base of the pawn-chain by 3...c5, followed by ...♘c6 and ...♛b6, when White finds himself defending a centre that has lost its flexibility.

There remains the third way, which is simple and consistent with common sense in chess – to support the e-pawn and bring a piece out on the scene.

3 ♘c3

Typical Tarrasch: he selects the method which furthers his development and maintains tension in the centre. This move brings a knight out, protects the e-pawn and increases the pressure on d5.

3 ... dxe4

Tarrasch disapproves of this exchange of pawns, as Black surrenders the centre without obtaining any compensation. If results are a measure of the merit of an opinion, Tarrasch proved his point in this match. Mieses played 3...dxe4 seven times with Black, with the consequence that two games were drawn and five were won by Tarrasch.

4 ♘xe4

Now White has a beautifully centralized knight, pressure on e5 and c5, and a superior pawn position (a pawn at d4 to one at e6) which assures him greater freedom of action.

4 ... ♘d7

Intending to support the g8-knight when it reaches f6. If Black plays 4...♘f6 at once, White can exchange knights by 5 ♘xf6+. Black's recapture either brings his queen too early into the game, or with 5...gxf6 allows his kingside pawn structure to be broken up.

5 ♘f3 (D)

This is where the king's knight is most useful, so why not place it there at once?

Even the greatest masters do not play startling, bizarre or 'brilliant' moves in the opening in an effort to be different, or to impress others with their ability to find extraordinary moves in commonplace positions. They are content to develop their pieces quickly, placing them on squares where they will operate to greatest effect, and then wait for Nature to take its course. When the time is ripe for combinative play, the odds are it will turn in favour of the player whose development is superior.

5 ...   ♘gf6

A sound developing move. Not only does the g8-knight move to the square most suitable for its powers, but it challenges the sovereignty of White's knight and disputes its hold on the centre.

6 ♗d3

Rather than retreat, White supports the knight by developing another piece. If Black exchanges on e4, White remains with a piece in the centre.

6 ...   ♗e7

The bishop is well placed at e7, and the decks are cleared for early kingside castling.

6...♘xe4 7 ♗xe4 ♘f6 8 ♗d3 is an interesting alternative, when the time lost by the bishop's retreat compensates Black for the tempo he lost when he played 3...dxe4.

7 0-0 (D)

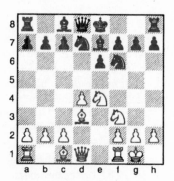

The king hides behind a pawn barricade while the rook moves in toward the half-open e-file.

7 ...   ♘xe4

Black exchanges to free his crowded position and let the queenside pieces get some air.

8 ♗xe4

The recapture gives White a monopoly on the important squares and poses Black the problem of attaining equality.

8 ...   ♘f6

This is always a fine square for the knight, and in this case the knight gets there with gain of time by attacking the unprotected bishop.

9 ♗d3

This mobile bishop is too valuable for White to allow its exchange. Any such transaction benefits Black as a reduction in the number of pieces on the board eases the pressure on him.

9 ...   b6

Understandably, Black wants his light-squared bishop on the job and intends developing it at b7. There is danger, though, in attempting this before the king has castled. Not only is there the risk of a check on the a4-e8 diagonal, which might compel the king to move and forfeit his right to castle, but there is also the possibility of White planting a knight on c6, a square weakened by the advance of Black's b-pawn.

10 ♘e5!

The knight occupies a wonderful outpost and will put a restraining hand on Black's ambition to expand.

10 ...   0-0 (D)

Black realizes that 10...♗b7 is refuted by 11 ♗b5+, to which he must respond either with 11...♔f8 losing the castling privilege, or with 11...c6 giving up a pawn.

Naturally, it would be silly to snatch a pawn by 10...♕xd4 and fall into 11 ♗b5+, losing the queen by a discovered attack.

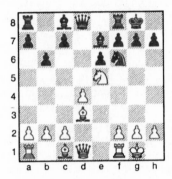

11 ♘c6

Immediately pouncing on the weakened square, with a view to removing Black's dark-squared bishop. But why give up the knight, which I said a moment ago was occupying a wonderful outpost, for a bishop that seems to have little potential?

There are at least three good reasons:

• The exchange deprives Black of one of his bishops, and the mere possession of both bishops is a formidable attacking weapon, no matter how placid the position.

• The reduction in material increases the dynamic power of White's pair of bishops, which have more space to work in. The emptier the board, the better they can sweep the area, one operating on light and the other on dark diagonals.

The third reason is rather subtle:

• Black's kingside position is stoutly defended by the knight, and the

knight in turn by the bishop and queen. In order to get at the knight, which must eventually be destroyed for a kingside attack to succeed, White first removes one of its firm supports, the bishop. The substitution of Black's queen for the bishop will make a pin on the knight a potent one – one which can not easily be shaken off.

11 ... ♕d6 *(D)*

As good as any other move the queen can make.

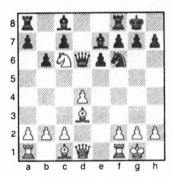

12 ♕f3!

A very important *zwischenzug* (in-between move). It is stronger than the immediate 12 ♘xe7+ and causes Black to modify his plans. Let us analyse both moves:

If White plays 12 ♘xe7+, then after 12...♕xe7 13 ♕f3 White attacks the rook. The rook evades the queen by escaping to b8, and Black's next move, 14...♗b7, drives the queen off the long diagonal, leaving Black's bishop in control of it.

After the actual move 12 ♕f3, Black is threatened with 13 ♘xe7+ ♕xe7 14 ♕xa8 – loss of a rook. This time the rook cannot run from the queen, as the flight square b8 is covered by White's knight, and the response 12...♗b7 (to interpose the bishop, meanwhile developing it on the long diagonal) fails after 13 ♘xe7+ ♕xe7 14 ♕xb7, and White wins a piece.

12 ...   ♗d7

The upshot of all this is that in order to save the rook's life the bishop must be content to move to d7, where it has little scope.

13 ♘xe7+

Strategically, this represents a triumph for White. Not only does he remain with the advantage of the two bishops against Black's knight and bishop, but he has also compelled Black's remaining bishop to take up an unfavourable post, while White retains control of the long light-squared diagonal.

13 ...   ♕xe7 (D)

Black recaptures with the impression that his position is solid enough, though defensive in character.

14 ♗g5!

White puts paralysing pressure on the knight with this powerful pin.

Before going any further, let's review the bidding:

By doing nothing more remarkable than making simple developing moves, White has an advantage in his pair of bishops, a better all-around position, more pieces in play, and an enduring initiative.

More pieces in play? Yes, his queen and both bishops are *actively* posted, while Black's knight is unable to move, his queen must hover about the knight (or lose a pawn after ♗xf6) and his bishop has little mobility, shut off as it is from the kingside by Black's own e-pawn. The pawn position in the centre also favours White, in that his d-pawn on the fourth rank has more to say about affairs than the enemy pawn at e6.

White now plans to create a breach in the line-up of pawns screening Black's king, by next playing the surprising but logical 15 ♕e4. Black could not reply 15...♘xe4 to this, as after 16 ♗xe7 (attacking two pieces) 16...♖e8 17 ♗xe4 he has no time to take the e7-bishop as his a8-rook is under attack. The idea underlying 15 ♕e4 is not to induce Black to snatch the queen, but by the threat of 16 ♗xf6 ♕xf6 17 ♕xh7# to compel him to play 15...g6. The effect of this pawn move would be to loosen the defensive structure shielding the king, remove a prop from under the pinned knight, and offer White points of entry on the weakened dark squares h6 and f6, which are no longer guarded by the g-pawn. One possibility, for example, is 15 ♕e4 g6 16 ♕h4 (attacking the knight) 16...♔g7

17 &h6+, and White wins the exchange.

14 ... Zac8

Black shifts the rook from the line of fire, so that 15 &e4 &xe4 16 &xe7 Zfe8 retains material equality.

Constructively, Black intends to follow up with 15...c5, coming to grips with White's centre pawn and opening the c-file for his rook.

15 Zfe1

A useful developing, restraining and preparatory move:

- It brings the rook out to a half-open file.
- It prevents any attempt by Black to free himself by prying open the e-file.
- It makes provision for utilizing the e1-rook in a kingside attack, somewhat like this: 16 &h3 (again threatening to win by 17 &xf6) 16...h6 17 &xh6 gxh6 18 &xh6, and the rook comes in decisively by way of e5 and g5 to inflict mate.

15 ... Zfe8

Vacating a square for the king. Black abandons the projected 15...c5, against which Tarrasch intended (according to his own comments) 16 &h3 (threatening 17 &xf6) 16...h6 17 &xh6 and now:

1) 17...c4 18 &xg7 &xg7 19 &g3+ &h8 20 &h4+ &g7 21 &g5+ &h8 22 &h6+ (pretty zigzagging by the queen!) 22...&g8 23 Ze5 with a quick mate.

2) 17...gxh6 18 &xh6 cxd4 (to meet 19 Ze5 with 19...Zc5) 19 &g5+ &h8 20 Ze4 and Black must give up his queen to avoid mate.

16 &h3! *(D)*

The winning move – although it appears that White has been playing a long string of winning moves.

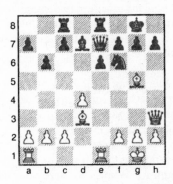

The pressure is now redoubled on the h-pawn, which White threatens to win either by 17 &xf6 followed by 18 &xh7+ or simply by taking it at once with the bishop, as Black's pinned knight dare not recapture, and his king may not take the bishop.

How does Black defend himself against White's threats?

If 16...h6, then 17 &xh6 gxh6 18 &xh6 &f8 (otherwise 19 Ze5 will lead to mate) 19 &xf6, when White, two pawns up, wins easily.

If 16...g6 (saving the h-pawn but depriving the knight of any real support), White wins by 17 &h4 &g7 18 Ze4!, followed by 19 Zf4, and the rook too hits out at the helpless knight.

If 16...e5 (uncovering an attack on the queen), then 17 &xf6 &xh3 (or 17...&xf6 18 &xd7, and White wins a piece) 18 &xe7 and White is a piece ahead.

Finally, after 16...c5 17 &xh7+ &f8 18 &e4 (threatening a devastating check at h8) 18...&g8, Black is a pawn down and still on the defensive.

All these variations are pleasant – especially if you are on the winning side!

16 ...   ♕d6

Hoping that 17 ♗xf6 gxf6 18 ♕xh7+, winning a pawn, will appease White.

17 ♗xf6

White removes the only defender in the neighbourhood of the black king, and...

17 ...   gxf6

...uproots the g-pawn, exposing the king.

18 ♕h6! *(D)*

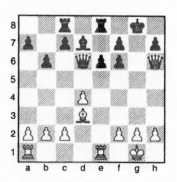

Holding the king fast! The idea is to keep him from escaping by way of f8 while facing him with deadly threats. The *modus operandi* after the text-move is 19 ♗xh7+! ♔h8 20 ♗g6+ ♔g8 21 ♕h7+ ♔f8 22 ♕xf7#.

If you can play this sort of move (18 ♕h6), you are a cut above the average player. Most young players (in a chess sense) have a tendency to try checking the king to death only to find after something like 18 ♕xh7+

♔f8 19 ♕h8+ ♔e7 that the king has escaped and the attack is exhausted. What is worse is that White's queen and d-pawn are threatened, and that saving both by 20 ♕h4 lets Black respond with 20...♖h8 and suddenly White is thrown on the defensive!

18 ...   f5

Intercepting the bishop's line of attack.

19 ♖e3 *(D)*

Obviously threatening check at g3, which would force Black to give up his queen in order to avoid instant mate.

Notice how the occupation of the partly open e-file by the rook enables the convenient use of e3 as a transfer point, allowing the rook to switch over to the open files on the kingside.

19 ...   ♕xd4 *(D)*

Guarding the g7-square, so that after 20 ♖g3+ ♔h8, White has no check there with his queen.

If instead 19...f6, to try escaping with the king, then 20 ♖g3+ ♔f7 21 ♕g7# is mate. Or if 19...♔h8, then 20 ♖h3 forces 20...♔g8, when 21 ♖g3+ is fatal.

20 c3!

A beautiful *coup de repos*!

Black is helpless: his queen dare not leave the diagonal leading to g7, and 20...♕g7 21 ♖g3 pins the queen, while 20...♕h8 succumbs to 21 ♖g3+, and the poor king's only flight square is occupied by his queen!

1-0

This game was awarded a brilliancy prize.

Game 15
Alekhine – Poindle
Simultaneous, Vienna 1936
Ruy Lopez

1 e4

With his first move, White gets a foothold in the centre and enables the development of his kingside pieces.

1 ... e5

Black must also establish a pawn in the centre, while preventing 2 d4 from being freely played.

What if White does continue 2 d4? After 2...exd4 3 ♕xd4 ♘c6 4 ♕e3 ♘f6 5 ♘c3 ♗b4 Black has three pieces in play with easy development. It is true that White has a pawn in the centre, but it will need constant care, and his queen meanwhile has lost valuable time. In short, after 1...e5 White may respond 2 d4 but not to advantage.

2 ♘f3

The knight is posted without delay on its most effective square in the opening. The move is ideal, as the knight develops with a threat. This limits the opponent's choice of replies, since he must do something to meet the threat before going about his business.

2 ... ♘c6

The best way to protect the pawn. The knight's development is natural, and no time is lost meeting the threat.

3 ♗b5

The strongest move on the board here, this characterizes the Ruy Lopez, the most powerful of kingside openings. As Reuben Fine puts it, "One reason why the Ruy Lopez is so strong is that the most natural sequence of moves leads to an ideal position for White."

3 ... ♘f6

Black brings his g8-knight out toward the centre with an attack on the e4-pawn.

Lasker favoured the knight's development at this point, but modern theory inclines to interpolating 3...a6 first, to make the bishop declare its intentions, and in any case to dislodge it from its fine position.

4   0-0 *(D)*

Very much to the point: the king is whisked away into safety while the h1-rook is activated.

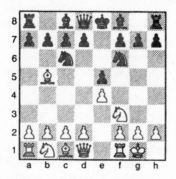

4   ...   ᐧxe4

Should Black capture this pawn? Lasker's view was: "When you are conscious not to have violated the rules laid down, you should accept the sacrifice of an important central pawn. If you do not, as a rule, the pawn which you have rejected will become very troublesome to you."

5   d4

This is stronger than 5 ᕦe1. Black's e-pawn is doubly attacked, while lines are opened up for White's queen and dark-squared bishop.

5   ...   ᐧd6

Puts the question to the bishop, which apparently must capture the knight or retreat.

An alternative course was 5...ᐩe7, developing another piece instead of moving the same one twice. Black must not waste time holding on to the extra pawn but should continue bringing pieces into play.

6   dxe5!

Initiating an attack which is troublesome to meet. White temporarily offers a piece, but he can be sure of regaining it quickly. This is superior to the less dynamic 6 ᐩa4, which gives Black time to reply 6...e4 with good counterplay.

6   ...   ᐧxb5

The knight's excursion has cost Black valuable time, as the knight has made four moves to capture a bishop that has only moved once.

7   a4 *(D)*

White attacks the knight at once to recover the piece he lost.

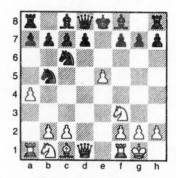

7   ...   ᐧd6

A fifth move by the same knight! White will surely have a strong attack in return for the pawn he intends to sacrifice.

Black should have played 7...ᐧbd4 8 ᐧxd4 ᐧxd4 9 ᐱxd4 d5, a better way of returning the piece as it frees his bishops.

8   exd6

White's first dividend comes in the form of an open centre file leading straight to Black's king!

    8 **...**   **♗xd6** *(D)*

Not a happy recapture, as the d-pawn is blocked, but certainly better than taking with the pawn, when Black's position is even more awkward.

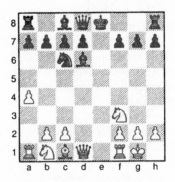

    9 **♘g5!**

This move is superior to the natural 9 ♖e1+. It is, as we shall see, both energetic and subtle.

One finesse is directed against Black's castling. After 9...0-0, White would play 10 ♕d3 threatening 11 ♕xh7#. Black would be forced to reply 10...g6 (not 10...f5 11 ♕d5+ ♔h8 12 ♘f7+, winning the exchange) and weaken the defensive formation of pawns. Once the line of pawns is disturbed, the king is vulnerable to direct attack.

    9 **...**   **♗e7**

An interesting move. In its retreat, the bishop not only attacks the knight but also manages to unblock the d-pawn.

Black hopes either to force the knight to leave or to bring about an exchange of pieces, ridding himself of the attacking knight.

    10 **♕h5!**

En avant! The obvious threat of mate camouflages the real purpose of this move.

White's last two moves are those of a beginner – or perhaps of a great master! The knight has moved twice to assist the queen in an attack, which the books say is premature, since White's development is not complete. Why does Alekhine violate elementary opening principles?

The reason he does so is that routine development ("You get your pieces out quietly and I'll do the same with mine") would give Black time to reorganize his position. Black has committed some indiscretions (such as moving one knight five times in the opening!), and the way to punish these lapses is to keep him occupied – face him with problems at every point and give him no time to recover. If it requires unconventional moves to force weaknesses in his position, then play these unorthodox moves! Moves are good or bad by one standard only – their effect on the position at hand.

    10 **...**   **g6**

What other choice was there?

If Black castles in order to avoid 11 ♕xf7#, he falls into 11 ♕xh7#, or if he exchanges by 10...♗xg5 then 11 ♗xg5 forces 11...♘e7, when the pin 12 ♖e1 wins a piece – as a start!

    11 **♕h6!**

White anchors the queen on this square, which is no longer guarded by Black's g-pawn, as the first step in controlling the dark squares.

White now threatens to penetrate further into the heart of the position by 12 ♕g7, attacking the rook. This would force 12...♖f8 in reply, when 13 ♘xh7 wins the exchange, a rook for a knight.

11 ...   ♗f8

Not only must further invasion be prevented, but the queen must be driven back.

Black has little choice, as castling is against the law, while 11...♗xg5 loses to 12 ♗xg5 f6 13 ♕g7 ♖f8 14 ♖e1+ ♘e7 15 ♗h6 ♖f7 16 ♕g8+ ♖f8 17 ♕xf8#.

12 ♖e1+

Forcing Black to tie himself up in knots.

12 ...   ♘e7 (D)

Certainly not 12...♗e7, when 13 ♕g7 ♖f8 14 ♘xh7 (threatening 15 ♕xf8#) 14...d5 15 ♘f6# is mate.

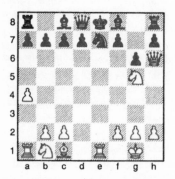

At this point, in spite of White's disregard of conventional methods of development, he has three pieces in active play, while Black has none! Black does have one piece off the first rank, but it is held fast by a pin and unable to move.

13 ♘e4!

Threatening to deliver mate on the move!

13 ...   f5

The only move to stay on the board! If Black continues 13...♗xh6 White wins by 14 ♘f6+ ♔f8 15 ♗xh6#, or if 13...♘f5 with a double attack on the queen, White retaliates with 14 ♘f6# – double check and mate!

14 ♘f6+

One way to get at the king is to make him come out into the open.

14 ...   ♔f7

Moving the king forfeits the privilege of castling, but unfortunately it's Black's only move.

15 ♕h4

White's queen and knight were both attacked, so the queen moves where she protects the knight.

15 ...   ♗g7

Now threatening 16...♗xf6. The alternative attack by 15...♘g8 pins the knight and strikes at it with two pieces, but is refuted by 16 ♕c4+ ♔xf6 (or 16...♔g7 17 ♘e8+ and Black must give up his queen) 17 ♕h4+ and White wins the queen.

16 ♗g5

Protecting the knight, which had no flight square.

16 ...   h6

Threatening the knight again by hitting out at one of its defenders.

If 16...♘g8 instead, White has a pretty combination in 17 ♘xg8 ♕xg8 18 ♖e7+ ♔f8 19 ♗h6 followed by 20 ♕f6+, forcing mate. Or he may prefer to win by 17 ♕c4+ d5 18 ♘xd5 ♕xg5 19 ♘xc7+ ♔f6 20 ♘e8#.

17 ♕c4+!

A happy diversion, as the check compels the opponent to drop everything and save his king.

17 ...   ♔f8 *(D)*

Practically forced, as 17...d5 18 ♘xd5 ♕xd5 19 ♖xe7+ costs Black his queen.

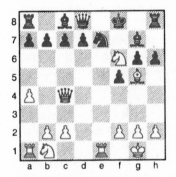

18 ♖xe7!

The hallmark of an Alekhine combination is the kick at the end of a series of apparently innocuous moves.

White's threat is obvious: mate on the move.

18 ...   ♕xe7

On 18...♔xe7, the only other way of preventing mate at f7, White replies 19 ♘d5++, and wins the queen next move.

19 ♘h7+

Direct attack on the king and discovered attack on the queen.

19 ...   ♖xh7

Black takes all the material he can get for his queen.

20 ♗xe7+

The point of the combination: in return for his rook and bishop, White gets the queen – and a lasting initiative!

20 ...   ♔xe7 *(D)*

Black must take the bishop.

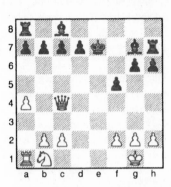

21 ♕xc7

White could win more simply by 21 ♕g8 ♔f6 22 ♕xh7 ♔f7 23 ♘c3 d6 24 ♖e1, followed by 25 ♖e7+, but the text-move is good enough. The queen remains active while Black's queenside is immobilized.

21 ...   ♗xb2

Black makes trouble. He takes a pawn and attacks the rook.

22 ♖a2

The rook steps aside nimbly and turns on his attacker.

22 ...   ♗f6

The bishop retreats to (comparative) safety.

23 c4!

Clears the way for the rook, which now can get to the open e-file – and the king!

23 ...   ♔f7

The king flees from the line of fire. Black hopes to free himself by 24...♖h8 and 25...♗d8, driving the queen off, followed by the advance of his d-pawn to release his queenside pieces.

24 ♖e2

White seizes the open file. Controlling it gives the rook a clear road and access to the enemy camp.

24   ...   ♜h8 *(D)*

Black intends either to evict the queen by 25...♝d8 or to dispute ownership of the e-file by 25...♜e8.

25 ♛d6!

Nailing down the d-pawn and paralysing Black's forces on the queenside.

25   ...   a5

What else is there? 25...♜e8 26 ♜xe8 ♚xe8 27 ♛xf6 wins a piece, or if 25...b6, then 26 ♛d5+ catches the a8-rook.

Black's idea is to follow up with 26...♜a6, dislodging the queen and getting his queenside pieces rolling.

26 ♞c3!

Excellent! White brings another piece up to join in the attack. Notice how the master player selects the move he would like to make, sees that it can't be made (here the knight is left *en prise*) and then makes the move!

26   ...   ♜a6

Black does not grab the knight with 26...♝xc3, as White mates by

27 ♜e7+ ♚f8 (or 27...♚g8 28 ♛d5+ and mate next move) 28 ♜xd7+ ♚g8 29 ♛d5+ ♚f8 30 ♛f7#.

27 ♛d5+ *(D)*

White's queen must retreat from the rook's attack, but she gains time by checking.

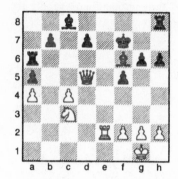

27   ...   ♚g7

Or 27...♚f8 28 ♞b5 (threatening 29 ♞d6) 28...♜e6 29 ♜xe6 dxe6 30 ♛c5+ ♚g7 31 ♛c7+ and a bishop falls with check.

28 ♞b5 *(D)*

Ready to switch over to d6 in order to support the queen in a mate threat at f7.

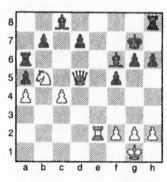

28   ...   ♜e6

Otherwise the knight goes to d6 and cuts the rook off from participating in the defence.

29 ♘d6!

The knight goes there anyway, settling down on this fine outpost where it will either take a hand in a decisive combination or simply stay there and choke Black to death.

29 ... ♖d8

Naturally, 29...♖xe2 is unthinkable, as 30 ♕f7# would come in a flash.

30 ♔f1

White protects the rook and declares his intention of winning by 31 ♘xc8 ♖xc8 32 ♕xd7+, followed by taking a rook or two.

1-0

There is no fight left.

Game 16
Tarrasch – Kurschner
Nuremberg 1889
Queen's Gambit Accepted

1 d4

One of the merits of beginning a game with 1 d4 is that the pawn standing in the centre is protected. It is safe from attack, whereas in openings starting with 1 e4, the e-pawn is more vulnerable.

In queen's pawn openings, with the queen firmly backing up the centre pawn, White dictates the tempo. He has the initiative and keeps it for a long time against any defence, any line of play that Black may select. Right from the start, White is given the opportunity to build up his position, with little danger of being bothered by a counterattack, while Black struggles to achieve equality. If Black plays timidly – if he fails to dispute the centre by ...c5 at some stage – his queenside pieces, especially the c8-bishop, will be badly cramped and unable to develop decent activity. If he develops carelessly – moving the same piece several times in the opening or bringing his bishops out

before the knights – punishment will come swiftly.

The purpose of chess being to win, not to entertain the gallery with pretty pictures on the chessboard, it is no wonder that many players prefer the 'dull, safe Queen's Gambit' to the romantic but risky adventures of the kingside gambits.

I venture to say (and this opinion has forty years of research behind it) that the queen's pawn openings have contributed as many masterpieces and as many genuine brilliancies as did any of the kingside openings.

1 ... d5

This is the best way for Black to stabilize the pressure in the centre.

Each side now has a pawn firmly stationed in the middle of the board, occupying one square and attacking two others; each side has released two pieces for action.

2 c4

The object of this move is to destroy Black's pawn-centre. First,

White offers a pawn to induce Black to surrender the centre. If that does not work, White threatens to dissolve it by 3 cxd5 ♕xd5 4 ♘c3 ♕a5 5 e4, and White controls most of the centre.

$$2 \quad \ldots \quad \text{dxc4} \ (D)$$

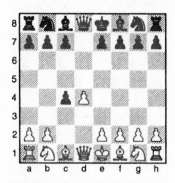

Black's idea with this capture is to avoid the constricted positions that are normally his lot in the Queen's Gambit Declined, but in doing so he has given up a beautifully centralized pawn for a less central one.

Accepting the gambit is perfectly sound, but the resulting play requires great care on Black's part. Above all, he must not hold on to the extra pawn for too long.

3 e3

A good move, but more to the point is 3 ♘f3 to prevent the counterthrust 3...e5.

White plays to release his light-square bishop and recover the pawn at once.

$$3 \quad \ldots \quad \text{♗f5}$$

By this, Black hopes to solve the problem of the shut-in c8-bishop, one of the evils the defence is heir to. However, the solution is not quite so

simple! The bishop's absence from the queenside weakens that section of the board and leaves the b-pawn vulnerable. Another drawback in Black's move is that it violates one of the precepts for sound development:

Bring out your knights before the bishops!

Instead of the text-move, Black's best bet is in counterattack, viz.: 3...e5 4 ♗xc4 (or 4 dxe5 ♕xd1+ 5 ♔xd1 ♗e6) 4...exd4 5 exd4 ♗b4+.

Attempting to hold on to the extra pawn might lead Black into one of the traps prepared for the greedy: 3...b5 4 a4 c6 5 axb5 cxb5 6 ♕f3, and White wins a piece.

4 ♗xc4 *(D)*

The recovery of the pawn equalizes the material, but White's position is slightly superior.

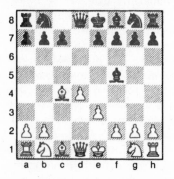

$$4 \quad \ldots \quad \text{e6}$$

A pawn move that contributes to the development of a piece, in this case the f8-bishop, is always in order.

Developing one of the knights first is somewhat risky. For instance, 4...♘f6 5 ♕b3 threatens to win a pawn by 6 ♕xb7 or 6 ♗xf7+, or if 4...♘c6 5 ♕b3 ♘a5, then 6 ♗xf7+ ♔d7 7 ♕d5+ ♔c8 8 ♕xf5+ ♔b8 9 ♕xa5, and White wins two pieces.

Even at this early stage White is directing events.

5 ♕b3

Why does White move his queen instead of getting his knights out?

His purpose is to punish Black for faulty development. Black's play has not been normal procedure, and the way to take advantage of his sins is not with routine moves.

White's move, developing a piece with a threat (6 ♕xb7) keeps Black on the run. It does not give him time to consolidate his position.

5 ... ♗e4

This looks attractive, since Black protects his b-pawn, and at the same time threatens to play 6...♗xg2, winning a rook.

Black's move, however, is abnormal and a serious infraction of the opening principle which states:

Move each piece only once in the opening; place it at once on the square where it exerts most power and where it has the greatest freedom of movement.

6 f3

This move is justified on more than one count. Not only does it parry a threat in an economical way, but it also forces Black to lose a move in the retreat of his bishop. Incidentally, the pawn at f3 will firmly support a later advance of the e3-pawn.

6 ... ♗c6 *(D)*

Now we see the results of the bishop's ill-timed expedition. It stands at c6, depriving the b8-knight of its natural square of development in the opening. Worse yet, it obstructs the c-pawn. If this pawn cannot get to c5 to dispute control of the centre and to open the c-file for Black's pieces, there is a danger that Black will be smothered.

7 ♘e2

"But the knight belongs on f3!" you must be protesting. So it does, but if it cannot develop at f3, get it into the game somehow! Move it, if only to get it off the back rank! Of course, the same comment applies to the other three knights, too.

White is ready to castle and get the h1-rook working.

7 ... ♘f6

At last, a normal, reasonable developing move to which no exception can be taken! In nearly every variation of every opening, the king's knight does its job most effectively at f6 (or f3 for White).

8 e4

This move has a threefold purpose:

1) to control the centre, by occupying it with pawns;

2) to clear a path for the development of his c1-bishop;

3) to limit further the activities of Black's c6-bishop.

8 ...   ♗e7

The only square open to the bishop. If instead 8...♗d6, the reply 9 e5 wins a piece for White.

The back rank is cleared and Black is ready to castle – if White lets him!

9 ♘bc3

Bringing another piece into play with gain of tempo. The threat is 10 d5 exd5 11 exd5 ♗d7 12 ♕xb7, and White wins a piece.

9 ...   ♕c8

Black must guard the b-pawn and put aside any thought of castling for a while.

10 d5 (D)

In order to drive the bishop back to the second rank.

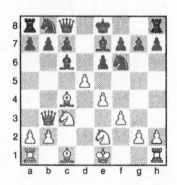

10 ...   exd5

This exchange of pawns is inferior to simply retreating the bishop. The opening up of lines favours the side that is better developed, and in this case White will benefit.

11 exd5

This recapture opens the e-file for the use of White's major pieces and compels Black's bishop on c6 to retreat.

11 ...   ♗d7

Anything else loses material.

Before making his next move, White must decide whether to continue bringing pieces into play or to try exploiting his present lead in development. Thus, he pauses to take stock before committing himself to a definite course of action.

He has a pawn stationed at d5, which at first glance is doing an excellent job. It prevents Black's b8-knight from developing at c6, keeps the d7-bishop from coming to e6, and restrains the f6-knight. The pawn does this single-handed, but at a price! In standing at d5 it occupies a square that should be reserved for pieces. Pieces have more mobility than pawns and can attack more readily. Pieces can utilize d5 as a jumping-off square, a point of departure to any part of the board. In fact, the wretched pawn does a disservice in obstructing the diagonal of the bishop and the supporting queen and takes up room on a file which should be open! Better that the d5-square be vacant than that a pawn block traffic there! (And in this last sentence, as we shall see, is the key to White's problem).

What about Black's prospects?

With the exception of the f6-knight, his pieces are confined to the first two ranks. His position is a bit crowded, but if he gets a chance to castle and reorganize his forces, it will be hard to subdue him.

White must not allow him time to do this. *White must not dawdle!*

12 d6!

This energetic thrust opens the diagonal leading to Black's tender spot, the f7-pawn, clears the d-file for later exploitation by a rook, and vacates the strategically important d5-square for the use of a piece. Meanwhile, the attack on Black's bishop leaves him no time to breathe!

12 ... ♗xd6

Better than 12...cxd6 hemming the bishop in.

13 ♗xf7+

This will smoke the king out! Once the king moves and loses the privilege of castling, he stands on insecure ground to the end of his days (which may not be far off).

13 ... ♔d8 *(D)*

Black prefers this to 13...♔f8 imprisoning the h8-rook.

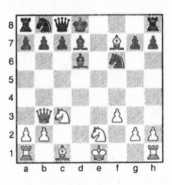

14 ♗g5

This pin paralyses Black's most useful piece. Meanwhile – and this sums up the miserable state of his game – Black's mighty queen is smothered by his own pieces!

14 ... ♘c6

Black's idea is to develop a piece and give the queen and a8-rook freedom to move – if only to the next square! It is hard to suggest a better move, as every move is inadequate in a losing position. Black might have ventured on a more active defence, such as 14...♗e8 followed by 15...♖f8, 15...♕d7 or 15...♕f5. He must try to beat back White's attacking pieces or get rid of them by exchanges.

The formula in such cases is:

In a cramped position try to relieve the pressure by forcing exchanges of pieces.

15 ♘e4

White puts more strain on the pinned knight. The threat (and there always is a threat when a pinned piece is attacked more than once) is 16 ♘xf6 gxf6 17 ♗xf6+, and White wins a rook.

15 ... ♗e7

Protecting the knight once again, and at the same time unpinning it. This is a better defence than 15...♗e5, which helps guard the knight but does nothing to relieve the pin. In such situations, the extra defender itself may be on shaky ground and apt to be disturbed. For instance, after 15...♗e5 16 f4 ♗d4 17 ♘xd4 (removing one of the knight's protectors) 17...♘xd4 18 ♕c3 Black is embarrassed for a plausible continuation.

16 ♗xf6

White does well to remove this rock of defence.

16 ... gxf6 *(D)*

Black takes with the pawn, as he wants to keep both his bishops.

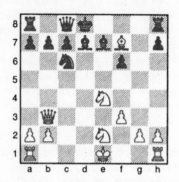

With his king so well sheltered by pieces, it looks difficult to penetrate Black's barricades.

17 0-0-0!

Much more energetic than castling on the other side. White's king is somewhat exposed, but as compensation his a1-rook has an instant and powerful grip on the open d-file, putting particular pressure on the unfortunate bishop, which now is pinned. The manoeuvre of castling on the queenside gains a tempo for the attack, while White's king is in little danger, since Black's development is so backward.

White threatens 18 ♗e6 or 18 ♕e6, either of which adds pressure to the pin.

17 ...   ♘e5

Not only to help the bishop but also to play 18...♘xf7, removing one of his tormentors.

18 ♘f4

Threatening sudden death by 19 ♘e6#.

18 ...   ♕b8

An unhappy situation for Black's queen, but the king needs a flight square.

What else was there? If 18...♗f8 to free the e7-square for the king, then 19 ♕e6 (threatening 20 ♕e8#) 19...♗e7 20 ♕xe5! fxe5 21 ♘e6# mates neatly.

19 ♕e6

With the queen's entrance into the enemy camp, the attack gains momentum. White plans a win by 20 ♘xf6 (striking once more at the hapless bishop and threatening 21 ♖xd7+ and quick mate) 20...♗xf6 21 ♕xf6+ ♔c8 22 ♕xh8+ and mate next move.

19 ...   ♖f8 *(D)*

Hoping to scare off the bishop, when his f-pawn would be protected by the rook. The alternative 19...♕c8 runs into 20 ♕xe5 and the previous win.

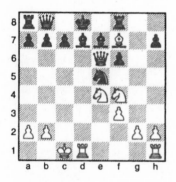

20 ♘xf6

Isn't it remarkable how threats are summoned up as if by magic against a piece that is pinned?

20 ...   ♗d6

Interfering with the rook's action on the open file and thereby threatening to take the queen.

Other defences promise no favourable results:

1) 20...♖xf7 21 ♖xd7+ and mate in two.

2) 20...♗xf6 21 ♕xf6+ ♔c8 22 ♕xe5 ♖xf7 23 ♕h8+.

3) 20...♕c8 21 ♕xe5 ♖xf7 22 ♘e6#.

With the text, Black unpins his d7-bishop, guards the e5-knight, attacks the queen and threatens the f7-bishop.

21 ♘xd7

This one hurts a bit. The knight captures one piece and attacks three others.

21 ... ♘xd7

Black recaptures and disposes of a troublesome piece.

22 ♖he1

The doubling of heavy pieces on the open e-file, with the consequent threat of 23 ♕e8+ ♖xe8 24 ♖xe8#, is enough to break anyone's spirit.

1-0

The c-pawn cannot move to give the king room because of the reply 23 ♖xd6, and if 22...♘c5, then 23 ♕e7+ ♔c8 24 ♕xf8+ ♗xf8 25 ♖e8# is the finishing touch.

The Queen's Pawn Opening

At some time in his life, almost every chess player makes a happy discovery – the Queen's Pawn Opening.

The Queen's Pawn offers White a great many advantages, and all of them can be summed up in one word – pressure!

White gets opportunities to control and exert pressure on the c-file, and in particular on the c5-square. So powerful can it be as to cause, by itself, the collapse of Black's game.

Against its dire effects there is only one antidote: the advance ...c5, which Black *must* get in, sooner or later. Without it, he may be choked to death; with it, he frees his position on the queenside, establishes a state of tension in the centre, and can put up a fight for possession of the c-file.

The game Pillsbury-Mason (No. 17) is a classic example of White controlling the c-file, while Black fails to free himself by ...c5. Pillsbury fixes the c-pawn so it dare not move, and then proceeds to attack it with more pieces than Black can summon to its defence. The pawn falls, of course, and White's continuing control of the vital c-file, extending into the ending, makes the winning process look easy.

In Noteboom-Doesburgh (No. 18), neglect of the freeing manoeuvre ...c5 allows White to restrain and prevent forever the advance of the c-pawn. Eventually, the pawn is nailed down so that Black's queenside is held in an iron grip. The weaknesses on the queenside lead to collapse on the kingside.

Similar difficulties beset Black in Grünfeld-Schenkein (No. 19), where delay in challenging the centre leads to a sealing in of Black's c-pawn, and with it his queenside, by an unprotected pawn! White's sudden shifting of the attack to the kingside leaves Black helpless to resist.

Positional play on a grand scale is seen in the Rubinstein-Salwe (No. 20) game. This again shows the consequences of Black's omission of the key defensive move in this opening, namely ...c5. White's control of the c-file and the c5-square enables him to demonstrate a remarkable bit of strategy. He blockades c5 with a bishop (stopping Black's c-pawn dead in its tracks) and then switches blockaders about, so that this square is occupied in turn by a bishop, a knight, a rook and the queen! Rubinstein eventually captures the c-pawn that was marked for doom and swings into the final movement, a triumphal march of his own passed pawn.

In the Chernev-Hahlbohm (No. 21) game, Black gets in the important counterthrust ...c5, but his centre, with an unprotected knight at d5, lacks solidity. Chernev gains time for his attack by threats against Black's exposed pieces, and it is these gains of tempo that lend the game its interest.

Pillsbury-Marco (No. 22) is an ideal Queen's Gambit game. In it, we see the classic demonstration of what came to be known as the Pillsbury Attack. It is a beautiful example of the power of a knight outpost at e5, and the impetus it furnishes to a whirlwind kingside attack.

In the game between Van Vliet and Znosko-Borovsky (No. 23), it is Black who wrests control of the c-file by a counterattack at the second move with 2...c5. It leads to more advantages, culminating in a rook invasion of the seventh rank and the establishment of a knight outpost at e4. Eventually, Black doubles rooks on the c-file and manoeuvres his king in among the enemy pawns. This leads to his winning a pawn, and the rest is a delightful little lesson in the art of simplification.

Game 17
Pillsbury – Mason
Hastings 1895
Queen's Gambit Declined

1 d4

White opens with one of the strongest possible first moves:
- The d-pawn occupies an important square in the centre and attacks two valuable points, e5 and c5.
- Control of these squares keeps the opponent from making use of them for his pieces.
- The queen and dark-squared bishop can now leave the first rank.
- The king is safe from some of the surprise attacks that occur in king's pawn openings. These come about when Black develops his f8-bishop at c5 and sacrifices it for White's f2-pawn to force the king out into the open and subject him to assault by the other pieces.

1 ... d5

Black equalizes the pressure in the centre, prevents White from continuing with 2 e4, and also releases two of his own pieces for action.

2 c4

This is a threat and an offer! The threat, a positional one, is 3 cxd5, when after the recapture 3...♛xd5, 4 ♞c3 drives the queen off and leaves White dominating the centre.

The offer of a pawn has as its purpose the removal of Black's d-pawn from its fine position in the centre. This offer, unlike the one in the King's Gambit, involves no risk. White regains the pawn easily and retains an advantage. It is in effect an exchange of a flank pawn for Black's centre pawn. The point of playing 2 c4 so soon is that *it disputes the centre at once, without endangering the safety of the king.*

There is also another purpose – a strategic one. An exchange of pawns must come, sooner or later, resulting in the opening of the c-file. *Owner-ship of this file is of paramount im-portance in the Queen's Gambit.* White generally tries to get full pos-session of it by posting his queen at c2, and developing his queen's rook at c1.

Control of this file and of the c5-square on this file is equivalent to control of the game. Of such pecu-liar significance is this c5-square that it is almost enough simply to plant a piece securely there to get a paralysing grip on Black's game.

2 ...   e6

Black defends the centre pawn by supporting it with another pawn.

He does not care to capture by 2...dxc4 as that means surrendering the centre to gain a pawn which he cannot hold on to. White, in reply to this, would play 3 ♘f3 (to prevent 3...e5), follow up with 4 e3, and then get the pawn back by 5 ♗xc4, with a central superiority.

Defending the d-pawn by 2...♘f6 is weak. White would play in re-sponse 3 cxd5, *and Black would have to recapture with a piece.* On 3...♕xd5, 4 ♘c3 banishes the queen from the centre and costs Black time, while 3...♘xd5 lets White seize the centre with 4 e4 and evict the knight in the process.

After the actual move, Black is set to meet 3 cxd5 by 3...exd5, keeping his hold on the centre by maintain-ing a pawn there.

3 ♘c3

This is a commendable develop-ing move, as it settles a minor piece on its most suitable square without loss of time. The knight bears down

on the e4-square and adds its pres-sure to that of the c-pawn in the at-tack on d5.

3 ...   ♘f6 (D)

This knight carries out his part of Black's opening strategy by simply leaving the back rank. Naturally, his development is toward the centre, where he counteracts the influence of White's knight on two of the im-portant squares there.

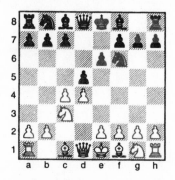

4 ♗g5

A highly efficient move as it com-bines rapid development of a piece with a threat. This latter consists of 5 cxd5 exd5 6 ♗xf6 gxf6 (or 6...♕xf6 7 ♘xd5, and White wins a pawn) and Black's kingside pawn position is shattered.

The opening thus far had been given sporadic earlier trials by vari-ous players, but Pillsbury was the first to appreciate its enormous win-ning possibilities. He pictured the bishop move (most masters brought the bishop quietly into the game at f4) as a sort of Ruy Lopez on the other side of the board! With this particular sequence of moves, which he perfected and popularized, he achieved some remarkable victories, notably in his debut at the Hastings 1895 tournament.

In this game, we see him applying the great power of the Queen's Gambit to crush an opponent who is not familiar with its fine points and who puts up less than flawless defence. He beats Mason 'like a child', as Marshall used to express it.

4 ...   **♗e7** *(D)*

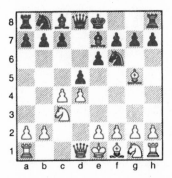

If nothing else, the development of the bishop *anywhere* furthers Black's progress, as the decks are cleared for kingside castling. At e7, the bishop is happily placed for defence, and, if the need arises, can be transferred quickly to a more aggressive position. Incidentally, the knight is unpinned and White's threat nullified.

5 ♘f3

In queen's pawn openings the king's knight's job is the control and sometimes the occupation of the outpost e5. In fact, entrenching the knight at this square and supporting it solidly with the d-pawn and the f-pawn is the motif of what later came to be known as the Pillsbury Attack,

a tremendously effective assault on the kingside.

5 ...   **b6** *(D)*

At first glance, this seems to be a simple and natural way to develop the c8-bishop, as it is hemmed in on the other side by the e-pawn. It took many years, and a great many losses by Black, to discover that an early fianchetto of the bishop was not an easy solution to the problem of the bishop's development.

After a great deal of trial and error, a reasonable defence was hit upon, which consisted of playing ...dxc4 at an early stage, followed after suitable preparation by an attack on White's d-pawn by ...c5 or ...e5. The first of these moves (...c5) is intended to dispute control of the centre, open the c-file for the use of Black's pieces and in general free his cramped position. The attack by ...e5 is meant to take away the control of e5 from White's d-pawn, and to open a diagonal for Black's c8-bishop.

In short, Black first puts up a fight for the centre before he thinks of developing the bishop.

It is of almost vital importance that Black play ...c5 sooner or later. This move strikes at White's d-pawn, establishes tension in the centre, opens the c-file for his own major pieces and frees the crowded position on the queenside. Failure to make this move permits White to seize control of the c-file and the c5-square. Should White manage to post a piece on that square, it will exert terrific pressure on Black's entire position, and this one factor alone may be enough to cause Black's downfall.

6 e3

White strengthens his centre and clears a path for his f1-bishop.

6 ...   ♗b7 (D)

Black completes the fianchetto development of the c8-bishop.

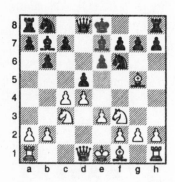

7 ♖c1

The rook hurries over to the important c-file. This is only partly open now, but an exchange of pawns will clear the file and accentuate the rook's power along its whole length.

7 ...   dxc4

Black usually waits until White moves his f1-bishop before making this capture, as then the bishop loses a move in recapturing. Apparently Black is anxious to give his b7-bishop more scope on the long central diagonal.

8 ♗xc4 (D)

White recaptures the pawn and gets another piece into play.

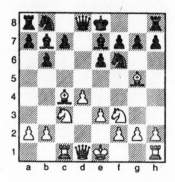

8 ...   ♘bd7!

This disposition of the knight is characteristic in queen's pawn openings. The knight must not go to c6, blocking the c-pawn. *The pawn must be free to advance and challenge the centre.*

At d7, the knight is situated ideally: it supports an advance by ...c5 or ...e5, attacking the centre, it participates in the fight for possession of these squares, and it cooperates with the knight on f6.

9 0-0

The king disappears from the scene while the rook is made available for duty.

9 ...   0-0

The advantage of castling is that the king is safer in the corner, where he is sheltered by three pawns and a stalwart knight, than in the centre of the board, while the rook is brought toward the centre files in the most convenient way possible.

10 ♕e2

The two most effective squares that White's queen can occupy in this opening are e2 and c2. At c2, the queen supplements the rook's action in exploiting the c-file, while in another direction guards the strategically important e4-square from invasion by Black's f6-knight. At e2, the queen prevents Black from breaking up the kingside pawn position by 10...♗xf3, supports an advance of the e-pawn which would monopolize the centre, and clears the way for the f1-rook to reach d1.

Developing the queen to e2 offers another advantage: attack on the queenside. By playing 11 ♗a6, White can force an exchange of bishops and then bring pressure to bear on Black's light squares, weakened by the removal of the bishop controlling those squares.

10 ...   ♘d5 *(D)*

Black's purpose in this is to free his cramped position by bringing about an exchange or two.

11 ♗xe7

White is willing to simplify by clearing away some pieces, as he can then return to his theme of exerting painful pressure on the c-file.

The alternative, retreat by 11 ♗f4, offers Black a choice of too many good continuations. He could play 11...♘xf4 (leaving himself with the two bishops) 12 exf4 ♘f6 followed by 13...♘d5, keeping a piece permanently on a square where no enemy pawns could dislodge it, or Black might attack the centre at once with 11...c5. Finally, he could swing the d7-knight over to f6 with a respectable game.

White's actual move has the merit of restricting Black's choice of reply.

11 ...   ♕xe7 *(D)*

This is preferable to capturing by 11...♘xe7 as Black gets his queen into play and unites his rooks. Naturally, he cannot go in for 11...♘xc3 12 ♗xd8 ♘xe2+ 13 ♗xe2 ♖fxd8 14 ♖xc7 (triumph of the rook on the open file) as it loses a pawn and the game.

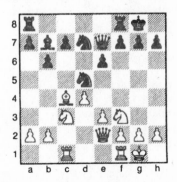

12 ♘xd5

This time the knight exchange suits White, who now can dictate the course of events.

12 ... exd5 *(D)*

Forced, as 12...♗xd5 13 ♗xd5 exd5 14 ♖xc7 costs a pawn.

In forcing Black to take with the pawn, White has compelled the closing of the long diagonal, so that Black's bishop is now terribly limited in scope.

13 ♗b5!

Presto! The file is suddenly open, and the c-file action begins with the rook's attack on the c7-pawn.

13 ... ♕d6

Black guards the pawn and prepares to dislodge White's bishop by 14...c6.

It is already too late to advance the pawn to c5 as after 13...c5 (seemingly a safe move as the pawn is triply defended and only twice attacked) 14 ♗xd7 ♕xd7 (note how White disposes of two of the defenders with one stroke) 15 dxc5 bxc5 16 ♖xc5 White wins a pawn.

14 ♖c2

White makes room for the other rook at c1, to add to the pressure.

The device of doubling rooks on an open file more than doubles their strength on that file.

14 ... c6

Black tries to evict the annoying bishop.

15 ♗d3 *(D)*

This is much stronger than 15 ♗a4, when Black gets some troublesome counterplay by 15...b5 16 ♗b3 a5 (threatening to win the bishop by 17...a4) 17 a3 ♘b6, and the knight settles itself firmly at c4.

15 ... ♘f6

Blissfully unconscious of the impending danger, Black goes about his business, which in this case consists of bringing the knight over to attack, and perhaps to occupy e4. Ordinarily, this is commendable procedure, but all strategy must be conditioned by the circumstances, the position at hand. All moves must be made with respect to the threats of the opponent, not to arbitrary judgements which declare that certain moves are always 'good' or 'bad'. *All moves must be measured by their worth in the particular position being played.*

White has declared his intention of piling up as much pressure as possible on the c-file and on the c6-pawn. Black must meet that threat by bringing all his resources to bear for defence of the file, or institute a counterattack vigorous enough to divert White's forces from the assault.

Black must do something to resolve his immediate difficulties, and he must do it at once, before his opponent gets a death grip on the open file.

With his last move, Black misses a golden opportunity – his last chance to play 15...c5, establish a state of tension in the centre, and give his pieces more room to move around in.

16   Zfc1

This fixes Black's c-pawn by preventing it from moving; if 16...c5, then 17 dxc5 bxc5 18 Zxc5 and White wins a pawn.

16   ...   Zac8

Rushing to the defence of the c-pawn and renewing (now that Black realizes his peril) the possibility of pushing the pawn.

17   Za6!

Very fine strategy! White wants to remove Black's bishop, since minor pieces are excellent defenders of pawns that are attacked by the heavy pieces. White's rooks could never seriously threaten the c-pawn while the bishop protected it.

17   ...   Zxa6

Was there anything else Black could have done? If 17...Zc7, White wins by 18 Zxb7 Zxb7 19 Zxc6 or if 17...Wc7, then 18 b4 further restrains the pawn, after which White

intensifies the pressure by 19 De5, simplifies by exchanging bishops and then takes the pawn off.

18   Wxa6 (D)

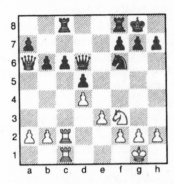

The queen comes closer, attacking not only the a-pawn directly, but also the c-pawn indirectly by the threat 19 Wb7 Zc7 20 Zxc6 Zxb7 21 Zxd6, and White wins.

18   ...   Zc7

Looks good, as Black saves the a-pawn, keeps the queen out of b7, and prepares to double rooks and to supply the wretched pawn with another defender.

19   De5

White's strategy is simple: he piles up more pressure on the c-pawn. It is now attacked by three pieces and defended by two.

19   ...   c5

The planned 19...Zfc8 lets White win nicely by 20 Dxc6 Zxc6 21 Wxc8+! Zxc8 22 Zxc8+ Wf8 23 Zxf8+ &xf8 24 Zc7 a5 25 Zb7 and the rest is child's play.

20   Zxc5

From now on, White simply removes anything that isn't nailed down.

20   ...   ☐xc5

Black is not wild about exchanging pieces when he is a pawn down, but what can he do? If he disputes the c-file by 20...☐fc8 then 21 ♕xc8+ wins, as in the earlier note, while on 20...☐e7 (the c7-rook's only flight square) 21 ☐c6 ♕d8 (or 21...♕b4 22 ♘d3 ♕d2 23 ☐6c2 ♕a5 24 ♕xa5 bxa5, and the forced exchange of queens leaves Black's position in ruins) 22 a3 White's threat of winning the queen by 23 ☐c8 ♕d6 24 ☐1c6 is hard to meet.

21   ☐xc5

The rook recaptures, disdainful of the pinned pawn which is helpless to remove it, and remains in control of the valuable open file.

21   ...   ♘d7

This looks attractive as the knight attacks two pieces. If White replies 22 ♘xd7, then 22...♕xd7 leaves a queen and rook ending which is not easy to win. White would eventually have to advance his pawn majority on the kingside and expose his king to a possible drawing perpetual check.

If the rook retreats, Black continues 22...♘xe5 23 dxe5 ♕xe5, again with drawing chances.

22   ☐c6

Neatly side-stepping the knight exchange, the rook gains time by attacking the queen.

22   ...   ♘b8

Black is forced into making this 'combination' as the retreat by 22...♕e7 is disastrous after 23 ☐c7 (pinning the knight) 23...☐d8 24 ♕b5 (triple attack!), and White wins a piece.

23   ☐xd6

Simplify! That's the magic word to remember in endings where you have an advantage in material.

With you are a pawn ahead, reduce the material (and your opponent's chances) by exchanging pieces, if it does not weaken your position.

23   ...   ♘xa6 *(D)*

Forced, of course.

24   ♘c6!

A master move! You or I might grab the d-pawn in order to be two pawns ahead. This could win, but why complicate matters? Why let Black seize the c-file with 24...☐c8 and start a counterattack?

Note that Pillsbury retains his attack on the d-pawn with the text-move, adds to it a threat against the a-pawn and prevents Black from playing 24...☐c8, when the knight check at e7 would annihilate him!

It is subtle moves in apparently simple positions and not queen sacrifices that mark the master player.

24   ...   g6

Sooner or later, the king will need some air. The king is also anxious to lend a hand in the ending by moving toward the centre, by way of g7.

25 ♘xa7

Another pawn falls, while two more are threatened by the rook.

25 ... ♖a8

Unable to get to c8, the rook makes frantic efforts to enter the fight.

26 ♘c6

The knight withdraws, still in position to punish 26...♖c8 by 27 ♘e7+ winning the rook.

26 ... ♔g7

Black moves the king out of range of the knight check and closer to the centre.

27 a3

There is no hurry about taking the d-pawn. White guards his a-pawn from any discovered attack on it by the rook hidden away at a8, and also prevents Black's knight from later emerging at b4.

Note that White avoids 27 ♖xd5 ♖c8 28 ♖d6 (the knight cannot move due to the mate threat) 28...♘b4, when Black wins the helpless knight.

27 ... ♖c8 *(D)*

Finally posting his rook on the coveted file, but can Black make use of it?

28 g4

White's king also needs an escape square. Black was threatening to win a piece by 28...♘b8, twice attacking the knight which could not run away.

The break-up of the pawn position around the castled king is of no consequence in the ending. It is in the opening and middlegame that these moves endanger the health of the king, as then he may be assaulted by every piece on the board.

28 ... ♘c7

Black protects his d-pawn, but at the cost of blocking the rook. There was little choice because White was threatening 29 ♘e7 (attacking the black rook and a couple of pawns) 29...♖c1+ 30 ♔g2 ♖b1 31 ♖xb6, and the two connected passed pawns assure White an easy win.

29 ♘e7 *(D)*

Once again chasing the rook from the open c-file. White threatens the rook, attacks the b-pawn and doubly attacks the d-pawn.

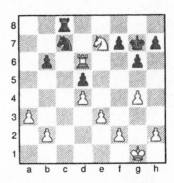

29 ... ♖b8

Black must hang on to the b-pawn as long as possible, as with its loss White's pawns on the queenside are free to go on to queen.

30 ♖d7!

The pressure must not be relaxed! Pillsbury prefers this to the rook ending resulting from 30 ♘xd5 ♘xd5 31 ♖xd5, though that would also win.

30 ...   ♘e6

The knight must leave, as the effort to protect it by 30...♖b7 fails after 31 ♘xd5 winning a piece.

31 ♘xd5 (D)

The d-pawn falls at last, giving White a passed pawn on the d-file and a rook on the seventh rank (in addition to the pawns he picked up).

31 ...   ♖c8

Rather than be gradually crushed to death, Black gives up another pawn to get some sort of counterplay on the open file. If his rook can get behind White's pawns, it might gather up a couple of them.

32 ♘xb6

White can play safe and keep the rook out by 32 ♘c3 but capturing the b-pawn leaves him with three passed pawns – an offer hard to resist!

32 ...   ♖c2

Occupation of the seventh rank is the logical consequence of play on

an open file by a rook. This could mean trouble for White except that he has powerful antidotes in all those pawns ready to rush up the board to become queens!

33 b4

The pawn lightly evades the rook's attack.

33 ...   ♘g5 (D)

White's pawns are not readily hindered from advancing, but perhaps White's deserted king might be sensitive to an attack by knight and rook.

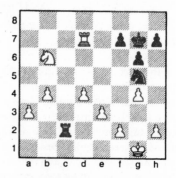

34 a4!

White goes calmly about his business of pushing the passed pawns and getting a queen.

It was tempting to drive the knight off with 34 f4 but this move, believe it or not, enables Black to draw the game! After 34 f4 ♘f3+ 35 ♔f1 (definitely not 35 ♔h1 ♖xh2#) 35...♖d2! 36 ♘c4 ♘xh2+ 37 ♔g1 ♘f3+ 38 ♔f1 ♘h2+ 39 ♔e1 ♘f3+ Black draws by perpetual check.

34 ...   ♘e4

Black tries another means of entry.

35 a5

Again, Pillsbury resists the impulse to get in a dig at the knight. If 35 f3, then 35...♘g5 again threatens 36...♘xf3+ and a draw by perpetual check.

35 ...   ♘xf2

Can Black conjure up a mating attack?

36 a6

White demonstrates the futility of his opponent's gestures by paying no attention to them! The passed pawn has only two more squares to cover and cannot be stopped in its march.

1-0

Black decides that it would be too much to hope for this bit of luck: 36...♘h3+ 37 ♔h1? ♘g5 38 a7? ♘f3 39 a8♕ ♖xh2#! Of course, White would play 37 ♔f1, when he wins easily.

Game 18
Noteboom – Doesburgh
Netherlands 1931
Queen's Gambit Declined

1 d4

In the opening, it is advantageous to occupy the centre with a pawn and to develop the pieces with a view to controlling the centre.

White begins by placing a pawn where it takes complete possession of one important square and attacks two others. Control of the two squares e5 and c5 makes it impossible for Black to place pieces there. White can hope to use e5 and c5 as outposts for his pieces, which will have the support of the d-pawn.

The advance of the d-pawn serves an additional purpose in opening lines for White's queen and c1-bishop.

1 ...   d5

This is the simplest way for Black to get an equal grip on the centre and to prevent White acquiring more territory with 2 e4.

2 c4

White offers a pawn to divert Black's d-pawn from the centre. In effect, it is an offer to exchange a flank pawn for a centre pawn, as White can regain the pawn without any trouble.

Concealed in White's proposal is a threat of destroying Black's pawn-centre by 3 cxd5 ♕xd5 4 ♘c3 (gaining a tempo, as White develops a piece while Black must move the same one again) 4...♕a5 5 e4, and White's control of the centre is imposing.

2 ...   e6

Black defends the centre by supporting the d-pawn with another pawn. If White plays 3 cxd5, Black can recapture with a pawn and maintain a pawn in the centre.

Black does not capture White's c4-pawn as that means surrendering the centre and his grip on e4.

The shutting in of his c8-bishop (after 2...e6) and the consequent difficulty in developing that piece effectively is one of the reasons for the popularity of the Queen's Gambit – for White.

3 ♘c3

A good move, as the knight attacks the two central squares e4 and d5, adding its influence to the pawn's pressure on the latter.

3 ...   ♘f6 (D)

Black's knight develops toward the centre, where its mobility is greatest and where it can counter the pressure exerted by White's knight.

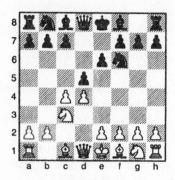

4 ♗g5

A pin which threatens 5 cxd5 exd5 6 ♗xf6, when Black must either submit to being left with a badly doubled pawn by 6...gxf6 or lose a pawn after 6...♕xf6 7 ♘xd5.

The threat is actually of minor importance. White's real aim in pinning the knight is not to institute a threat that can so easily be parried. What White is interested in is the most effective placement of his pieces, and the development of the bishop at g5 is extremely strong. The restraint it places on Black's knight and the cramping effect it has on Black's whole game is not easily shaken off.

4 ...   ♘bd7 (D)

In queen's pawn openings, Black's queen's knight does its best job at d7, not c6. At d7 it supports the other knight and helps prepare the advance of the c-pawn to c5. The b8-knight must not move to c6, where it obstructs the c-pawn. *The c-pawn must be free to advance and attack White's centre.*

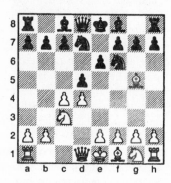

Black incidentally sets a trap with the text-move, which is designed to catch the greedy player.

5 e3

Why not win a pawn by 5 cxd5 exd5 6 ♘xd5 instead? There would then follow 6...♘xd5! (the knight breaks the pin by brute force) 7 ♗xd8 ♗b4+ 8 ♕d2 ♗xd2+ 9 ♔xd2 ♔xd8 and Black has gained a piece.

White could not fall into the trap if he followed the principle which covers these cases:

Do not chase after pawns at the expense of your development.

White's last move supports the central d4-pawn and creates an outlet for the f1-bishop.

5 ...   c6

Black strengthens his d-pawn and opens a diagonal for his queen's use.

He plans a counterattack beginning with 6...♕a5 and 7...♗b4.

6 a3

This puts a stop to any such manoeuvre, as Black's bishop can never get to b4 to pin the knight.

6 ... ♗e7

Black develops a piece, unpins the knight and clears the back rank for castling.

7 ♕c2

An ideal development for the queen in this opening. At c2, the queen exerts pressure on the c-file (which will be strongly evident after centre pawns are exchanged) and controls the e4-square. The latter circumstance is the reason for the queen coming into play at this point, instead of the expected mobilization of the kingside pieces. It is vital to guard the e4-square so that Black cannot free himself easily by playing 7...♘e4 and exchanging some pieces.

7 ... 0-0

Black moves his king to safer quarters. He cannot free his crowded position by the Lasker manoeuvre 7...♘e4 as White responds 8 ♗xe7 ♕xe7 9 ♘xe4 dxe4 10 ♕xe4 and wins a pawn. Notice that White's pawn at a3 prevents Black from regaining the pawn by 10...♕b4+, showing that White's sixth move was not a waste of time.

Instead of the passive kingside castling, Black should have tried for counterplay by 7...dxc4 8 ♗xc4 e5!, which disputes control of the centre and helps clear a diagonal for his c8-bishop.

8 ♘f3

White brings his king's knight to its best post and attacks the e5-square again, putting an end to any contemplated break by ...e5.

8 ... a6 *(D)*

Preparation for the manoeuvre 9...dxc4 10 ♗xc4 b5 11 ♗d3 ♗b7, followed by an eventual ...c5. This would serve to develop the c8-bishop, free his queenside and start action against White's pawn-centre.

9 ♖d1!

If Black is going in for an attack on the wing, White is prepared to meet it with the recommended antidote – play in the centre!

The position of the rook at d1 acts as a deterrent to central pawn exchanges by Black, as any clearances on the d-file increase the pressure of the rook on that file.

9 ... ♖e8

Black brings his rook to the e-file, as the centre is usually the theatre of action.

10 ♗d3

With the entrance of this bishop, White's development is nearly complete. Notice that he plays no combinations of any sort, either to win material or to start an attack on the king, until most of his pieces are brought off the back rank and into play. It is only after these pieces are posted where they are most effective – where they control the centre, enjoy their greatest mobility, and take possession of a good part of the important territory – that White looks around for a combination, a stroke that will decide the game quickly.

10 ...   dxc4

Black has delayed taking this pawn until White's f1-bishop made a move, so that the bishop will now lose a move in recapturing.

11 ♗xc4

The recapture is forced.

11 ...   b5 (D)

Black makes the bishop lose time in retreating and vacates the b7-square, ready for the development of the c8-bishop.

12 ♗d3!

From this square, the bishop manages to be remarkably useful:

It reaches out in two directions to attack, it helps guard e4 from invasion, it threatens Black's kingside and, by attacking h7, prevents Black

from freeing himself by means of 12...c5.

12 ...   h6 (D)

If 12...c5, then 13 dxc5 ♗xc5 (certainly not 13...♘xc5 14 ♗xh7+ and White wins the queen by discovered attack) 14 ♗xh7+ and White wins a pawn, as the pinned knight is helpless to take the bishop.

With the text-move, Black moves the h-pawn out of the attack of White's queen and bishop. Now he hopes to free his queenside and establish a state of tension in the centre by 13...c5. Incidentally, he would like White's g5-bishop to declare its intentions.

13 ♗xf6!

A very fine concept! White does not waste time holding on to the two bishops but plays to prevent any counterplay by ...c5. If he can keep the c-pawn from advancing, Black's game will be fearfully cramped, and he may never solve the problem of getting his light-squared bishop settled on a decent square.

The immediate object of 13 ♗xf6 is to divert one of Black's recapturing pieces, the knight or the bishop, from its surveillance of the c5-square and the support of a pawn moving to that square.

13 ... ♘xf6

This is probably better than taking with the bishop, as Black's queen and c8-bishop now have more freedom.

14 0-0

The king (who must be secure from danger at all costs) goes into hiding, while the rook (that must take part in the fighting) comes closer to the scene of action.

14 ... ♗b7 *(D)*

With rook and queen on the same file, it would be foolhardy to venture on 14...c5. White simply takes the pawn, 15 dxc5, and punishes the recapture 15...♗xc5 with 16 ♗h7+ winning the queen.

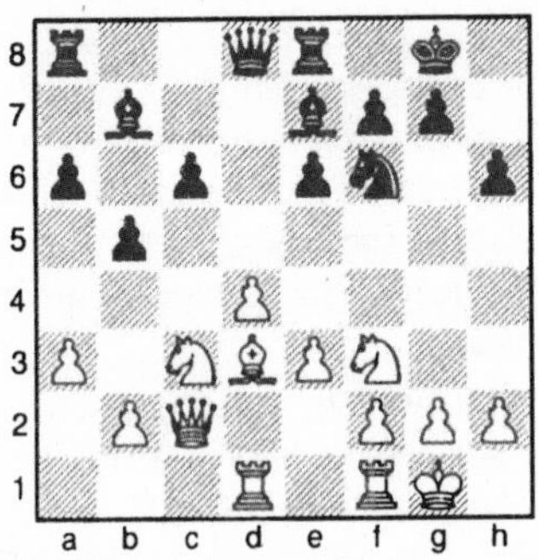

Black's idea, besides that of developing the light-squared bishop, is to bring his rook to c8 and then push the c-pawn.

15 ♘e4!

White clears the c-file so that he now has three pieces (queen, knight and d4-pawn) concentrating their power on c5, with the aim of making an advance of Black's c-pawn to that square impossible.

Notice too how White has resisted the temptation to play e4, filling up the centre with pawns. Instead he keeps the e4-square free and utilizes it as a springboard for his pieces.

15 ... ♘xe4

Otherwise, White might swing the knight over to c5 and completely smother Black's queenside.

16 ♗xe4 *(D)*

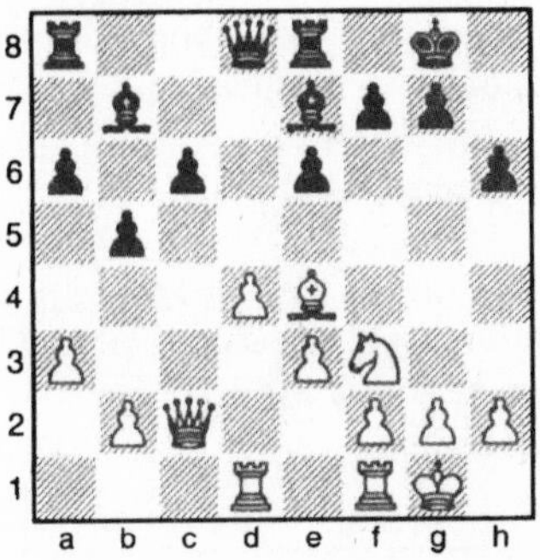

Still keeping Black under restraint: he may not play 16...c5 as his b7-bishop would be snapped up.

16 ... f5

Black must drive the bishop off at once, even at the cost of weakening the pawn position on his kingside. A delay gives White time to play 17 ♘e5 (intensifying the pressure on the c-pawn and incidentally providing the f3-square for a bishop retreat) followed if need be by 18 ♖c1.

17 ♗d3

The third visit of the bishop to this square.

White must not be hasty and play 17 ♗xc6 as the reply 17...♖c8 pins the bishop.

17 ... ♕b6

Once again preparing the liberating pawn-push.

18 ♖c1

The position demands that White devote all his efforts to sustaining the blockade of Black's c-pawn. White must acquire undisputed control of the c5-square, so that the pawn may never advance. He must not relax for a moment, as *domination of the key c5-square virtually assures him of a positional win.*

18 ... ♖ac8 (D)

Black persists in his plan to push the pawn. If he does not get this move in, his b7-bishop will never have any air.

19 b4!

White nails the pawn down! White has a won game, strategically. What remains is to apply the proper tactical touches to compel the opponent to yield. The time is ripe for the combinations to appear!

19 ... ♕d8

Ready to parry 20 ♕b3 (threatening 21 ♕xe6+ or 21 ♗xf5) with 20...♕d5.

20 ♘e5

A powerful blow! White attacks the unfortunate c-pawn (which must stay where it is) a third time. Against passive resistance, White plans 21 f4 (to give his knight additional support and to stabilize the centre), followed by 22 ♗e2 and 23 ♗f3, after which the c-pawn must perish.

20 ... a5 (D)

Black attacks one of the pawns hemming in his queenside.

Against 20...♗f6 White sticks to the script with 21 f4, followed by 22 ♗e2 and 23 ♗f3.

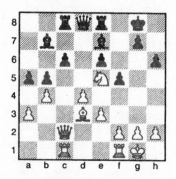

21 ♕b3!

Again threatening 22 ♕xe6+ or 22 ♗xf5.

White probably gave no more than a glance to 21 bxa5, to which Black can reply 21...♕xa5, 21...♗xa3 or 21...c5, any of which gives him far too much freedom – from White's point of view!

21 ... ♗d6

The defence that Black had relied on is ruled out: if 21...♕d5, then 22 ♕xd5 and White wins a pawn after 22...exd5 23 ♗xf5 or 22...cxd5 23 ♗xb5.

22 ♗xf5

The first bit of actual violence brings in a pawn.

22 ...   ♕f6

With an attack on the bishop and a double attack on the knight, Black hopes to get his pawn back.

23 ♗b1

The idea of this withdrawal to the back rank is to support the queen in an attack along a diagonal, either by moving the queen to c2 or by shifting the bishop to a2 behind the queen.

23 ...   ♗xe5

Black does not care to part with the services of an active piece, but he must do so in order to recover the pawn he lost.

24 dxe5

Forced.

24 ...   ♕xe5

Material is even, and Black seems to have survived the worst.

It is true that White can win a pawn by 25 bxa5, but he would be left with doubled and isolated pawns on the a-file, and it is doubtful that he could get any advantage from the extra pawn. There must be a better reward for fine positional play than this dubious bounty!

25 ♖c5!

White spurns the pawn, in favour of piling on more pressure. The rook now holds Black's queenside in a paralysing grip. The strength of White's move is evident in the fact that the rook can never be dislodged!

25 ...   a4 *(D)*

An intermediary move, whose purpose is not only to save the pawn, but also to gauge White's plans by his next queen move.

26 ♕a2!

A remarkable retreat! One would expect 26 ♕c2 so that the queen, backed up by the bishop, might penetrate Black's kingside position. However, Black refutes this cleverly by 26...♕f6 and now:

1) 27 ♕h7+ is met by 27...♔f7, when White has no means of furthering the attack.

2) 27 e4 (intending to banish the queen by 28 e5 and then pierce the position) 27...e5 and Black repels any invasion.

26 ...   ♕d6

The defence 26...♕f6 succumbs to 27 e4! (now we see the point of 26 ♕a2 – it is to pin Black's e-pawn and prevent 27...e5 at this point) 27...♖cd8 28 e5 ♕f4 29 ♕c2 (threatening 30 ♕h7+ ♔f8 31 ♗g6 ♖e7 32 ♕h8#) 29...♕g5 30 f4 ♕g4 31 ♖c3, when the entrance of the rook at g3, followed by 33 ♕h7+, is conclusive.

Notice that the move 31 ♖c3, relaxing the pressure on the queenside, is not an infraction of principle. An attack that leads to a forced win takes precedence over positional considerations.

27 ♕c2

Now this grouping has more effect! White threatens 28 ♕h7+ ♔f8 29 ♗g6 ♖ed8 30 ♕h8+ ♔e7 31 ♕xg7#.

27 ... ♖cd8 (D)

If 27...e5 to guard the g6-square with the queen, then 28 ♕h7+ ♔f7 (on 28...♔f8, 29 ♗g6 wins easily) 29 f4 (threatening 30 fxe5+) 29...e4 30 ♗a2+ ♔f6 31 ♕f5+ ♔e7 32 ♕f7+ and White wins the bishop, as a start.

28 ♕h7+

Control of the light squares leading to Black's king renders this a decisive invasion; the cramping of Black's queenside and the smothering of his bishop make it difficult for Black to hold out.

28 ... ♔f8

On 28...♔f7 White can either win the exchange by a bishop check or pursue the attack by 29 f4, when the continuation might be 29...♖h8 30 ♕g6+ ♔f8 31 f5 e5 (or 31...♕e7 32 f6) 32 f6 and White wins.

29 ♗g6

Further confines the king while attacking the rook. The threat is 30 ♕h8+ ♔e7 31 ♕xg7#.

1-0

Black can only delay the execution at great cost in material.

White's play is a fine example of the value of preventive strategy. In paralysing Black's queenside, he demonstrates the extraordinary fact that weaknesses on one wing can lead to complete collapse on the other! Once Black is held in restraint, his efforts to make some sort of stand seem little more than feeble flutterings.

Game 19
Grünfeld – Schenkein
Vienna 1915
Queen's Gambit Declined

1 d4

Beginning the game with this pawn move releases two pieces at one stroke. This is as much as White can achieve in one move in the way of getting the pieces off the back rank and into play. The pawn itself plays an important part in the struggle for domination of the centre and the control of key squares.

1 ... d5

Probably Black's best reply. With it, he offsets White's pressure on the centre.

2 c4

This is an attack, as well as an offer of a pawn. It is an attack in that White threatens by 3 cxd5 ♕xd5 4 ♘c3 ♕a5 5 e4 to establish two pawns abreast in the centre. It is an offer, since Black can gain a pawn (temporarily, it is true) by 2...dxc4.

Either way you look at it, White's purpose is to destroy Black's pawn-centre, either by removing Black's d-pawn from d5, or enticing it away from there.

2 ... c6 *(D)*

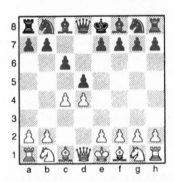

Black is ready to meet 3 cxd5 with 3...cxd5, *recapturing with a pawn* in order to maintain a pawn in the centre.

Black's second move has the merit of not shutting in the c8-bishop, as the alternative 2...e6 does. On the debit side though, if Black does develop his bishop freely, he must be prepared to beat off troublesome attacks on his d-pawn and his b-pawn, occasioned by the absence of the bishop. Another and more important consideration is that while the c-pawn standing at c6 represents a fine support for the d-pawn, it is not

fulfilling its main purpose in life, which is to challenge White's control of the centre. It must be available to advance to c5 in order to attack White's d-pawn and to open the c-file for the use of Black's heavy pieces.

3 ♘f3

Why doesn't White play 3 c5 and stifle his opponent completely on the queenside? These are some of the reasons he does not do so:

1) It is good strategy to maintain tension in the centre – to keep the pawn position fluid, not static.

2) In advancing to c5, White gives up his attack on the enemy centre, and the option of exchanging pawns when it is worthwhile to do so. Such an exchange might be the means of demolishing Black's whole centre!

3) The c5-square should be an outpost for a piece, not a pawn. A piece posted there exerts a tremendous effect on Black's whole queenside.

4) Placing a pawn at c5 closes the c-file and makes it useless for the operations of the queen or the rooks.

5) In the opening, pieces, not pawns, should be moved.

All the foregoing explains why a chess master 'instinctively' finds the right moves. It is not that he can analyse twenty moves ahead, or that he bothers to examine the effects of every possible move. Sometimes he does not even look one move ahead! He saves time by dismissing from consideration any move which his instinct (or more accurately his experience and judgement) warns is contrary to principle and cannot possibly lead to favourable results. By discarding moves which offend his feeling for what is proper, by avoiding artificial expedients which are distasteful to his positional judgement, he plays stronger, sounder chess at ten seconds a move than does the average amateur in his serious tournament games.

3 ...   e6

This quiet move strengthens his centre and frees the f8-bishop.

Black's intentions are still unclear. He might capture the c4-pawn next move and then try to hold on to it by ...b5, or he might go in for the Stonewall formation, by playing 4...f5 followed by 5...♘f6 and possibly 6...♘e4.

4 e3 *(D)*

White plays safe by protecting the c4-pawn. He releases one bishop at the expense of another, but one cannot have everything.

4 ...   ♘f6

The knight takes up a good post, extending powerful influence on d5 and e4, two of the four strategically important squares in the centre.

5 ♗d3

The bishop occupies a diagonal where it can operate with great effect, while the kingside is cleared for speedy castling.

Broadly speaking, it is good policy to develop the kingside pieces first, so that the king can find safer quarters. Most players are familiar enough with this procedure and its benefits to carry it out faithfully, some even to the extent of completely forgetting about releasing the queenside pieces!

5 ...   ♘bd7

Excellent, as the knight supports an eventual thrust at White's centre by ...c5 or ...e5. Being in touch with the other knight also has its uses, as it can replace the f6-knight.

6 ♘bd2

The chief object of this move is to back up an advance of the e-pawn as in the Colle System. A second purpose of the knight's development at d2 instead of c3 is to recapture with the knight if Black plays 6...dxc4, and then anchor one of the knights at e5, strongly supported by the other.

6 ...   ♗e7

A good defensive move – perhaps too much so! The bishop is well placed at e7, and progress is made toward castling, but no attempt is made to prevent White from expanding and acquiring more territory. Black must get in the counter-thrust ...c5 or be slowly crowded back and confined to a small area.

7 0-0

The king flees to a safer part of the board, while the h1-rook takes a more active position.

7 ...   ♛**c7** *(D)*

Another quiet developing move, which might better have been replaced by the aggressive 7...c5. Black cannot temporize but must fight for equal rights. Chess is no game for cowards!

8 e4!

This resembles the Colle device for breaking up the position in the centre and opening lines of attack for the pieces crouched in the background.

8 ...   **dxe4**

Black cannot allow the pawn to go to e5. There it would drive away his f6-knight and put it completely out of action.

9 ♘xe4

More energetic than recapturing with the bishop. The knight gets out of the way of the c1-bishop and puts the question to the enemy knight.

9 ...   ♘**xe4**

Black must exchange to relieve his constricted position.

10 ♗xe4

The exchange of pieces suits White too. The more material disappears from the board, the more scope

there is for the activities of his pieces, especially the wide-ranging bishops.

10 ...   ♘**f6**

The attack on the bishop gains a tempo for Black while giving his queenside pieces a bit more room.

11 ♗c2 *(D)*

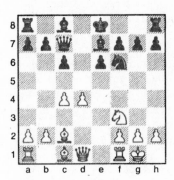

The bishop retreats, but to a fine vantage point. It is poised for a kingside attack but can quickly shift to the queenside if necessary.

White's position is distinctly superior. He enjoys these advantages:
- His bishops have a great range of attack.
- He dominates the centre with his pawns.
- He controls the strategically important e5-square.
- His major pieces can operate with great effect on the centre files.

11 ...   **b6**

To develop the bishop at b7, since it is shut in by the e-pawn on the other diagonal.

12 ♛e2

White develops another piece and intensifies the pressure on e5. Control of this square will make it difficult, if not impossible, for Black to free his position by advancing the e-pawn.

12 ...   ♗b7

With the development of this bishop, Black seems to be finding a way out of his troubles. He is now set to play ...c5 next move, operate on the long diagonal with his light-squared bishop and establish a proper state of tension in the centre. Will he have time for this, or has he missed the right moment to hit out with ...c5?

13 ♘e5!

A magnificent outpost for the knight! From this central station, the knight radiates power in eight directions, accentuating Black's difficulties in gaining freedom for his pieces.

13 ...   ♖d8

This looks plausible, since Black mobilizes the rook while attacking a pawn.

It is too late, alas, to play the liberating 13...c5; White's reply 14 ♗a4+ would force Black's king to move (interposing the knight or bishop instead costs a piece) and forfeit the right to castle.

14 ♖d1

White defends without loss of time. The rook guards the pawn and develops simultaneously, going to the file it would have chosen in any event.

Rooks belong on open files, or on files likely to be opened.

14 ...   0-0 (D)

The advance 14...c5 is still premature, being met by 15 ♗a4+ and Black must either move the king and lose the castling privilege, or play 15...♘d7 losing the exchange after 16 ♗xd7+ ♖xd7 17 ♘xd7.

Before White makes his next move, let us sum up his advantages:

- His pawn position in the centre, restraining the free movements of the enemy pieces, is definitely superior to Black's.
- His queen attacks nine squares while Black's is limited to five.
- His bishops control thirteen squares, whereas Black's are limited to seven.
- His knight enjoys wonderful mobility, while Black's knight can only retreat.

Clearly, White has established a definite positional superiority. His pieces have greater mobility, as simple arithmetic shows, and their power to attack is definitely greater than that of Black's army. White has earned the right to look for a decisive combination that will exploit to the full his positional advantages.

It is interesting to see what form of attack will succeed in breaking through Black's strongly entrenched position.

15 ♗f4!

The bishop develops with a threat against the queen. White intends to play 16 ♘g6 next move, discovering an attack on the queen by the bishop. After the queen moves away, White will capture the f8-rook, winning the exchange.

15 ... ♗d6

The alternative 15...♕c8, moving the queen out of the bishop's range, does not look appetizing. With the text, Black prevents the knight from moving and uncovering an attack.

16 c5!

This begins a series of vigorous blows which do not let up until Black surrenders. White's idea is twofold: he will dislodge the bishop and permanently seal up Black's queenside position.

16 ... bxc5

This is forced, as on 16...♗xe5 White can win by 17 ♗xe5 ♕c8 18 ♗xf6 gxf6 19 ♕g4+ ♔h8 20 ♗xh7 ♔xh7 21 ♖d3 followed by 22 ♖h3#.

17 dxc5 *(D)*

Another pawn springs up to stab at the bishop.

Or 17...♗xc5 18 ♘g6 and White wins the exchange.

18 ♗xe5

This recapture attacks the queen and keeps Black on the run.

18 ... ♕a5

If 18...♕c8 White wins by 19 ♗xf6 gxf6 20 ♕g4+ ♔h8 21 ♕h4 (threatening mate) 21...f5 22 ♕f6+ ♔g8 23 h4 (intending to push the pawn to h6 and then to mate at g7) 24...♖d7 (to follow with 24...♕d8 driving White's queen off) 24 ♖xd7 ♕xd7 25 ♖d1 ♕c7 26 h5, when the two threats of 27 h6 and 27 ♖d3 (followed by 28 ♖g3+) are decisive.

19 ♗xf6!

White does away with the knight, the best defender of a castled position, as a prelude to breaking into the stronghold of the king.

19 ... gxf6 *(D)*

After this, Black's position on the kingside is torn apart, where it should be barricaded. On the queenside, where his pieces need room for their movements, his position is nailed up – and by an unprotected pawn at that!

17 ... ♗xe5

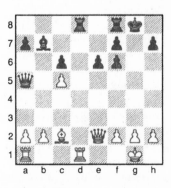

20 ♕g4+

This is more accurate than 20 ♕e4. It leaves Black with only one reply.

20 ...   ♚h8

The king must go to the corner.

21 ♕h4

Now threatening mate on the move.

21 ...   f5 (D)

Black's only defence.

22 ♕e7!

Penetrating into the heart of the enemy's position. The attack on the black bishop is a device whose purpose is to occupy the opponent, even if only for a moment, with the problem of saving the bishop. This will give White the time he needs to carry out his real threat, an attack on both the black rooks.

22 ...   ♗c8

If Black plays 22...♖b8 to protect the bishop, White wins this way: 23 ♕f6+ ♚g8 24 ♖d3 f4 25 ♖h3 (threatening 26 ♗xh7#) 25...♖fd8 26 ♖xh7 and mate follows.

23 b4!

A knockout blow! The queen is forced off the diagonal leading to the rook at d8 – which needs her protection!

What can Black do?

1) 23...♕xb4 24 ♖xd8 ♖xd8 25 ♕xd8+ wins.

2) 23...♖fe8 is met by 24 ♕f6+ followed by 25 bxa5.

3) 23...♖xd1+ 24 ♖xd1 leaves two strong threats on tap: 25 ♕xf8# and 25 bxa5, which cannot both be parried at the same time.

1-0

Game 20

Rubinstein – Salwe
Lodz 1908
Queen's Gambit Declined

1 d4

A hundred and forty years ago, players began their games almost automatically with 1 e4, and if they could offer a gambit, they did so.

Today, when everyone wants to win with the minimum of risk, 1 d4 has become equally popular. The queen's pawn openings lead to positions which are safe and sound. They offer security, and as additional inducement let White have a slight advantage right from the start.

With his first move, White occupies and exerts pressure in the centre with a pawn *which is protected* and simultaneously frees his queen and dark-squared bishop.

1 ... d5

The classical reply, this equalizes the pressure in the centre. It also prevents White from playing 2 e4 and monopolizing most of the best squares.

2 c4

With several objects in mind:
- To induce Black to surrender the centre, by offering him a pawn.
- To exchange pawns (if Black does not) and open the c-file for his rooks.
- To institute an attack on Black's d-pawn, and the d5-square.

2 ... e6

Black supports the d-pawn with another pawn. He is prepared, if White plays 3 cxd5, *to recapture with a pawn* and maintain a pawn in the centre.

3 ♘c3 *(D)*

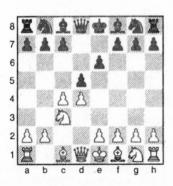

A good development for the knight, now that it does not block the c-pawn and the opening of the c-file. It is a bit sharper than 3 ♘f3 since it steps up the pressure on d5, an important square in this opening.

3 ... c5

This move had the unqualified endorsement of Tarrasch. He held that Black had no better means of developing his pieces freely and easily, even if pawn exchanges in the centre leave him with an isolated pawn.

One advantage of 3...c5 is that it disputes possession of the centre at once by the attack on the d4-pawn. Another is that it enables Black to post his queen's knight at c6, instead of at d7 where it interferes for a long time with the career of the c8-bishop.

4 cxd5! *(D)*

The best way to keep the initiative! This exchange aims to saddle Black with an isolated d-pawn.

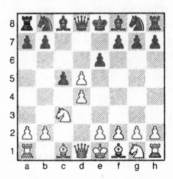

4 ... exd5

The safest recapture. Black can offer a pawn by 4...cxd4 5 ♕xd4 ♘c6 6 ♕d1 exd5 7 ♕xd5 ♗e6 but this gambit is dubious.

5 ♘f3

White's knights now have all four of the strategically important central squares (e4, e5, d4 and d5) under surveillance.

5 ... ♘f6 *(D)*

It makes little difference whether Black plays this or 5...♘c6 first.

6 g3!

Probably the best of the many good moves White has at his disposal. He can also play the placid 6 e3 or 6 ♗f4, either of which gives him a safe, substantial position, or he can attack at once by the aggressive 6 ♗g5, with which Alekhine beat Kussman brilliantly in a 1924 simultaneous exhibition.

With the quiet text-move, Rubinstein intends to fianchetto his light-squared bishop and increase the pressure on d5.

6 ...   ♘c6

Black attains one of the objectives that motivated him to select the Tarrasch Defence. His queen's knight enjoys some influence in the centre, while the light-squared bishop (usually restrained by a knight at d7) is free and unrestrained.

7 ♗g2

The bishop commands the long diagonal and will devote special attention to Black's d-pawn. For the moment, the knight obstructs its path, but a knight can readily leap aside.

7 ...   cxd4

Black exchanges to give his pieces more scope (note the increased mobility of his dark-squared bishop) but this is not without its dangers. Open lines favour the player whose development is superior, and in this case it is White.

Somewhat better is the quiet move 7...♗e7, developing a piece or, if Black feels pugnacious, the sharp 7...♗g4 putting more pressure on the d4-pawn by striking at one of its defenders.

8 ♘xd4 (D)

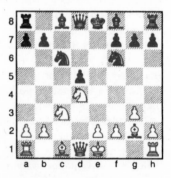

The recapture leaves Black with an isolated pawn in the centre of the board. Such a pawn must depend on pieces to defend it from attack, as there are no pawns on either side that can come to its support. Another consideration is that an enemy piece can be posted firmly on the square directly in front of the isolated pawn, in this case d4, without any fear of being driven off by a pawn.

All this is very discouraging, but in return for these shortcomings, the possessor of the isolated pawn is rewarded with open files and diagonals

– room for the activities of his pieces. The pawn itself, in spite of its forlorn appearance, often becomes the spearhead that pierces and breaks up a fortified position.

The theorists themselves are not in complete agreement on the merits or demerits of an isolated pawn. Many years ago, Philidor said in his *Chess Analysed: or Instructions by Which a Perfect Knowledge of This Noble Game May in a Short Time Be Acquired:* "A pawn, when separated from his fellows, will seldom or never make a fortune." For the defence, we have Tarrasch, who said, "He who fears possession of an isolated d-pawn should give up chess."

There are arguments for both sides:

- Black has in his favour: increased mobility for his pieces, possible outposts for his pieces at e4 and c4 (supported by the d-pawn) and open files for his major pieces (the e- and c-files).
- White has advantages in the fact that he can station a piece permanently at d4 and can keep Black busy warding off threats to the d-pawn. Not that the pawn can easily be captured, since the number of pieces attacking it can always be equalled by the number of pieces defending it, but by virtue of the fact that the pawn needs constant care, White can switch the attack to another section of the board. Black must not only be prepared to fight back there but also keep in close touch with the weak pawn.

8 ...   ♕b6 *(D)*

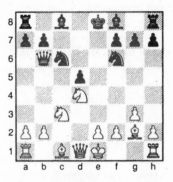

Urging his opponent to exchange knights or defend by 9 e3, blocking the path of his dark-squared bishop.

9 ♘xc6!

A suggestion White is delighted to fall in with! He relieves Black of the isolated pawn, but in return fixes him with other weaknesses. From now on White will forget about the d5-square and turn his attention to dominating d4 and c5 completely. By anchoring pieces on those squares he can prevent Black from advancing his d-pawn or his c-pawn. The effect of blockading these pawns will be to shut in all of Black's pieces behind the pawns.

9 ...   bxc6

The alternative capture 9...♕xc6 loses the d-pawn at once.

10 0-0

Before pursuing the attack, White conveys his king to safer quarters. The king's rook meanwhile becomes available for action on the centre files.

10 ...   ♗e7

Unfortunately, Black may not advance either of the pawns marked for doom: if 10...c5, then 11 ♘xd5 wins a pawn, or if 10...d4, then 11 ♘a4 forces the queen to desert one of the threatened pawns.

There were better chances of resistance with 10...♗e6, protecting the d-pawn once more so as to get in the freeing ...c5 as quickly as possible. Black cannot rely on passive measures or he will be crushed to death.

11   ♘a4!

White is not interested in scaring the queen. The knight does not move to attack but to get a grip on the c5-square so that a white piece may settle itself securely there.

11   ...   ♛b5 (D)

The queen stays in the neighbourhood to help ward off the invaders.

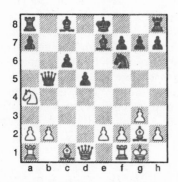

12   ♗e3!

You would expect this bishop to go to f4, where its range is long and where it does not obstruct the e-pawn's movements; or you might consider g5 where it cramps Black's game. These are good and natural moves, but they do not fit in with the strategic concept governing this position. Once there is a definite, logical plan to follow, we must play

moves that conform to that plan, so that the improvement of our own position or the undermining of the opponent's is conducted systematically and not as a result of accidental circumstances. Development, at this point, must not be carried out for its own sake.

It may seem strange that control of one square can cause a position to collapse, but it is true. It is one of the fine points in the Queen's Gambit that such domination (resulting from Black's neglect to dispute the centre and also free his queenside by ...c5) enables White to confine his opponent's pieces to a small area and drive them back step by step, while he (White) either starts escorting a pawn to the queening square or turns to the other side of the board and beleaguers the enemy king.

12   ...   0-0

Not having read the previous note, Black is content to make 'good' developing moves.

He should concentrate his energies on advancing the c-pawn one square before it is permanently fixed at c6. Pushing the pawn at once is premature, as after 12...c5 13 ♗xd5 ♘xd5 14 ♛xd5 ♛xa4 15 ♛xa8 White has won the exchange, but Black could put up more fight with 12...♗e6 (protecting the d-pawn and preparing to move the c-pawn) followed by 13...♘d7 and 14...♖c8, all of which is designed to help the c-pawn to advance one square.

13   ♖c1

White seizes the half-open file, brings more pressure to bear on c5, and prepares to post a piece there.

13 ... &g4 *(D)*

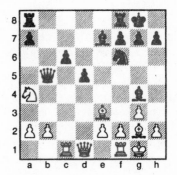

A double attack on the e2-pawn, which may be embarrassing to meet. How does White answer it?

If 14 &e1, the rook's development is wretched.

If 14 &c3, then 14...&xb2 wins a pawn.

If 14 &c2, Black snaps up the knight.

If 14 f3, White loosens the pawn position around his king and hems in his own bishop.

In spite of all these arguments in favour of Black's move, Tarrasch used to dismiss such demonstrations with: "Beginning of an attack...

14 f3

...and end of attack!"

The hemming in of the g2-bishop is only temporary, and as for the weakness of the kingside pawns, it is of no consequence if Black cannot exploit it.

14 ... &e6

The bishop finds the right square, but it is too late – much too late!

15 &c5!

Now that the strategically important d4- and c5-squares are under his control, White stations a piece where it will immobilize Black's pawns and restrict the movement of his pieces.

15 ... &fe8 *(D)*

Black must either protect his bishop or submit to an exchange of pieces. The latter option does not appeal to him, as after 15...&xc5+, the reply 16 &xc5 replaces one block-ader with another and gains a tempo by the attack on the queen.

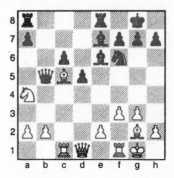

16 &f2!

A very fine move! After White plays e3, the rook can switch over to c2 to help exploit the c-file. It also vacates f1, so that the bishop can occupy a more useful diagonal.

16 ... &d7

Black attacks the bishop a third time, with the hope of forcing it to retreat.

17 &xe7

The bishop does not withdraw, as that lets Black get in the thrust 17...c5, breaking the bind on his position. Nor does White support the bishop by 17 b4, the kind of move many players would make instantly. The consequence would be 17...&xc5,

forcing the pawn to recapture, since 18 ♖xc5 costs the exchange, and 18 ♘xc5 allows 18...♕xb4. However, after 18 bxc5 the pawn stationed at c5 is not only immobile and useless but itself closes the c-file to White's pieces. This would negate the whole strategy of the position, which is to occupy the weak squares in the opponent's position with pieces, not pawns. Pieces can be freely moved about, so that lines are kept open for the attack, and one blockader can make room for a different one, if occasion demands it.

17 ...   ♖xe7 *(D)*

Black must recapture.

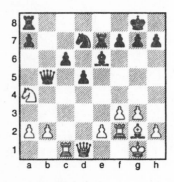

18 ♕d4!

Excellent! The centralization of the queen is tremendously effective. Not only does the queen exert its influence on every part of the board, but it also both prohibits Black from getting in the freeing ...c5 move and prepares the posting of the knight at c5. Notice how, from its new position, the queen still guards the knight and keeps an eye on the b-pawn. The knight is free to move, while the e2-pawn, abandoned by

the queen, is now under the rook's care.

18 ...   ♖ee8

This rook retreats to help defend the c-file against White's attack, since a move by the a8-rook costs a pawn.

19 ♗f1

A subtle means of activating the bishop. The alternative 19 f4 is not nearly as good, as it gives Black's pieces much more room in which to manoeuvre, his bishop and knight then having access to the e4-square.

19 ...   ♖ec8 *(D)*

Reviving the possibility of playing 20...c5. Black must have realized by this time that if he does not get this move in, he might just as well sit back and wait for the axe to fall.

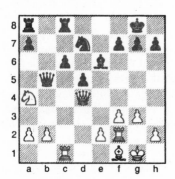

20 e3!

Such a little move, but it accomplishes a great deal! It gains a tempo or two as it uncovers an attack on the queen (forcing Black to lose a move by its retreat), opens up a diagonal for the bishop, and clears a pathway on the second rank, so that the rook can switch from f2 to c2 and increase the pressure along the c-file.

20 ...   ♕b7 *(D)*

Discretion is the better part of valour, as Beaumont and Fletcher said, anticipating Shakespeare.

The desperate thrust 20...c5 is refuted by 21 ♖xc5, when Black dare not take the rook as his queen is still under attack.

21 ♘c5!

Blockade! The knight settles down on c5 and barricades Black's position.

21 ...   ♘xc5

Black removes the knight, not only to get rid of an active blockader but also on the theory that exchanges help relieve a cramped position.

22 ♖xc5

Not so agile as its predecessor, the new blockader enjoys the privilege of immunity to harassment by pawns or the enemy bishop, which is confined to squares of opposite colour to the one the rook occupies.

22 ...   ♖c7

Black cannot counterattack; all he can do is sit tight and await events.

But how does White profit by his opponent's lack of mobility? How does he overcome passive resistance?

23 ♖fc2

First by doubling rooks on the open file, *which more than doubles the strength of the rooks.*

At present, the rooks seem to be biting on granite, but there are ways and means! Have faith!

23 ...   ♛b6 *(D)*

Black sticks to noncommittal moves, until his opponent declares himself by a threatening gesture.

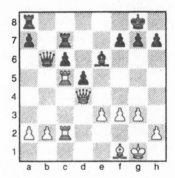

24 b4!

This is the point! While the rooks keep a grip on the enemy, the pawn will spearhead an attack on the position.

White's immediate threat is 25 b5, striking a third time at the immobilized c-pawn.

24 ...   a6

Black must not allow the pawn to advance.

25 ♖a5!

Shifting the attack so as to keep Black occupied guarding all the weak points (the new target is a6). Transferring the rook does not relinquish the pressure on the c-pawn, which must remain where it is.

25 ...   ♖b8

Black protects his queen, which was threatened with capture. Other courses offer bleak prospects:

1) If 25...♕xd4 26 exd4 ♗c8 (to save the a-pawn), then 27 ♖xd5 wins a pawn for White.

2) If 25...♕b7, then 26 ♕c5 followed by 27 a4 and 28 b5 engineers a decisive breakthrough.

26 a3

Protecting the valuable b-pawn (which is destined to bring the enemy to his knees) before proceeding with the attack.

26 ... ♖a7 (D)

Black saves the a-pawn, which was under double attack, but loses a different pawn. However, there was no way for Black to safeguard all the vulnerable points. Had he tried 26...♗c8, White would have won a pawn by 27 ♕xb6 ♖xb6 28 ♖xd5, exploiting the pinned c-pawn.

27 ♖xc6!

This bit of plunder is the first material evidence of the merit of White's positional strategy. It is no more than justice that the c-pawn, the cause of Black's troubles, should be the first to fall.

27 ... ♕xc6

Better than retreating to b7 or exchanging queens: if 27...♕b7, then 28 ♖axa6 wins another pawn and leaves White with two connected passed pawns ready to race up the board. Or if 27...♕xd4 28 exd4, then White will gather up the triply attacked a-pawn.

28 ♕xa7 (D)

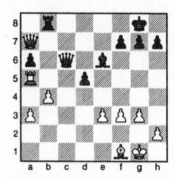

The recapture keeps Black on his toes. His rook is attacked and so is the a-pawn.

28 ... ♖a8

Rescues the pawn, as 29 ♖xa6 ♖xa7 30 ♖xc6 ♖xa3 nets Black a pawn in return.

29 ♕c5

Again taking possession of the c-file and the key square, this time with the queen.

29 ... ♕b7

Black avoids the exchange of queens, since after 29...♕xc5 30 ♖xc5 ♔f8 31 ♖a5 Black can save the a-pawn only by abandoning the d-pawn.

30 ♔f2

Not only to fortify the kingside but to move the king closer to the centre for the endgame, in the event that the queens are exchanged.

30 ... h5

This demonstration does not intimidate White or divert him from his purpose of effecting a decision on the queenside.

31 ♗e2

White shelters the king from any annoying checks that might ensue once the position is opened up.

31 ... g6

Black's pieces are tied down to the defence of the two isolated pawns, so he makes a waiting move with a pawn.

32 ♕d6

White responds vigorously by attacking the a-pawn with a third piece. The queen's further infiltration into Black's territory also clears the c5-square so that the rook can use that as a springboard to get to the seventh rank.

32 ... ♕c8 *(D)*

Black cannot guard all his pawns (if 32...♗c8, then 33 ♕xd5), so he deserts the a-pawn to try to get at White's king via the open c-file.

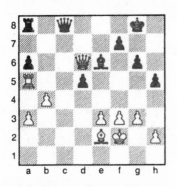

33 ♖c5!

Not through the Iron Duke! It is more important to retain control of the c-file and to keep Black's pieces off it than to pick up stray pawns.

33 ... ♕b7

The queen hasn't a wide choice of squares to flee from the rook's attack.

34 h4

This immobilizes Black's kingside pawns and also guards against any surprise attack on that wing.

34 ... a5

Black tries to open a file for his queen by main force.

What else is there? After 34...♔g7 35 ♖c7 ♕b8 36 ♗xa6 ♔g8 (or 36...♖xa6 37 ♖xf7+ winning the queen) 37 ♗b7! ♖a7 38 ♖c8+ ♗xc8 39 ♕xb8 White wins easily.

35 ♖c7

This reduces the queen's flight squares to the minimum – just one square!

White is now in full control of all the strategically important areas – the c-file, the all-important c5-square, the d-file, the sixth rank and the seventh rank.

35 ... ♕b8

The only hiding place! The queen is driven further and further back.

36 b5

A new source of trouble! White has a passed pawn moving up the board.

36 ... a4

Black must give his rook more room.

37 b6

Threatening to continue with 38 b7 ♖a7 39 ♖c8+ ♗xc8 40 ♕xb8, winning everything in sight.

37 ...   罝a5
The rook accomplishes nothing here, but there is no real defence.
38 b7!
Renewing the threat of winning the queen by 39 罝c8+.
1-0
There is no holding out any longer:
1) 38...♔g7 39 罝xf7+ wins the queen at once by discovered attack.
2) 38...♕e8 39 ♕b6 wins the rook in an odd way.

3) 38...♕a7 39 ♕d8+ ♔g7 40 b8♕ leaves White with an extra queen.

The whole game is a remarkable example of the systematic exploitation of a positional advantage. The manner in which the c5-square is used as a springboard for White's pieces – the bishop, knight, rook and then the queen occupying it in turn – contributes a bit of sleight of hand to an artistic achievement of the highest sort.

Game 21
Chernev – Hahlbohm
New York 1942
Colle System

1 d4
This is one of the best moves on the board – and so is 1 e4!

Either move establishes a pawn in the centre, while permitting two pieces to come into play.

Which move should you adopt? The choice is a matter of taste. Broadly speaking, 1 e4 leads more often to wide-open attacking games, while 1 d4 tends toward a struggle for positional advantage. Blackburne says, "The first piece of advice I would offer to the young student who wishes to improve his chess is that in the formation of his style he should try to follow his own aptitude and temperament. One player derives pleasure in working a game out accurately like a sum in mathematics; another cares for nothing but ingenious combinations and brilliant attacks. It is by far the best

for each to develop his own qualities."

1 ...   d5
An excellent reply, as it prevents White from continuing with 2 e4, when the two pawns abreast dominate the centre. Black, too, frees his queen and a bishop.

2 ♘f3
Instead of this, White often plays 2 c4, offering a pawn. This is a gambit only by the grace of definition, since White recovers the pawn easily while maintaining a strong position.

The knight move has the virtue of developing a piece to its most useful post while retaining the option of transposing into the Queen's Gambit.

2 ...   e6
Perfectly safe, but somewhat modest. I would prefer 2...♘f6, which

does not commit Black to defensive play and does not interfere with the c8-bishop's development.

The text-move is the best way to support the d-pawn *after White has attacked it by c4*, but White has not yet made this threatening gesture!

3 e3!

This quiet move is the prelude to the Colle Attack, a vicious kingside assault.

The general plan of the Colle is to advance the e-pawn to e4, *after suitable preparation*. This consists of the following manoeuvres:

1) developing the f1-bishop at d3, to reinforce the pressure on the vital e4-square and to attack Black's h-pawn, a tender point after he castles;

2) posting the queen's knight at d2 (not at c3, as the c-pawn must not be obstructed), to bear down on e4 and lend support to the e-pawn when it reaches that square;

3) castling on the kingside, to mobilize the h1-rook;

4) developing the queen at e2 and/or the rook at e1, to add further weight to the contemplated pawn push;

5) advancing the pawn to e4.

The pawn moves only one square, but it sets all the machinery in motion: the position in the centre will be ripped apart and lines opened for White's attacking forces.

3 ... c5

This thrust at the pawn-centre is practically compulsory for Black in queen's pawn openings.

• Black *must fight* for an equal share of the centre.

• Black *must dispute* possession of the important squares.

4 c3

Supporting White's centre and making ready for ♗d3, since it prepares the retreat square c2 in case Black should attack this bishop by ...c4.

4 ...   ♘f6 (D)

Natural and strong. This is the best possible disposition of the king's knight. It is developed *toward the centre*, so as to take part in the events there. It is in the centre that most of the fighting takes place, and whatever happens there affects the rest of the chessboard. Superiority in the centre is essential for a positional advantage, and control of the centre is indispensable to the successful conduct of a kingside attack.

All development should therefore be conducted with a view to the effect on the centre.

A plausible move, instead of the text, is the advance 4...c4 to prevent White from placing his bishop at d3. It is the kind of move many players find irresistible, but it must be avoided. It is an error in strategy, as it relaxes the pressure on White's d-pawn and the centre.

- *It is important to keep the pawn position in the centre fluid.*
- *It is important to maintain pressure on White's d-pawn in the centre.*
- *It is important to retain the option of exchanging pawns in the centre.*

5 ♗d3 (D)

An ideal development for the bishop: it controls the b1-h7 diagonal leading to Black's king (after he castles) and bears down on the key e4-square, where the break will come.

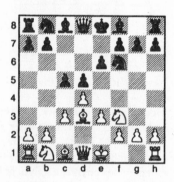

5 ...   ♘c6

The knight comes into play toward the centre, as prescribed. Black has an eye to freeing his game by an early ...e5. A good alternative is 5...♘bd7 in order to recapture with the knight, instead of with the bishop, if White should play 6 dxc5.

6 ♘bd2

Offhand this looks unnatural, as the knight seems awkwardly placed and blocks the path of the c1-bishop. In reality the knight performs its two assigned tasks: *it gets into the game,*

even if it is only at the modest d2-square, and it also lends support to the coming action at the critical point e4. The c1-bishop is inconvenienced, but only temporarily.

6 ...   ♗e7

This is preferable to the aggressive development at d6. The bishop is needed closer to home for defence of the king.

7 0-0 (D)

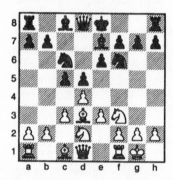

This remarkable *coup*, by means of which the king is spirited away to safety while the rook magically appears on the scene, is probably the most significant contribution to civilization since the invention of the wheel.

7 ...   0-0

Black also hurries to safeguard his king and put the king's rook to work.

8 ♕e2

A perfect spot for the queen in nearly every form of queen's pawn opening. The queen supports the contemplated advance of the e-pawn and will add a great deal of weight to the consequent attack.

8 ...   ♖e8 (D)

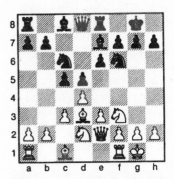

Rooks must seize open files! What if there are none? Then bring your rooks toward the centre! They will then be at the head of files most likely to be opened. That is why the king's rook is usually developed at e8 or d8, while the queen's rook goes to d8 or c8.

9 dxc5!

The thrust 9 e4 would be premature: after 9...dxe4 10 ♘xe4 cxd4 White would lose a pawn. The text-move was made with these further considerations in mind:

1) Black's bishop, which has moved once, will have to waste a move in recapturing the pawn;

2) this bishop, needed for the defence of the kingside, will find itself on the wrong side of the board;

3) at c5, the bishop will stand unprotected and subject to a surprise attack;

4) White's knight at d2 will gain a tempo later by moving to b3, where it threatens the exposed bishop while simultaneously clearing a way for his own dark-squared bishop;

5) in the ending, if it comes to that, White will have the favourable arrangement of three pawns to two on the queenside.

9 ...   ♗xc5 *(D)*

Black must recapture or be a pawn down.

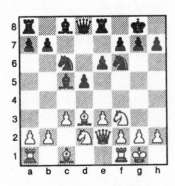

10 e4!

The key move in the Colle Attack! It is the forcible break which releases all the fury of the pent-up pieces.

How should Black reply? If he exchanges by 10...dxe4, then after 11 ♘xe4 ♘xe4 12 ♕xe4, he is threatened with the devastating 13 ♕xh7+. No longer does he have a knight at f6 (the best defender of a castled position) so he would have to weaken himself by moving one of the pawns in front of the king.

If he avoids exchanging pawns and plays 10...d4 instead, then comes 11 ♘b3 ♗b6 (the bishop must stay in touch with the d-pawn) 12 e5 ♘d5, and White should win "accurately like a sum in mathematics", as Blackburne puts it, by 13 cxd4. The attempt to win through "ingenious combination and brilliant attack" by 13 ♗xh7+ ♔xh7 14 ♘g5+ succeeds after 14...♔g6 15 ♕e4+ f5 16 exf6+

♔xf6 17 ♕f3+ ♔e7 (if 17...♔e5,
then 18 ♘f7#) 18 ♕f7+ ♔d6 19
♘e4+ ♔e5 20 ♕h5+ g5 (20...♔xe4
21 ♘d2+ ♔d3 22 ♕g6+ ♔e2 23
♕g4+ ♔d3 24 ♕e4#) 21 ♗xg5, leading to mate in a few moves. However, 14...♔g8 15 ♕h5 ♘xe5 is a
dash of cold water, after which White
would be hard-pressed to justify his
sacrifice.

10 ... e5

Black avoids both pitfalls and
plays to prevent 11 e5, which would
dislodge the knight. Meanwhile, the
rook has more elbow-room, and the
c8-bishop can now take part in the
action.

11 exd5

Work in progress! White continues the process of opening lines for
the attack. The e4-square is now
available as a jumping-off spot for
his pieces.

11 ... ♘xd5

Black did not care to capture with
his queen, as after 11...♕xd5 12 ♗c4
these lines are possible:

1) 12...♕d6 13 ♘g5 (threatening
14 ♗xf7+, winning the exchange)
13...♖e7 14 ♘de4 ♘xe4 15 ♘xe4,
and White wins the bishop.

2) 12...♕d7 13 ♘g5 ♖e7 14 ♘de4
♘xe4 15 ♕xe4 (threatening the h-
pawn) 15...g6 16 ♕h4 h5 17 ♘e4,
and Black must give up his bishop to
avert loss of his queen by a knight
fork.

3) 12...♕d8 13 ♘b3 ♗b6, and
White will have a happy time weigh-
ing the effects of various attacks beginning with 14 ♗g5, 14 ♖d1 or 14
♘g5.

12 ♘b3

Gaining a tempo by the attack on
the exposed bishop. Note too that
White's c1-bishop now has lots of
room.

12 ... ♕b6 (D)

A move with deceptive aspects. It
is true that the queen has made a developing move and that the bishop is
now protected, but other factors appear in the reckoning. Black's kingside lacks pieces for defence, and his
knight at d5 is loose (unguarded by
another piece or a pawn).

Is there a combination? Is there a
check or capture – a move that does
some damage? Yes, indeed there is!

13 ♗xh7+!

Such opportunities must be seized
at once, before the opponent has a
chance to catch his breath.

13 ... ♔xh7

Refusing to capture is even worse:
the bishop can run away with his
booty or stay put while the attack
continues with 14 ♕c4, and the queen
pounces on the stranded pieces in
the centre.

14 ♕e4+

The point! By means of a double
attack White regains his piece, with

an extra pawn as interest on his investment.

14 ...   &g8

There is nothing to be gained by interposing a pawn by 14...f5 or 14...g6, either of which moves further disrupts the kingside pawn position.

15 ♕xd5

White wins the piece back and gains another tempo by the double attack on the bishop. Black is kept busy defending and is given no time to consolidate his position. Without having made any moves that were obviously bad, Black has a theoretically lost game.

15 ...   ♗f8 *(D)*

Abject retreat, but the alternative 15...♗e7 lets White take the poorly defended e-pawn.

16 ♘g5

Threatening 17 ♕xf7+, and mate in two more moves. Black must be given no respite!

16 ...   ♗e6

At last, the light-squared bishop comes into the game. Black's move looks effective as mate is warded off, the enemy queen driven back, a piece developed, and another one (the a8-rook) released.

17 ♕e4

The queen retreats, but no time is lost as mate is threatened at h7.

17 ...   g6

Black has little choice, and this is a better defence than 17...f5, after which 18 ♕h4 ♗d6 (or 18...♗c5 19 ♘xe6 ♖xe6 20 ♕c4 winning a piece) 19 ♕h7+ &f8 20 ♕g6 ♘d8 (if the e6-bishop moves, then its colleague on d6 falls) 21 ♘h7+ &e7 22 ♕xg7+ leads to a catastrophe.

18 ♕h4

Again threatening mate on the move. Black is kept on the run and has to place his pieces where White's mating threats compel them to go.

18 ...   ♗g7

White cannot be kept from checking at h7, but this prevents the queen's further inroad at h8. Failure to keep the queen out, for instance by 18...♗d6 instead, would lose after 19 ♕h7+ &f8 20 ♘xe6+ ♖xe6 (if 20...fxe6, then 21 ♗h6#) 21 ♕h8+, and White wins a rook.

With the actual move, Black seems to have built a bomb-proof shelter for his king.

19 ♗e3

So White brings up the reserves! The dark-squared bishop comes into active play with gain of tempo. The attack on the queen is incidental to the bishop's real purpose, which is to gain control of c5 for itself or the knight. A knight planted there would dominate the centre and the queenside; a bishop would be useful to prevent Black's king escaping by way of f8.

19 ...   ♕a6

Black rejects 19...♕c7 as he visualizes the continuation 20 ♕h7+ ♔f8 21 ♗c5+ ♘e7 22 ♕xg6! fxg6 (or 22...♕xc5 23 ♘xe6+ fxe6 24 ♕xe8+ ♔xe8 25 ♘xc5 winning easily) 23 ♘xe6+ ♔g8 24 ♘xc7, when Black's rooks are impaled on a knight fork.

20 ♘c5!

Once more one of White's pieces invades the enemy's half of the board by the timesaving expedient of attacking the queen.

20 ...   ♕c4

Hoping to get some peace by effecting an exchange of queens.

21 ♕h7+

With the object of smoking the king out and ripping away his pawn protection.

21 ...   ♔f8 *(D)*

The only move left.

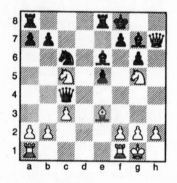

22 ♘cxe6+

There is often more than one way to win, *once a positional superiority has been established.* A pretty finish would be 22 ♘gxe6+ fxe6 23 ♗h6 ♖e7 (or 23...♗xh6 24 ♘d7#!) 24 ♕h8+ (if only to show that the queen *can* get to h8) 24...♔f7 25 ♕xg7+ ♔e8 26 ♕g8#.

22 ...   fxe6

If Black sacrifices the exchange by 22...♖xe6 then he may prolong but not alleviate the suffering.

23 ♕xg6 *(D)*

Threatening 24 ♕f7#.

23 ...   ♘d8

I was hoping for 23...♖e7, when I could have forced the win by the 'excelsior' idea, a pawn march up the board, as follows: 24 f4 (threatening 25 fxe5+ ♔g8 26 ♕h7#) 24...e4 25 f5 (again threatening to deliver discovered check) 25...e5 26 f6 and White wins.

24 ♘h7+

Here I was sorely tempted to go in for the flashy win by 24 f4 e4 25 f5 e5 26 f6 ♗h8 27 ♘h7#, but common sense prevailed. One must win in the quickest possible way and play the simple, brutal move if thereby it shortens the struggle.

1-0

If 24...♔g8, then 25 ♘f6+ ♔h8 (or 25...♔f8 26 ♕xe8#) 26 ♕h7#, or if 24...♔e7, then 25 ♖ad1, and mate follows after 26 ♗g5+ or 26 ♕xg7+.

Game 22
Pillsbury – Marco
Paris 1900
Queen's Gambit Declined

1 d4

Whether for fun, honour or blood, this is one of the best ways to begin the fight. Outlets are created for the queen and a bishop, while the d-pawn itself takes an active part in the struggle for control of the centre. It occupies d4 and stands guard over e5 and c5, making those squares unavailable for the opponent's pieces.

1 ... d5

The simplest way to stop White gaining more ground in the centre. If White is permitted to play 2 e4 freely, the two pawns abreast in the centre will give him the balance of power in that important area.

2 c4

White offers a pawn in order to eliminate Black's strong point in the centre. It is necessary to play this move before developing the b1-knight at c3, as the c-file must not be obstructed.

2 ... e6

Black is set to reply to 3 cxd5 with 3...exd5, maintaining a pawn at d5. If he were to recapture with a piece, White could attack it, drive it off and create a strong pawn-centre by playing e4.

Accepting White's pawn offer by 2...dxc4 is not recommended policy. Black could not hold on to the extra pawn, so that in the end it would amount to exchanging a centre pawn for a side pawn. It is true that the text-move limits the c8-bishop's scope, but it is a necessary evil of what is probably Black's soundest defence. In this lies the great strength of the Queen's Gambit (for White) and its popularity with the majority of players who feel happy with an opening which lets them exert pressure from the very first move.

3 ♘c3 (D)

The knight develops aggressively, moving in toward the centre and intensifying the attack on Black's d-pawn.

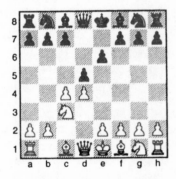

3 ... ♘f6

An excellent move: it brings the g8-knight to its most suitable square in the opening, exerts pressure on d5 and e4 (to neutralize the influence of White's knight on those squares), helps defend the central d5-pawn and facilitates early kingside castling.

4 ♗g5! (D)

This powerful move develops a piece, pins one of Black's and threatens by 5 ♗xf6 gxf6 (if 5...♕xf6, then 6 cxd5 exd5 7 ♘xd5 and White wins a pawn) to dislocate Black's pawn position on the kingside.

Strangely enough, although Pillsbury used this move to great effect in a magnificent victory over Tarrasch at Hastings in 1895, the comment on it by Gunsberg, who annotated the game for the tournament book, was, "No good results from this early sortie of the bishop. The attack, or perhaps better speaking, would-be attack differs from similar play in the French Defence, inasmuch as White has not the move e5 at his command. Generally speaking, both the first and the second player in this opening require their queen's bishop on the queenside."

This view, it turned out, easily qualified for 'the clouded crystal ball department'. Pillsbury utilized the attack stemming from 4 ♗g5 for some of his most marvellous triumphs, defeating such masters of the game as Steinitz, Maroczy, Janowsky,

Burn, Marco and Tarrasch. Others who evaded this line, such as Lasker, Marshall and Chigorin (to name a few) fell victims to other forms of the Queen's Gambit. Gunsberg, who criticized this form of attack so severely, chose what Lasker called "a peculiar, but not altogether sound, manner of development", with the result that Pillsbury defeated him in an ending which is one of the most beautiful in the literature of chess. In short, it was Pillsbury's great success with the Queen's Gambit that revealed its terrific strength to the other masters and gave it a popularity that has continued to this day.

4 ...   ♗e7

The simplest: Black develops the bishop where it is best placed for defence – close to home. Incidentally, he neutralizes the pin of the knight.

5 e3 (D)

Pawns should be moved sparingly in the opening, but moves which help pieces come into play are developing moves. In playing 5 e3, White develops because he creates an outlet for his f1-bishop.

5 ...   0-0

The king finds safer quarters while the rook prepares to make itself useful.

6 ♘f3 *(D)*

With the development of this piece, White's knights now exert pressure on all the four squares in the centre. Moreover, the f3-knight has an eye to utilizing e5 as an outpost. Once firmly stationed there, it will get a death grip on Black's position.

6 ... b6

It is natural to develop the bishop at b7, especially as it is hemmed in on the other side, and indeed this is one of Black's soundest plans – however, it would have been more accurate to precede it by 6...h6, so as to remove the h-pawn from the vulnerable h7-square with gain of tempo.

An alternative continuation was 6...♘bd7 to support a thrust at White's centre by ...c5 or ...e5. The knight move would also curb White's ambition to anchor his f3-knight at e5.

7 ♗d3

An ideal spot for the bishop: it commands an important diagonal

and aims at Black's h-pawn. This pawn is in no immediate danger, but it does stand in the line of fire.

7 ... ♗b7

Black expects to control the long diagonal with his bishop by means of this fianchetto. However, Pillsbury's next move puts Black in a dilemma.

8 cxd5! *(D)*

White removes a pawn and lets Black recapture in any of four ways – none of them satisfactory!

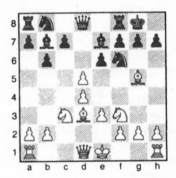

8 ... exd5

Black wants to maintain a pawn in the centre, but this pawn blocks the path of his b7-bishop and prevents it from accomplishing anything useful on the diagonal.

Black could have captured with a piece instead, but that amounts to an eventual surrender of the centre. White would evict the piece by e4 and remain in control of all the strategically important central squares.

9 ♘e5!

This is the key move in the famous 'Pillsbury Attack'. The knight anchors itself on a square from which its striking power is terrific!

Its attack extends in all directions, affecting the queenside as well as the kingside.

9 ...   ♘bd7

This knight does what it can: it develops, it threatens to do battle with White's knight, and it stands ready to support a break by 10...c5, disputing control of the centre.

10 f4

This pawn not only strengthens the position of the knight by providing it with a firm base, but it discourages Black from exchanging pieces. On 10...♘xe5, the recapture by 11 fxe5 opens wide the f-file for an attack by the heavy pieces. The capturing pawn itself will then stab at Black's f6-knight and drive it away from its strong defensive post.

10 ...   c5

This demonstration on the queenside is either too soon or too late. Black wants to attack on the queenside where, after playing 11...c4, he will have a three to two pawn majority. What he underestimates is the speed and vigour with which White can get an attack rolling on the kingside. It will strike faster and with more force than any action of Black's on the queenside. Black must deprive White's attack of some of its strength by effecting some exchanges and then counterattacking in the centre. One possibility was 10...♘e8 11 ♗xe7 ♕xe7 12 0-0 ♘xe5 13 fxe5 f6. This would comply with two important principles in defence:

- An exchange relieves a crowded position.
- An attack on a wing is best met by play in the centre.

11 0-0 (D)

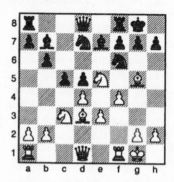

A defensive measure (the king should be sheltered) but primarily to put the rook immediately to work on the partly open f-file.

11 ...   c4

With the idea of securing a queenside pawn majority. This is commendable strategy for the ending, but Black has not yet survived the middlegame!

The move 11...c4 is a strategic error. It removes the pressure on White's d-pawn and relieves the tension. As long as Black has the option of capturing the d-pawn and disturbing White's centre, it is difficult for White to stabilize the centre. And until the centre is stabilized, the success of a kingside attack for White is doubtful.

The moral is clear: *keep the pawn position in the centre fluid; reserve the option of capturing the central pawn.*

12 ♗c2

The bishop retreats but does not relax its grip on the diagonal leading to Black's kingside.

12 ...   a6

Preparing a sweeping advance of queenside pawns, beginning with 13...b5 and 14...b4.

13 ♕f3

White brings up the heavy artillery. White's object with the queen move is to start a direct attack on the king, and he gains time because he forces Black to deal with the threat to win a pawn by 14 ♘xc4 dxc4 15 ♕xb7. To defend himself against White's threats, Black will be forced to move some pawn near his king. This change in the pawn formation will loosen the structure and create an irreparable weakness in the king's defences.

13 ... b5 *(D)*

Marco protects the c-pawn and proceeds with his counterattack on the queenside. Note how Black's last three moves, filling up light squares with pawns, further reduce what little mobility his light-squared bishop has.

14 ♕h3!

Threatening 15 ♘xd7 ♕xd7 (certainly not 15...♘xd7 16 ♕xh7#), after which White has a choice of three winning continuations:

1) 16 ♕xd7 ♘xd7 17 ♗xe7, and White gains a piece.

2) 16 ♗xh7+ ♔h8 (if 16...♘xh7, then 17 ♕xd7 wins) 17 ♗f5+, and White wins the queen.

3) 16 ♗f5 ♕d8 17 ♗xf6 ♗xf6 18 ♕xh7#.

"All this is very interesting," you might say, "but how does White plan this series of moves? What makes him look at even so much as the first move in the combination?"

Very well! Let's try to follow his line of reasoning:

White attacks the critical point, Black's h7-pawn, with queen and bishop.

If this pawn were protected only by the king, White could capture it and announce mate.

But the pawn has another protector, a knight.

How about removing the knight?

That would not do. It would only be replaced by another knight.

How about getting rid of the other knight? With that knight disposed of, wouldn't the whole structure collapse?

Once White thinks in this direction and sees the first move in the combination, the rest of it plays itself. In fact, once he finds the key – removing the knight which protects the knight which protects against mate – he can win any way he pleases.

14 ... g6 *(D)*

Black avoids being mated by making a simple pawn move. What then has White accomplished, if his mating combination can so easily be frustrated?

It is true that White has not in-flicted mate, but the threat of doing so has enabled him to achieve his real objective – a disturbance in the line-up of pawns near Black's king. *This change in the pawn configuration weakens the entire defensive structure.* After Black's actual move, his f6-knight, deprived of its pawn support, is a vulnerable object of attack, notwithstanding the fact that it is protected by three pieces.

What other defence did Black have? If 14...h6, then 15 ♗xh6 gxh6 16 ♕xh6 ♘e4 17 ♖f3 (threatening 18 ♖g3+ ♘xg3 19 ♕h7#) 17...♘df6 18 ♖h3, is winning for White. Or if 14...♘xe5 (to avoid moving the king-side pawns), then 15 dxe5 ♘e4 16 ♗xe4 dxe4 17 ♖ad1 ♕e8 18 ♗xe7 ♕xe7 19 ♖d7 and the b7-bishop per-ishes.

15 f5!

A pawn is a wonderful weapon of attack! This one threatens to break up Black's pawn cordon by 16 fxg6. The capture will also uncover an at-tack on Black's f6-knight by the rook, an attack which could be aug-mented by doubling rooks.

15 ...   b4 *(D)*

Clearly 15...gxf5 is out of the question. White could recapture with the bishop with a tremendous game.

Black hopes, with his threat on the c3-knight, to divert White's at-tention from the course of events on the kingside. If he can persuade White to delay the attack for even a moment, he might put up a fight. If, for example, White prudently re-treats the knight to e2, then 16...♘e4 complicates White's task.

16 fxg6!

Ripping right into Black's posi-tion! The rook's attacking range is lengthened – he has the whole f-file to work on – while the bishop's at-tack leads straight to the enemy king!

16 ...   hxg6

Let's dispose of the alternatives:

1) 16...bxc3 17 ♗xf6 ♘xf6 18 ♖xf6 fxg6 (or 18...♗xf6 19 ♕xh7#) 19 ♗xg6 hxg6 20 ♖xg6#.

2) 16...fxg6 17 ♕e6+ ♔h8 18 ♘xd7 ♘xd7 (or 18...♕xd7 19 ♗xf6+ followed by 20 ♕xd7) 19 ♖xf8+ ♘xf8 20 ♕e5+ ♔g8 21 ♗xe7, and White wins.

17 ♕h4!

Concentrating his fire on the f6-knight, whose position has been weakened by the loss of his pawn support.

17 ... bxc3 *(D)*

Black might as well take the knight. The alternative 17...♘xe5 loses to 18 dxe5 bxc3 19 exf6 ♗d6 20 ♕h6.

Before White makes his next move, let us look at the object of his attack, the knight at f6. Although it has lost the protection of the g7-pawn, which has had to move to g6, it is still immune from capture, since it has a defender for every piece that attacks it. In fact, if White tries something like 18 ♗xf6 ♗xf6 19 ♖xf6 ♕xf6 20 ♕xf6 ♘xf6, he finds himself a rook down. So direct assault doesn't do it! The answer must then lie in indirect means. We have lured away one of the knight's defenders, the pawn. Can we get rid of its other protectors? Indeed we can!

18 ♘xd7!

This removes one of the props supporting the knight.

18 ... ♕xd7

And this recapture draws another one away! Notice the technique of besieging a heavily guarded objective by doing away with the pieces that protect it. In this case, two of the knight's defenders have disappeared – one removed bodily, and the other lured away by the compulsion to recapture.

Black had no better defence in 18...♘xd7 as 19 ♗xe7 ♕a5 20 b4 (faster than 20 ♗xf8) 20...cxb3 21 axb3 ♕b6 22 ♖f3, followed by 23 ♖h3, forces a quick mate.

19 ♖xf6!

Stronger than 19 ♗xf6 as Black dare not take the rook.

19 ... a5

If 19...♗xf6, then 20 ♗xf6 threatening 21 ♕h8# is conclusive.

Black's actual move prepares 20...♖a6, to help defend the vulnerable g-pawn and perhaps to beat off White's rook.

20 ♖af1

Doubling the rooks institutes two new winning threats: 21 ♗xg6 fxg6 22 ♖xg6# and 21 ♖1f3, followed by 22 ♖h3 and 23 ♕h8#.

20 ... ♖a6 *(D)*

Hoping to induce an exchange of rooks which would divert one of White's pieces from the attack. White could still win, but the play would require care. It might go like this: 21 ♖xa6 ♗xg5 22 ♕xg5 ♗xa6 23 ♖f6 (23 ♗xg6 at once is risky and might even lose) 23...cxb2 24 ♗xg6 fxg6 25 ♖xg6+ ♔f7 26 ♖g7+ ♔e8 27 ♕e5+ ♔d8 28 ♕b8+ ♗c8 29 ♖xd7+ ♔xd7 30 ♕xb2, etc.

But Pillsbury is not to be swayed! He carries out the motif of the attack with admirable consistency by annihilating the g-pawn that stepped out of line and weakened the defensive formation.

21 ♗xg6!

Logic and poetic justice dictate that this pawn be destroyed!

21 ...   fxg6

White was threatening mate on the move.

Pillsbury now showed a forced mate in seven moves by 22 ♖xf8+ ♗xf8 23 ♖xf8+ ♔xf8 24 ♕h8+ ♔f7 25 ♕h7+ ♔f8 (25...♔e8 26 ♕g8# or 25...♔e6 26 ♕xg6#) 26 ♕xd7 followed by 27 ♗h6+ ♔g8 28 ♕g7#.

1-0

More than any other, this game made the chess world aware of the terrific potential of the Queen's Gambit, a positional opening, as an instrument of attack. The assault on the kingside is carried out with speed and power, and unlike attacks stemming from speculative king's pawn gambits, it is founded on a position sound to the core.

Game 23
Van Vliet – Znosko-Borovsky
Ostend 1907
Stonewall Attack

1 d4

The queen's pawn opening, to paraphrase George Bernard Shaw, "offers the maximum of security with the maximum of opportunity."

With the first move, White occupies the centre with a pawn and frees two of the queenside pieces.

His general plan of development runs somewhat as follows:

He will establish and maintain at least one pawn in the centre.

This pawn will act as a support to a knight outpost at e5 or c5.

The bishops are to take charge of key diagonals or pin enemy pieces.

The rooks are to control the open or partly open files.

The queen should stand at c2 or e2, close to home but off the back rank.

The king should find safety in castling, preferably on the kingside.

Basically, White's aim is to gain space and crowd Black to the wall. With less room to move around in, and with the consequent difficulty of manoeuvring his pieces effectively, Black will be forced to weaken his position. He will have to make some poor moves, because good moves are not easily available in a cramped position. The weaknesses will come to light, and the opportunity to exploit them will come in the form of a combination, resolving the issue at one stroke.

1 ... d5

This is a more forthright move than 1...♘f6. Either of these moves prevents White from playing 2 e4 and establishing two pawns in the centre. The text-move offsets White's pressure in the centre and creates a state of equilibrium there.

2 e3

A strangely passive move in an opening where every single moment counts.

Usually, White strikes at Black's d-pawn by 2 c4 to weaken his grip on the centre. Or, if White does not want to show his hand too soon, he simply develops a piece by 2 ♘f3.

2 ... c5

So Black takes the initiative and plays this all-important freeing move. It opens the c-file for the use of the rooks and gives the b8-knight more scope by letting it come out at c6. The c-pawn itself puts up a fight for possession of the centre by its attack on White's d-pawn.

3 c3

Indicating that he intends to reply to 3...cxd4 with 4 cxd4. This would keep his pawn position in the centre intact and open the c-file for his major pieces.

3 ... e6

Black must protect the c-pawn. Otherwise White might play 4 dxc5, and then hang on to the extra pawn by supporting it with 5 b4.

4 ♗d3

The bishop develops to a useful diagonal, where it exerts pressure on the centre and is ready to participate in a kingside attack.

4 ... ♘c6 (D)

A rare opportunity for this knight, who seldom gets good breaks in queen's pawn openings. From its post at c6 the knight brings considerable influence to bear on e5 and d4 and, as it later turns out, on another important sector.

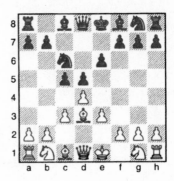

5 f4

White has made four out of five moves with pawns in order to secure a particular arrangement known as the Stonewall Attack. Aside from the fact that making so many pawn moves in the opening is a flagrant violation of principle, the adoption of a system which calls for the launching of an attack by a preconceived formation of pieces, without regard to the advisability of an attack and without reference to the requirements of the particular position, is contrary to the concept of proper strategy and to the spirit of chess itself. What such an expedition amounts to is undertaking the risk of assuming the offensive against an enemy whose force is equal, whose line-up of power is unknown and who has betrayed no vulnerable points. Under these conditions, an attack is premature and is sure to be repulsed and turned into a disorderly retreat. If any such system worked, it would be fine for White, who would always win, but then who would want to play Black?

5 ...   ♘f6

An excellent development while awaiting developments! Both Black's knights are poised beautifully, with one watching over e5 and d4, while the other keeps the two remaining central squares under observation.

6 ♘d2

This knight has the unhappy choice of making its entrance at this square or at a3. At d2, it blocks the bishop and itself has no bright prospects in view. At a3 it is only half a knight, since it reaches at most in four directions instead of eight.

6 ...   ♕c7

Very good, since the heavy pieces (the queen and the rooks) fulfil their functions best when placed on open files, or files likely to be opened.

The queen develops with gain of tempo since a positional threat is involved – which White either overlooks, or disregards.

7 ♘gf3 (D)

Routine and in this case thoughtless development. White is so intent on carrying out the basic theme of the Stonewall attack (posting of a knight at e5, stoutly supported by pawns) that he fails to stop at every move to ask himself, "What does my opponent threaten with his last move? Has he any checks or captures that cut down my choice of reply?"

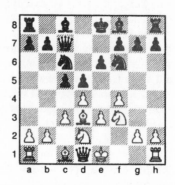

7 ...   cxd4!

Black wrenches the c-file open at one blow!

8 cxd4

The point of Black's move is revealed in this forced recapture. White could not take by 8 exd4 (hoping to maintain strong pawn support for the prospective stationing of a knight at e5) as that permits the brutal reply 8...♕xf4 winning a pawn for Black. The alternative, 8 ♘xd4, conflicts with the system White had determined to follow before lines of battle were drawn up. In that scheme of things, the knight belongs at e5, not d4, while the d4-square should be occupied by a pawn.

8 ...   ♘b4!

A disturbing attack on the bishop! Without the services of this piece, White can never hope to work up an effective kingside attack.

9 ♗b1

An unusual square of retreat, but the only one available if the bishop wants to stay on the diagonal leading to Black's kingside.

White is not too troubled by this setback. He expects to drive the enemy knight off with 10 a3 and then reorganize his troops.

9 ...   ♗d7

A quiet move, but a subtle one. The bishop will make its presence felt, even from this modest start.

Black is now prepared to shift his rook over to c8 to strengthen his grip on the c-file.

10 a3

Before going about his business, White must dislodge the annoying knight, which disconcerts his entire queenside.

10 ...   ♖c8 *(D)*

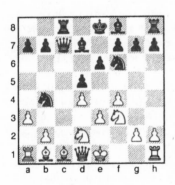

This counterattack must have come as a surprise to White.

What shall he do against the threat of 11...♕xc1? If he plays 11 axb4, there comes 11...♕xc1 12 ♖xa7 (certainly not 12 ♕xc1 ♖xc1+, and Black wins a rook) 12...♕xb2 (threatening 13...♖c1, pinning the queen) 13 0-0 ♕xb4, and Black is a pawn ahead – and a passed pawn at that.

11 0-0

Now the bishop is guarded by queen and rook, and so safe from capture. The king meanwhile goes into hiding.

11 ...   ♗b5!

The bishop seizes a fine diagonal with gain of time, as White must move his rook out of range.

12 ♖e1

Clearly forced, since 12 ♖f2 loses on the spot to 12...♕xc1, while 12 axb4 ♗xf1 (threatening to continue with 13...♕xc1) costs the exchange.

12 ...   ♘c2! *(D)*

An attack on both rooks which leaves White no choice of reply. He must remove this terrible knight.

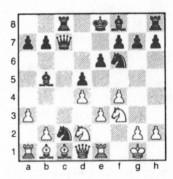

13 ♗xc2

After the alternative capture 13 ♕xc2, Black plays 13...♕xc2 14 ♗xc2 ♖xc2 and has a rook on the seventh rank, as in the actual game.

13 ...   ♕xc2

Black penetrates into the vitals of the enemy's position – the seventh rank.

White is almost paralysed:

His e1-rook and queen are prevented from moving by Black's b5-bishop.

His bishop cannot move at all.

One knight must stay at d2 to prevent 14...♘e4.

The a1-rook can move – but to no avail.

14 ♕xc2

So he exchanges his helpless queen for Black's active one.

14 ... ♖xc2

The upshot of Black's positional combination is that it has given him full control of the open file and a grip on the seventh rank with his rook. The position of the rook at c2 has a terribly constricting effect on White's game. It is especially troublesome as the rook is not easily driven off, while White's pieces are still in each other's way.

15 h3

To prevent 15...♘g4, an invasion by another piece.

15 ... ♗d6

The bishop develops to a useful diagonal.

16 ♘b1 (D)

White's idea is to rearrange his forces so as to get some freedom of movement. He plans the continuation 17 ♘c3 ♗a6 18 ♖d1, followed

by 19 ♖d2, to get rid of Black's annoying rook. By this means, his bishop might eventually see some action.

16 ... ♘e4!

The knight immediately pounces on this excellent outpost! Not only does this throttle any freeing advance of the e3-pawn, but it also sweeps aside White's plan of reorganization. If White tries 17 ♘c3, then 17...♘xc3 18 bxc3 ♖xc3 wins a pawn for Black.

17 ♘fd2

White therefore tries to exchange or otherwise dispose of Black's powerfully placed knight. After that, he might arrive at some reasonable development.

17 ... ♗d3

Black falls in with this offer, with the stipulation that if knights are to be exchanged, he wants another piece occupying the outpost e4.

18 ♘xe4

White has no option but to clear the board of as many pieces as he can, otherwise he will never be able to extricate his forces from their tangled position. The move 18 ♘c3, which earlier would have lost a pawn, is even worse now because after 18...♘xd2 19 ♗xd2 ♖xd2 Black wins a piece.

18 ... ♗xe4

Black recaptures with the threat of 19...♖xg2+, so White has no time to play 19 ♘c3.

19 ♘d2 (D)

White saves the g-pawn by blocking the rook, but he cuts off his own bishop as well – and White's back to the previous entanglement.

Unfortunately, nothing else is promising. If 19 ♗d2, then 19...♖xb2 20 ♖c1 (getting an open file for the pawn and threatening 21 ♖c8+) 20...♔d7, and White will be driven off the file by the threat of 21...♗xb1 winning more material, or 21...♖c8 opposing rooks on the file.

19 ...   ♔d7

Much more energetic than castling. Mating threats are not likely with so few pieces on the board, hence the king comes out into the open. The king's power increases with every reduction of force, and, as befits a fighting piece, the king heads for the centre to assist in the attack. Meanwhile, a new avenue has been opened for the benefit of the h8-rook.

20 ♘xe4

White's only hope is to keep clearing the board.

20 ...   dxe4

After this recapture, a survey shows the inferiority of White's position:

The bishop is undeveloped, preventing communication between the rooks.

The pawn cluster in the centre is completely immobilized.

All the pieces are still on the first rank.

Aside from the features of this particular position, it is important to appreciate the peculiar strength with which a rook is imbued when it dominates (as Black's does) the seventh rank:

- It attacks the pawns still remaining on the rank, striking all along the line, so that defending them is difficult.
- The rook can get behind pawns that have moved off the rank and maintain constant pressure, since the pawns are always under attack by the rook, no matter how far up the file they move.
- The rook restrains the enemy king from coming out to take a hand in the ending, by guarding the line of exit.

The moral is:

In the opening, shift the rooks toward the centre, on files likely to be opened.

In the middlegame, seize the open files and command them with your rooks.

In the ending, post your rooks on the seventh rank. Doubled rooks on the seventh rank are almost irresistible in mating attacks. If there is little material left on the board, the seventh rank is a convenient means of manoeuvring a rook behind enemy pawns.

21 ♖b1

Preparing to play 22 b4 followed by 23 ♗b2, to let the bishop finally see daylight.

It is useless to attempt to dislodge Black's rook, for example after 21 ♔f1 ♖hc8 22 ♖e2 ♖xc1+ Black wins a piece.

21 ...   ♖hc8

The doubling of rooks on an open file more than doubles their strength on that file.

Their power is manifest here, where they reduce White's resistance to the feeble hope of developing his bishop. White's rooks may not leave the first rank unless the bishop does so first.

22 b4

This makes the b2-square available to the bishop.

22 ...   ♖8c3

Discouraging that project! Against 23 ♗b2, Black plays 23...♖b3, with a double attack on the bishop. This forces 24 ♗a1, when 24...♖xa3 wins a pawn for Black, who then doubles rooks on the seventh rank for an easy win.

23 ♔f1 (D)

The king comes closer to guard the rook, which will protect the bishop when it comes off the first rank. Stated in chess language, White

intends 24 ♗b2 ♖b3 25 ♖e2 (a move previously impossible) when all points are at least temporarily secure.

23 ...   ♔c6

The king takes a hand in the ending, making its way in along the weakened light squares.

Tarrasch's recipe in similar cases is "The king must be moved (in the ending) as far as is compatible with his safety, right into the enemy camp, where he can capture pawns, hold up hostile pawns and lead his own pawns on to queen."

Reuben Fine says clearly and simply, "The king is a strong piece – use it!"

24 ♗b2

The bishop manages to emerge, but is it too late?

24 ...   ♖b3

Immediately attacking the bishop and forcing White's next move.

25 ♖e2

Clearly the only way to save the bishop without losing the a-pawn. If instead 25 ♖ec1, then 25...♖xb2 wins a piece for Black.

25 ...   ♖xe2

Black is happy to exchange rooks and simplify the ending. He retains a positional advantage in the superior mobility of his pieces, including his king, who plans to get in among the enemy pawns and wreak havoc there.

26 ♔xe2

White recaptures and threatens to extricate himself by 27 ♖c1+ ♔b5 28 ♖c2, and the bishop is unpinned while the rook (after 29 ♗c1) might even utilize the open file!

26 ... ♚b5

Lightly stepping aside, the king evades the check. He is headed for a4, to get a good grip on White's queenside before starting to undermine the pawns on that wing.

27 ♔d2

White's rook and bishop are immobilized, so he is reduced to king moves and not too many at that, as the e-pawn needs protection.

27 ... ♚a4

Before starting the decisive combination, Black renders the opposing pawns impotent.

28 ♔e2 *(D)*

All that White has left, aside from meaningless moves by the kingside pawns.

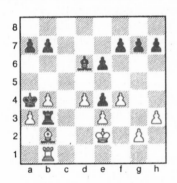

28 ... a5!

Pawns, as we shall see, are unexcelled as spearheads of an attack. They can break through almost any barrier.

Black's threat is 29...axb4 30 axb4 ♚xb4, winning a pawn.

29 ♔f2

On 29 bxa5, 29...♟xa3 regains the pawn and then wins the bishop, while after 29 ♔d2 axb4 30 axb4 ♣xb4+ 31 ♔c2 ♣a3 Black exchanges all the pieces to leave himself with an extra pawn and an elementary win.

29 ... axb4

The first bit of booty.

30 axb4

Otherwise Black's pawn continues to wreak havoc.

30 ... ♣xb4 *(D)*

Black does not take with the rook or the bishop. Either would give White time for 31 ♜a1+ and freedom for his bishop.

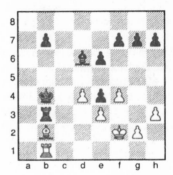

31 ♔e2

White is restricted to waiting moves.

31 ... ♚b5!

Here, too, moving the king to the a-file or the c-file allows a check by the rook.

Black now threatens to double the pressure on the pinned bishop by 32...♣a3 and win a piece.

32 ♔d2

The king moves closer to save the bishop.

32 ... ♣a3

Forcing the issue by attacking the bishop again.

33 ♔c2 *(D)*
The only move.

33 ... ♖xb2+!
Clearing the board of pieces and reducing to a pawn ending. This is the simplest way of winning an ending with an extra pawn.

34 ♖xb2+
White must recapture.

34 ... ♗xb2
Continuing the simplification.

35 ♔xb2
The only move.

35 ... ♔c4
Threatening to get at the kingside pawns by way of d3.

36 ♔c2
Preventing the planned invasion.

36 ... b5
Passed pawns must be pushed! This clinches the win, as White cannot stop the pawn without letting Black's king come in among his deserted pawns.

0-1

The continuation might be 37 g4 b4 38 h4 b3+ 39 ♔d2 b2 40 ♔c2 b1♕+ 41 ♔xb1 ♔d3 42 ♔c1 ♔xe3 43 ♔d1 ♔f2, and the new passed pawn moves up the board to become a queen.

The Chess Master Explains his Ideas

Let us imagine ourselves sitting beside a master player who reveals his thoughts in the course of a game. We can then thrill to the excitement of combinative play and revel in the pleasure of watching ideas come to life. We can see how the tactical themes, the pin, the knight fork, the double attack and the mating combination (the sort of thing we could always spot if similar opportunities only presented themselves) are prepared for by the strategy of setting the scene for their appearance.

The games that follow are not primarily displays of pretty fireworks, nor do they feature explosive (and sometimes unpredictable) attacks. They may not conform to the popular concept of brilliancy, but they do show how circumstances can be shaped by iron control of the forces involved. They also show what can be accomplished by applying the three great principles that Capablanca advocated and himself utilized so successfully:

1) in the opening, rapid and efficient development;

2) in the middlegame, coordination of pieces;

3) in the ending, accurate and time-saving play.

These games are wonderful illustrations of the efficacy of Capablanca's principles in practical play. In *my* book, games such as these are brilliancies.

In the game Capablanca-Mattison (No. 24) White does nothing but develop his pieces, but it's enough to summon up all sorts of piquant little combinations. What makes the feat impressive is that all the combinations are in White's favour, right up to the threat of mate in one (a smothered mate), which is enough to persuade Black to resign. A Capablanca jewel!

Janowsky-Alapin (No. 25) is undoubtedly the most beautiful game Janowsky ever played. His manoeuvring on the open d-file leads to the creation of a passed pawn. The pawn must be blockaded, and Black shows ingenuity in shifting blockaders so that a weaker piece keeps replacing a stronger one. Then comes an interesting phase where Janowsky's pawns reach out to the dark squares on the seventh rank, gripping them like so many fingers at the throat of an adversary. The finale includes an amusing shifting of attack to various files, which Black must try to imitate in defence.

"Étude on the Black Keys" might be a title for the Bernstein-Mieses (No. 26) game. Bernstein fastens on the weaknesses of his opponent's dark squares and plants pieces in these holes in his position. After a remarkable tour by his king, Black's pawns begin to fall and a pathway is cleared for the advance of Bernstein's passed pawns.

Chekhover-Rudakovsky (No. 27) is an unknown masterpiece in which the themes we discussed in the first two sections of the book (Kingside Attack and the Queen's Pawn Opening) are beautifully blended. Black omits the freeing ...c5 move, a circumstance which his opponent immediately exploits. Chekhover, who controls the c-file, restrains and then blockades the enemy c-pawn. With Black tied up on the queenside, he switches the attack suddenly to the kingside, giving his opponent the job of defending on both wings, to say nothing of the centre. Black is forced to play ...g6 and weaken his dark squares f6 and h6. White's queen pounces on one of the weak squares. Then begins a series of mating threats on the kingside, which culminates in winning the queen – on the queenside!

Tarrasch-Mieses (No. 28) is notable for Tarrasch's skilful refutation of a premature attack. His gains of tempo in the opening are carried over into the ending, so that what remains is a clear-cut demonstration of the technique for converting a pawn majority on the queenside into a passed pawn.

Marshall-Tarrasch (No. 29) is a little-known masterpiece, which features a duel between a genius of attack and a virtuoso of defence. The methods of the positional player prove superior, his continual acquisition of territory driving White to the wall. Against Tarrasch's steady accumulation of positional advantages, any attack by his opponent seems futile.

There follow three games in which the motif is: get a passed pawn, move it up the board, and win! In the first, Capablanca-Villegas (No. 30), White offers to sacrifice his queen, but where in most games such an offer is the high point of a combination, here it is subordinate to the grand strategy of securing a positional advantage. It leads to control of the d-file, and this in turn is converted to a queenside majority of three pawns to two. Skilful play resolves this into a lone passed pawn, heavily blockaded, until another queen sacrifice opens wide the gates.

Havasi-Capablanca (No. 31) is a superb specimen of positional play featuring the art of squeezing the most out of a tiny advantage. Capablanca secures a pawn majority on the queenside and sets to work to translate it into a passed pawn. This he does by getting control of the open c-file and then exploiting the weakness of his opponent's light squares. The rest consists of escorting the passed pawn safely to the queening square.

Canal-Capablanca (No. 32) is a game for the connoisseur. Canal surprises Capablanca by a combination that wins two pieces for a rook. Or was it a surprise? Apparently Capablanca anticipated the combination and, looking further into the position than Canal, saw resources that were not revealed to his opponent. The ending that follows is a fascinating study and illustrates a 'domination' theme rare in actual play. There is a pawn to be queened, but it would take an eagle eye to find the particular pawn that will be crowned.

Rubinstein-Maroczy (No. 33) is a splendid all-around performance. Rubinstein's economic development in the opening results in magnificent middlegame centralization, and this in turn is a prelude to a kingside attack in the ending. Not the least of this game's attractions is the remarkable use of d5 as a pivot for the manoeuvres of Rubinstein's knight, bishop, rook and queen, who each utilize this square in turn as a landing field!

Game 24
Capablanca – Mattison
Karlsbad 1929
Nimzo-Indian Defence

1 d4

The popular impression of king's pawn openings is that they offer all sorts of opportunities for whipping up a quick attack. A variety of gambits can be played, pieces may be sacrificed to open lines, combinations ventured on, and speculation indulged in – anything for the sake of mate. Sometimes these tactics succeed, but very often the gambit player finds himself at the wrong end of the attack, as wide-open positions are as dangerous for one side as for the other.

In queen's pawn openings, the ideal to strive for is development for its own sake. The attack is not the 'be-all and end-all'. It is not deliberately played for, but, strangely enough, the very fact that all the pieces are developed economically, that they are put to work as quickly as possible on the squares where they function best, seems to imbue them with marvellous powers of attack. Combinations come into life out of nothing! Can it be that the simple posting of pieces where they have the greatest freedom of movement and the greatest command of the board generates in them so much dynamic energy that it must be released somehow? And can it be that knowledge of this fact is what makes the virtuosi of positional play repress their instinct to attack until the time is ripe for an attack to be unleashed?

White's move of the d-pawn begins the process of getting *all* the pieces into play as quickly as possible. Two of them are now free to make their debut, while the pawn that released them occupies the centre of the stage.

1 ... ♘f6

A developing move, whose object (besides the commendable one of bringing a piece to its most suitable square) is to prevent White from gaining too much ground with 2 e4.

2 c4

This move does many things:

1) it begins an attack on the d5-square;

2) it keeps the c-file open for the use of the heavy pieces;

3) it offers the queen a diagonal;

4) it hinders Black from establishing a pawn in the centre by 2...d5, as White's reply 3 cxd5 compelling a recapture with a piece would leave Black with no pawn in the centre.

2 ...   e6

Black clears a path for the dark-squared bishop and indicates that he will go in for an active defence.

3 ♘c3

White's motive is evident: he develops the b1-knight first, to support an advance of the e-pawn.

3 ...   ♗b4 (D)

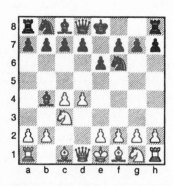

To this, Black counters by clamping a pin on the knight. If White were to play 4 e4, then 4...♘xe4 would leave him helpless to recapture.

4 ♕c2

With a twofold purpose: to meet 4...♗xc3+ with 5 ♕xc3, keeping White's pawn structure intact, and to threaten again the advance 5 e4.

There is a prevalent concept that in the opening there is a 'best move'

at every point. The belief is that the chess master memorizes every one of these best moves and its proper reply. That such reasoning is specious is obvious: the very fact that millions of games have been played without duplication of moves is proof enough in itself.

Let us consider the position on the board. Besides the text-move (4 ♕c2), there are at least seven excellent alternatives, each of which has enthusiastic advocates. They are: 4 ♕b3; 4 ♗d2; 4 a3; 4 ♗g5; 4 e3; 4 g3; and 4 ♘f3. Which of these is best? No one can say for sure, but the move that leads into positions congenial to your style is the best move, and the one you should play.

4 ...   c5

Black too can conduct the defence (or the counterattack) in the manner that suits his style and temperament. The move he plays immediately disputes White's control of the centre. It does other things, too: it gives the queen more scope, opens the c-file, protects the bishop, etc.

However, there are other moves, equally effective, at Black's disposal. He can select from these replies, each of which has something to recommend it: 4...♘c6; 4...d6; 4...d5; 4...0-0; and 4...b6. There is something for every taste.

5 dxc5

Strongest for various reasons:

White does not lose time in taking the pawn, as Black in recapturing will return the lost tempo. The open d-file resulting from 5 dxc5 will benefit White, who will occupy d1 with a rook and exert pressure along the length of it, especially endangering the backward d-pawn.

Other continuations are less energetic. For instance, after 5 e3, Black frees himself by 5...d5, while after 5 ♘f3 cxd4 6 ♘xd4 ♘c6 White has lost the initiative.

5 ... ♘c6

Black develops another piece before recapturing the pawn.

6 ♘f3

Somewhere about this stage, the amateur wants things to happen. He begins to look around for surprise moves. "There *must* be a brilliancy in the position!" The great master, in the same situation, is content to make simple moves. He knows that if he keeps on bringing pieces into play, there will be no need to look for winning combinations. They will evolve naturally out of the position and spring up all over the place!

6 ... ♗xc5 (D)

Further delay in recovering the pawn might be dangerous.

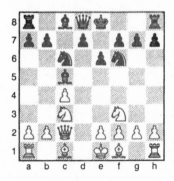

7 ♗f4

The aggressive 7 ♗g5 is more usual, to pin the knight and keep Black under pressure, but no fault can be found with this method of development. It looks mild, but the bishop surveys an important diagonal and bears down on d6, a tender spot in Black's position.

7 ... d5

Vigorously challenging White's possession of the centre.

8 e3

Another quiet move which liberates one bishop and strengthens the position of the other.

8 ... ♕a5 (D)

Black spies a chance to start an attack which will result in saddling White with an isolated c-pawn – a slight positional weakness, so he begins an action against the knight, but "such artificial manoeuvres," says Tartakower, "can hardly succeed against a Capablanca."

Black should instead do something to get his c8-bishop into play, for example 8...a6 9 ♗e2 dxc4 10 ♗xc4 b5 11 ♗e2 ♕b6 (not at once 11...♗b7 on account of 12 ♘xb5) 12 0-0 ♗b7.

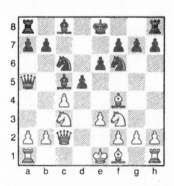

9 ♗e2

Yet another modest move, but it is packed with more energy than you might suspect. It accomplishes these objectives:

1) it activates a piece, by getting it off the first rank;

2) it develops the bishop at e2 so that it can move to f3 and attack the centre;

3) it clears away the kingside, making early castling possible;

4) it prepares the cooperation of the rooks on the first rank, subsequent to castling.

What was wrong with playing the more aggressive-looking 9 ♗d3? For one thing, the reply 9...♘b4 enables Black to force an exchange of knight for bishop. White would lose the services of a piece valuable for its potential influence on the centre. Why not then prepare to develop the bishop at d3 by playing 9 a3 first? The answer is that time is too valuable in the opening to waste on unnecessary pawn moves. *Only those pawn moves that are essential to the development of pieces should be made.* The additional circumstance that 9 a3 weakens the light squares on the queenside is more proof that such strategy is artificial and time-wasting.

9   ...   ♗b4 *(D)*

In contrast to White's classically simple method of development, Black moves the same bishop a third time in the opening, in order to inflict his opponent with an isolated pawn. Such an attempt is premature in view of Black's incomplete development.

Instead, a plausible continuation is 9...0-0 10 0-0 dxc4 11 ♗xc4 ♗d7, when Black has a fair game.

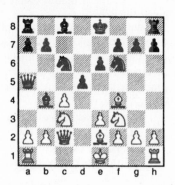

10   0-0

The king is made secure, while the h1-rook moves closer to the centre, the theatre of action. The rook, of course, will try to seize an open file, or, if none is available, one which is likely to be opened.

10   ...   ♗xc3

The bishop has moved four times to make this exchange for a knight that has moved only once! So much shifting around of one piece indicates that the strategy behind it must be faulty.

11   bxc3

Despite White's doubled c-pawn, he enjoys these advantages:

1) he has two active bishops against Black's knight and bishop;

2) all of his minor pieces are in play while Black still has a bishop on the first rank;

3) his rooks are in touch with each other and ready to seize the half-open b- and d-files;

4) his king is safely tucked away in a corner while Black's is out in the open;

5) his queen is ideally posted and has more influence on the centre

than does Black's, standing at the side of the board;

6) an exchange of pawns in the centre (which looks inevitable) will open lines of attack, a circumstance that favours the player whose development is superior – in this case, White;

7) he maintains the initiative.

11 ... 0-0 *(D)*

One of Black's difficulties is resolved with his king's escape to safer quarters.

Developing the bishop instead was somewhat risky, since after 11...♗d7 12 ♖ab1 (attacking the b7-pawn) 12...b6 13 ♗d6 White stops kingside castling and threatens 14 ♖b5 ♕a6 15 cxd5 exd5 16 ♖xd5, and the discovered attack on the queen wins a pawn for White.

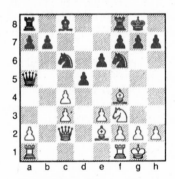

12 ♖ab1 *(D)*

Another of those subtle moves, whose purpose the average player usually fails to see. "What use is it," he says, "to waste a rook move in attacking a pawn that is adequately protected?"

True, the pawn is defended, but by a bishop which cannot develop

without abandoning the pawn. Sooner or later, Black will be compelled to play ...b6, or have three pieces on his first rank interfering with each other. There are drawbacks to ...b6, though, for example Black's queen will be cut off and prevented from returning to the kingside and the defence of the king. In addition, his c6-knight's position will be insecure, once the prop (the b7-pawn) is removed from under it.

White's move is simple and quiet, but it exerts uncomfortable pressure on Black's queenside, makes normal development difficult, and creates permanent weaknesses which lend themselves to exploitation.

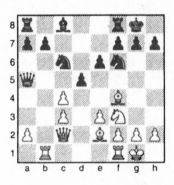

12 ... ♕a3

Black wants to develop his bishop, and for that purpose he must play ...b6, but to do so at once might endanger the queen by cutting off her line of retreat. For instance, 12...b6 13 ♗d6 ♖d8 14 ♖b5 ♕a6 15 cxd5 ♖xd6 (15...exd5 permits 16 ♖xd5 discovering an attack on the queen) 16 dxc6 ♖xc6 17 ♘d4 ♖c7 18 ♖e5 wins material, as 18...♕b7 loses after 19 ♗f3 ♘d5 20 ♗xd5 leading to a surprising back-rank mate following 20...exd5 21 ♖e8#.

13 ♖fd1! *(D)*

With the posting of this rook on the partly open d-file, White's development has been completed in an ideal way, every piece taking its best post in no more than one move. White has not so much as hinted at an attacking combination until every piece has been put to work.

13 ...   b6

To enable the bishop to come out, but the advance of the pawn takes away the c6-knight's support and weakens its position.

Guarding the b-pawn by 13...♕e7 instead does not help much, since the bishop cannot develop at d7 next move without cutting off the queen's protection of the pawn. Nor can Black try to simplify by 13...dxc4 as the reply 14 ♗d6 wins the exchange.

14 cxd5

The attack begins! The first blow destroys Black's pawn-centre.

14 ...   ♘xd5 *(D)*

The recapture with the pawn, 14...exd5, is bad in view of 15 c4!. Black could not then escape by

15...dxc4 since 16 ♗d6 attacks queen and rook, while protecting the pawn by 15...♗e6 yields to 16 cxd5 ♗xd5 17 ♖xd5 ♘xd5 18 ♕xc6, and White has won two pieces for a rook.

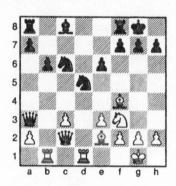

15 ♘g5!

A master stroke! The brutal threat of 16 ♕xh7# disguises the two real purposes of the move: the strategic concept of forcing Black to move one of his kingside pawns, thereby loosening the defensive structure; and the clearance of the f6-square for the benefit of the dark-squared bishop, who will bear down heavily on the long diagonal.

15 ...   f5

Black had two alternatives:

1) 15...♘f6 avoids moving one of the pawns, but 16 ♗d6 wins the exchange.

2) 15...g6 leaves Black's position riddled with weaknesses on the dark squares.

Therefore, Black moves the f-pawn, staving off the mate, but it weakens his e-pawn and ties the bishop down to its defence.

16 ♗f3!

This arrangement of bishops gives them tremendous raking power along the two parallel diagonals.

White's chief threat is 17 ♖xd5 exd5 18 ♗xd5+ ♔h8 19 ♗xc6 followed by 20 ♗xa8, sweeping away a good part of Black's army.

16 ...   ♕c5

The queen rushes to the aid of the vulnerable knights. This is what happens on other defences:

1) 16...♘de7 17 ♗d6 ♕a5 18 ♗xe7 ♘xe7 19 ♗xa8, and White wins a whole rook.

2) 16...♘ce7 17 c4 ♘b4 18 ♖xb4 ♕xb4 19 ♗xa8, and White wins a piece.

3) 16...♘xf4 17 ♗xc6 ♖b8 18 exf4, and White has won a piece.

4) 16...♕xc3 17 ♕xc3 ♘xc3 18 ♗xc6 ♘xd1 19 ♖xd1 ♗a6 20 ♗xa8 ♖xa8, and White is a piece ahead.

After Black's actual move, he seems to have escaped the worst, but White has an ingenious way to get at the knights:

17 c4! *(D)*

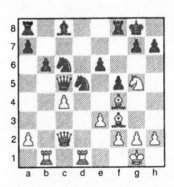

This stab at the knight looks harmless, the pawn being pinned and unable to capture, but the point of 17 c4 is to use the pawn to support an attack by 18 ♖b5. This will drive the queen off and make the capture 19 cxd5 possible.

The combinations now appear in quick succession.

17 ...   ♘db4

Counterattack on the queen. All other attempts at defence fail, viz.:

1) 17...♘f6 18 ♗d6 ♕a5 19 ♗xc6 and both Black's rooks are *en prise*.

2) 17...♘xf4 18 ♖b5! (a pretty 'in-between' move) 18...♕e7 (alternatively 18...♘b4 19 ♕d2 ♕xc4 20 ♖xb4 and White wins) 19 ♗xc6 ♕xg5 20 exf4, and the attack on the queen leaves Black no time to save his a8-rook.

3) 17...♘de7 18 ♗d6 ♕a5 19 ♗xe7 winning a whole rook.

18 ♕b3 *(D)*

White's queen must move, but the threat of 19 ♗d6 hangs over Black like the Sword of Damocles.

18 ...   e5

Not only because there is no other antidote to 19 ♗d6, but with the hope of curbing the terrible bishops by putting obstacles in their paths.

19   a3! *(D)*

This starts a beautiful combination at one end of the board which culminates in a queen sacrifice followed by a smothered mate over at the other end!

19   ...   ♘a6

The only other move, 19...exf4, allows White to force the win by 20 axb4 ♕e7 21 ♗xc6 ♖b8 22 exf4, and the extra piece wins easily.

20   ♗xc6

After the recapture 20...♕xc6, there comes 21 c5+ ♔h8 22 ♘f7+ ♔g8 (or 22...♖xf7 23 ♖d8+ and White forces mate) 23 ♘h6++ ♔h8 24 ♕g8+! ♖xg8 25 ♘f7#!

Black did not wait to be convinced by a demonstration over the board but turned down his king in surrender.

1-0

An exquisite game played with elegance and precision. Capablanca's own comment on it was "I made a few little combinations in this game."

Game 25
Janowsky – Alapin
Barmen 1905
Queen's Gambit Declined

1   d4

White opens by stationing a pawn in the centre. This pawn performs various services:

- It releases two pieces.
- It occupies an important square.
- It controls e5 and c5, hindering the opponent from placing pieces on those squares.
- It stands ready to give firm support to a friendly piece making use of e5 or c5 as an outpost.

1   ...   d5

Black follows suit, establishing a pawn in the centre, and prevents White from continuing with his intended 2 e4.

2   c4

White offers a pawn to induce Black to surrender the centre.

White's move is also an attack on the d-pawn, by means of which he hopes to uproot it and its hold on the centre.

2   ...   e6

The customary device for maintaining a pawn in the centre. In the event of White's playing 3 cxd5, *Black must be ready to replace the d-pawn with another pawn.* It would not do to recapture with a piece. The piece could be driven off by White's e-pawn, leaving White in full possession of the central squares.

For instance, after 2...♘f6 3 cxd5 ♘xd5 4 e4 ♘f6 5 ♘c3 White holds all the trumps.

3 ♘c3

This is more enterprising than the passive 3 ♘f3. Pressure is added to the attack on d5, and the knight also takes a hand in the battle for control of e4.

One of White's objects in queen's pawn openings is to effect a subsequent advance of the e-pawn, just as in king's pawn openings an effort is made to gain more ground with a later d4.

3 ... ♗e7 *(D)*

The usual move at this point is 3...♘f6 but Black transposes moves to prevent his knight being pinned.

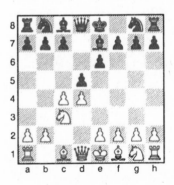

4 ♘f3

White is content with simple development and places the king's knight at its most suitable post.

4 ... ♘f6

Black postponed this move, excellent though it is, and now makes it

reluctantly, but how else can he develop the kingside and prepare to castle?

5 ♗g5 *(D)*

This is not really a pin, but its effect is somewhat similar. Pressure is exerted on the knight, the bishop behind it and even on the last in line, the queen.

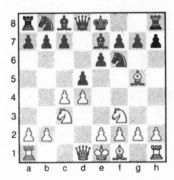

5 ... h6

Alapin can't stand pins or pseudo-pins! He attacks the bishop at once, to force it to a decision.

6 ♗h4

Whether objectively this is the strongest move is immaterial; the fact that the bishop's pressure bothers Black is enough reason for Janowsky to maintain the pin!

6 ... dxc4

Black opens the position to give his pieces more elbow room, but with this capture he gives up his hold on the centre.

7 e3

The simplest way to regain the pawn. The f1-bishop will capture it and make a developing move at the same time.

7 ... a6

Ready to counter 8 ♗xc4 with 8...b5, attacking White's bishop and gaining a tempo for the development of his own bishop.

8 ♗xc4

Material is now equal, but White's prospects are better: he has two more pieces in active play than Black, and his pawn position in the centre is superior.

8 ... b5 (D)

Black's chief purpose in this pawn attack is to vacate the b7-square for his light-squared bishop.

9 ♗b3

Nobody has yet decided whether this or d3 is the better retreat for the bishop. At b3 the bishop strikes at Black's centre, but those who favour d3 reason that from there the bishop helps control the vital e4-square and is aimed at the enemy king after a subsequent ...0-0.

9 ... ♘bd7 (D)

Naturally, the knight does not go to c6 where it would obstruct the c-pawn. The pawn must not be hindered from carrying out its mission in life, which is to attack White's centre and open a file for Black's rooks.

The knight's development looks clumsy, but it does back up the other knight, and it is ready to support a thrust at the centre by ...c5 or ...e5.

10 ♕e2

Notice how an expert player puts all his pieces to work before starting any decisive action! This does not look like much of a move for so powerful a piece as the queen, but the simple act of getting a piece off the back rank advances the cause of development and constitutes progress.

Two more points: in the early stages of the game, the queen is most happily placed close to home, for instance at c2 or e2. In getting off the back rank, the queen permits the rooks (after the king castles) to get in touch with each other. A more aggressive development (generally for the sake of picking up a stray pawn) is only courting danger.

10 ... c6

It is hard to tell exactly what Black had in mind with this move. He may have feared the advance 11 d5 by White, or perhaps he wanted to create an outlet for the queen on the queenside. In any case, the move is definitely inferior to 10...c5, disputing the centre without any more delay.

11 0-0

Castling by White is an aggressive measure, to press the rook into active service.

11 ... 0-0

Castling by Black is defensive in purpose, to get the king out of harm's way.

12 ♖ac1 *(D)*

The rook comes to the head of the c-file, control of which is one of White's main objectives in this opening.

12 ... ♗b7

With the development of the light-squared bishop, Black seems to have solved one of the problems that besets the defender in queen's pawn openings, but he isn't out of the woods yet!

13 ♖fd1

Excellent play! The rooks are now beautifully posted. The pressure on the d-file makes it dangerous for Black to try to free himself by 13...c5, as the reply 14 dxc5 opens a file for the d1-rook.

13 ... ♖c8 *(D)*

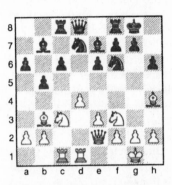

Black gives the c-pawn more support in an effort to get in 14...c5. This would free his position and let him put up a fight for the c-file.

14 ♘e5!

White is now ideally developed, with every one of his pieces taking an active part in the game. Black, on the contrary, is hampered by the restricted mobility of his pieces.

White's knight move prevents a freeing attempt by 14...c5, since 15 dxc5 ♖xc5 (15...♗xc5 16 ♘xd7 leaves Black unable to recapture) 16 ♗xf6 ♗xf6 17 ♘xd7 wins a knight and attacks a couple of rooks.

14 ... ♘xe5

Black tries to relieve the pressure by exchanging whatever pieces he can.

15 dxe5

This exchange suits White in that he has opportunities for attack along the newly opened d-file. Another effect arising from the pawn's recapture is the creation of a strong point at d6, a circumstance which White hopes to exploit by planting a piece on that square.

15   ...   ♘d5 *(D)*

The knight must block off the rook's attack on the queen. If instead 15...♘d7, then 16 ♗xe7 (in order to remove the guardian of the d6-square) 16...♕xe7 17 f4 and White will either entrench his rook at d6 and double rooks on the d-file or manoeuvre his knight to d6 by way of e4.

16   ♗xe7

In order to benefit from the weakness of d6 it is necessary to remove the bishop that defends the dark squares.

16   ...   ♘xc3

Black destroys the knight before it does him any damage. The alternative 16...♕xe7 lets White swing his knight over to e4 and then anchor it either at d6 or c5.

17   ♖xc3

Certainly not 17 ♖xd8 (nor 17 ♗xd8) 17...♘xe2+ 18 ♔f1 ♘xc1, and Black wins. The text gains a tempo for White in his plan to double rooks on the d-file.

17   ...   ♕xe7 *(D)*

Material is even after this recapture, but White has a slightly superior position. Is this enough of an advantage for a master to squeeze out a win?

White's specific advantage consists of his possession of the only completely open file, and the pressure he exerts on the strategically important d6-square.

18   ♖cd3!

Much stronger than the plausible continuation 18 ♖d6. The reply to that would be 18...c5 whereupon doubling the rooks by 19 ♖cd3 allows the pawn fork 19...c4 and Black wins a piece.

White's actual move doubles his rooks without loss of time and also threatens to win a piece by 19 ♖d7.

18   ...   ♖fd8

The dilemma which the weaker side always faces in this sort of situation is that if he does not dispute the enemy at every point and fight for control of every important file, diagonal or square, he will slowly be driven back and crushed to the wall; if he does oppose him at every turn, the resulting exchanges will simplify the position without improving his chances.

In this particular position, Black could hardly delay opposing rooks, as he was threatened with invasion on the seventh rank by 19 ♖d7, as well as 19 ♕d2, tripling the heavy pieces on the file. Such a massing of power on the open file would of course be overwhelming!

19 ♖d6!

White stakes out a claim to the d6-square by settling a piece firmly there.

19 ... ♖xd6

Otherwise, White plays 20 ♕d2 next, with intolerable pressure on Black's position.

20 exd6

This gives White a passed pawn, which exerts a terrific influence on the opponent's way of life. Nimzowitsch calls particular attention to "the lust to expand in a passed pawn" and says that it must be regarded as "a criminal who should be kept under lock and key".

To prevent any further advance of the passed pawn, Black must blockade it by placing a piece in its path. In effect, to keep the pawn under surveillance, he must lose the services of one of his four remaining pieces! If constant vigilance is necessary to keep the pawn quiescent, it is obvious that Black will be too busy defending to think of counterattack. On the other hand, White is free to switch the attack from one point to another!

20 ... ♕d7 *(D)*

This is practically forced, as the pawn must be blockaded, and at once! Another forward step by the pawn might be fatal! Witness this

possibility: 20...♕d8 21 d7 ♖c7 22 ♕d2 (threatening to win by 23 ♕d6 followed by 24 ♕xc7 and queening the pawn) 22...c5 23 ♕a5 ♖xd7 24 ♕xd8+ and White wins.

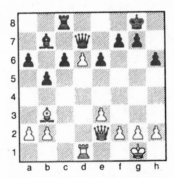

After Black's actual move, the pawn is stopped, but in blockading it, Black is tying up the queen, his strongest piece!

21 e4

Indicating that he intends to play 22 e5, supporting the d-pawn and further cramping Black's game. White's pieces, relieved of the necessity of watching over the d-pawn, could then move freely about the board.

21 ... c5

Black opens a diagonal for his bishop and gives his rook more air.

An effort to prevent 22 e5 by 21...f6 would have been met by 22 ♕g4 and now either 22...♔f7 23 e5 fxe5 24 ♕f5+ ♔e8 25 ♗xe6 ♕d8 26 ♕f7# or 22...♖e8 23 ♗xe6+ ♖xe6 24 ♕xe6+! ♕xe6 25 d7, and White wins.

22 e5

Assisting the d-pawn on to the next stage in its career: first, a pawn undistinguished from its fellows, then a passed pawn, now a protected passed pawn, and finally (if it fulfils its brilliant promise) a queen.

22 ...   c4

Back to sober reality! Black fights every step of the way to institute countermeasures which will keep his opponent busy on the queenside.

23 ♗c2

The bishop, though forced back, now overlooks a new diagonal with interesting prospects.

23 ...   ♕c6 (D)

Black does not like to have his strongest piece tied down to the job of watching a passed pawn, so he diverts White's attention by threatening mate. While White is occupied with stopping the mate, Black will have time to switch blockaders.

24 f3

This puts an end to attacks on the long diagonal, as it leaves Black's queen and bishop biting on granite.

24 ...   ♕c5+ (D)

The chief purpose of the check is to prevent White from playing 25 ♕e3, seizing control of the dark-squared diagonals.

25 ♔h1

White keeps the queens on the board. Apparently he wants to win the game by direct attack, in preference to offering an exchange of queens by 25 ♕f2.

Such decisions are a matter of style more than anything else. A player who has choice of more than one way of winning should select a method that is congenial to his temperament and aptitudes. In the present position, I imagine that a Rubinstein or a Capablanca would unhesitatingly offer the exchange of queens and simplify, confident in his ability to turn a small but safe advantage into a win; they would be happy to leave the brilliancies to other masters. It is to these varying techniques that we must be grateful for the creation of a wealth of masterpieces in so many colours and moods.

After 25 ♕f2, if Black avoids the exchange of queens and continues 25...♕xe5, White wins elegantly by 26 ♕b6 ♗c6 27 ♕xc6! ♖xc6 28 d7, regaining the queen by promotion and ending up a piece ahead.

25 ...   ♖d8 (D)

The rook takes over the job of keeping the pawn covered.

26 ♕e1!

A very fine move! The queen threatens to invade Black's kingside by way of 27 ♕h4 or his queenside by 27 ♕a5.

26 ... ♖d7

Nailing down the passed pawn for the time being.

27 h3

An outlet for the king in case of need. If White's queen and rook leave for the attack, his king must not be caught by surprise and mated on the first rank.

27 ... ♗c6

Another regrouping so that the rook may leave its post, and the bishop (a lesser piece) stand guard.

28 f4

Preparing a breakthrough by 29 f5 – pawns make excellent instruments of attack. They can break into almost any stronghold and make gaps wide enough for an invasion by the pieces.

28 ... ♖a7 *(D)*

The rook vacates d7 for occupation by the bishop.

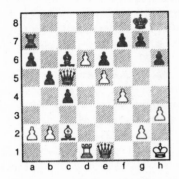

29 f5!

To this vigorous thrust Black may not reply 29...exf5 as 30 e6 fxe6 (otherwise White obtains two connected passed pawns on the sixth rank) 31 ♕xe6+ ♔h8 (31...♖f7 32 d7 wins) 32 ♕c8+ ♔h7 33 ♗xf5+ wins for White.

29 ... ♗d7

Black completes the changing of the guard. Since one of his pieces must act as blockader, he assigns the task to the least important, the bishop.

30 f6

This battering ram of a pawn will force a breach in Black's defensive structure. White's threat is 31 ♕g3 (intending 32 ♕xg7#) 31...g6 32 ♗xg6 fxg6 33 ♕xg6+, and mate in two.

30 ... g6 *(D)*

On 30...gxf6 White wins by 31 ♕g3+ ♔h8 (31...♔f8 32 ♗h7 mates) 32 ♕f4 f5 (or 32...♕xe5 33 ♕xh6+ ♔g8 34 ♕h7+ ♔f8 35 ♕h8#) 33 ♕xh6+ ♔g8 34 ♕g5+ ♔f8 35 ♕f6 ♔g8 36 ♖f1 ♗c6 (or else ♖f3 and ♖g3+) 37 ♗xf5 exf5 38 ♖xf5 ♗e4 39 ♖h5 with a quick mate.

After the actual move, the change in the pawn configuration provides White with fresh objects of attack. One thing he must watch out for, though, is the preservation of his invaluable e-pawn, which so stoutly supports the two advanced pawns. Note that the position of these pawns gives them a powerful grip on the dark squares c7, e7 and g7. These squares are in the enemy's camp and close to his king, but he (Black) cannot place pieces on those squares. With fewer facilities at his disposal, it will be difficult for Black to beat back the invaders.

The play for the win from this point comes under the heading of instruction and entertainment.

31 ♕g3

Threatening to win at once by 32 ♗xg6 fxg6 33 ♕xg6+, followed shortly by mate.

31 ...   ♔h7

The only way to protect the pawn. Advancing it instead by 31...g5 allows White a winning reply in 32 h4.

32 h4

The g6-pawn is pinned and White prepares to hit it again by 33 h5.

32 ...   ♕c8

Hastening to bring the queen over to the danger zone. If Black tries to stop the pawn's advance by 32...h5 then the queen works her way in by 33 ♕g5 (threatening 34 ♕xh5+) 33...♔g8 34 ♕h6 and 35 ♕g7#.

33 h5

Concentrating his fire on a vulnerable spot.

33 ...   ♕g8 (D)

Not 33...♗e8, which protects the pawn but blocks the queen. The queen is the only piece agile enough to defend against White's attack as it shifts from one point to another.

34 ♖d4

White makes use of all his resources. The rook will take part by switching over either to the h-file or the g-file.

34 ...   ♗e8

The bishop helps defend the g-pawn so that the queen is free to protect the h-pawn, White's next target of attack.

35 ♖h4

Revealing the plan: mate in three by 36 hxg6+ fxg6 37 ♖xh6+ ♔xh6 38 ♕h4#.

35 ...   ♕f8

The only possible defence.

36 ♖g4

A pretty manoeuvre! White's last move lured the queen away from the g-pawn. Now that this pawn has one piece less defending it, White attacks it with a fourth piece, the rook.

36 ...   ♕g8 (D)

The queen rushes back to defend.

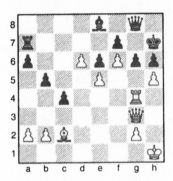

37 ♕e3!

The threat on the rook gains time for White's real purpose, an attack on the h-pawn at the other side of the board.

37 ...   ♖d7

The rook flees but cannot get over to help defend the king.

38 ♖h4

Renews (and shortens) the earlier threat: 39 hxg6+ fxg6 40 ♕xh6#.

38 ...   ♕f8

Once again, the queen shifts over to protect the h-pawn.

39 g4!

Bringing up the infantry! White throws everything into the attack and now threatens 40 g5 followed by 41 hxg6+ fxg6 42 ♖xh6+ ♔g8 43 ♕h3, with an easy win. If after 40

g5, Black tries 40...hxg5 then 41 hxg6++ ♔g8 42 ♖h8+ ♔xh8 43 ♕h3+ forces mate.

39 ...   ♔h8

Black unpins the g-pawn and prepares 40...g5 41 ♕e4 ♕g8, when White will have trouble breaking through the defence.

40 hxg6

Tearing apart the cordon of pawns guarding the king.

40 ...   fxg6

This capture is the lesser evil, as otherwise White's next move, 41 g7+, is fatal.

41 ♖xh6+

Killing off another bodyguard.

41 ...   ♖h7

If 41...♔g8, then 42 ♕h3, doubling pieces on the open file, is conclusive.

42 ♖xh7+

Certainly not 42 g5 ♖xh6+ 43 gxh6, when the h-file is closed and useless to White.

42 ...   ♔xh7 (D)

White is only one pawn up, but his attack has lost none of its virulence.

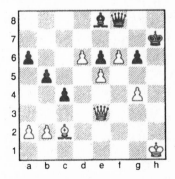

43 ♕g5

Now White plans to penetrate by 44 ♕h5+ (exploiting the plight of the pinned g-pawn) 44...♔g8 45 ♗xg6, and the last barrier is destroyed.

43   ...   ♕f7 *(D)*

Black avoids a queen exchange, as 43...♕h6+ 44 ♕xh6+ ♔xh6 45 f7 ♗xf7 46 d7 results in White getting a new queen.

44   ♕h5+

Beginning of the final movement!

44   ...   ♔g8

The king is driven back and the g-pawn loses a protector.

45   ♗xg6

White sacrifices a piece to bring about a position where the passed pawns will decide the issue.

45   ...   ♕xg6

An attempt to counterattack by 45...♕b7+ is futile. White simply replies 46 ♔h2 and the king, seemingly exposed, is not in the slightest danger.

46   ♕xg6+   1-0

White wins as 46...♗xg6 fails to 47 d7.

The whole game is a marvellous blend of clear-cut positional play and ingenuity in attack. The opening is sound and simple, the middle-game is a lesson in attacking technique, and the ending is artistic.

Game 26
O.Bernstein – Mieses
Coburg 1904
Sicilian Defence

1   e4

Regarded objectively, 1 e4 is one of the strongest possible opening moves. It establishes a pawn in the centre and permits two pieces to come into play. More could hardly be asked of one move.

1   ...   c5

This opening, the Sicilian Defence, is currently one of the most popular openings. Black's first move has the defect that only one piece is released, but in one respect it has a similar aim to 1...e5: it covers d4 and so makes it more awkward for White to form a 'two-abreast' pawn-centre by playing d4. If White insists on d4, then Black can reply ...cxd4, thereby exchanging White's central pawn for a less central one.

The Sicilian Defence is perfectly sound and leads to a fighting game in which Black has many counterattacking chances, especially against an over-ambitious opponent, too intent on a kingside attack.

Black aims at queenside counter-attack, and for this, control of the c-file is essential to offset White's superiority in the centre and on the kingside.

2 ♘c3

A normal developing move. White brings a piece to a square where it exerts influence on the centre – but what a placid move this is!

More to the point is the energetic 2 ♘f3. This develops a piece on the kingside (facilitating early castling) and prepares 3 d4 – action in the centre and release of the queenside pieces.

2 ...   e6 (D)

Black's move is quiet but effective! Diagonals are opened for the f8-bishop and the queen, and preparation is made to occupy the centre, if appropriate, with 3...d5.

3 ♘f3

This excellent move places the knight at once on its most suitable square, increases the pressure on the centre, and makes early kingside castling feasible.

Playing 3 d4 instead leads to 3...cxd4 4 ♕xd4 ♘c6, when Black gains a tempo by the attack on the queen.

3 ...   ♘c6

If Black plays 3...d5, then the reply 4 exd5 exd5 5 d4 opens lines to the advantage of the better developed player – in this case White, who has two pieces out to Black's none.

4 d4

The characteristic break in the Sicilian, by means of which the mobility of White's pieces is increased. A diagonal is opened up for the c1-bishop, while the queen gets some more air.

4 ...   cxd4

Black exchanges to kill off one of the two centre pawns in return for his c-pawn. Meanwhile, he opens the all-important c-file for the use of his queen and a8-rook.

5 ♘xd4

The recapture centralizes White's knight and increases the attacking range of White's pieces.

5 ...   ♘f6 (D)

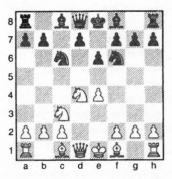

By a devious route, the players have arrived at the Four Knights

Sicilian, a tricky variation in spite of its classical appearance.

What should White play now? The choice is more a matter of style, mood and temperament than anything else – and this is what makes chess so fascinating.

White can decide to be methodical and stick to straightforward development by 6 ♗e3 or 6 ♗e2. He can be bold and combinative with 6 ♘db5, or cautious with 6 a3, preventing a powerful pin. He can be patient and devote his efforts to trying to build up a positional advantage after 6 g3 or 6 ♘xc6.

Whatever he does, the play will reflect something of his own personality. The way he directs the activities of his small army will mirror the thoughts, moods, and instincts of the individual.

6   ♘xc6 (D)

White is content with the slight positional advantage that results from the exchange of knights. Let us take a quick look at some of the alternatives:

1) 6 ♗e3 ♗b4 (pinning the knight and threatening 7...♘xe4) 7 ♗d3 d5! and Black has overcome all his difficulties.

2) The quiet 6 ♗e2 (certainly not 6 ♗d3, leaving the knight *en prise*) is also met by 6...♗b4 with good counterplay.

3) Preventing the pin by 6 a3 is not attractive. It is answered by 6...d5, and White must fight to retain the initiative. Time is too valuable in the opening to waste on pawn moves.

4) The double-edged 6 ♘db5 is not to everybody's taste, leading as it

does to wild complications after 6...♗b4 7 ♗f4 ♘xe4 8 ♘c7+ ♔f8 9 ♕f3 d5 10 0-0-0 or the sharp Pelikan variation after 6...d6 7 ♗f4 e5 8 ♗g5.

One merit of the text-move is that Black, in recapturing with a pawn, closes the c-file, his chief avenue of attack in the Sicilian.

6 ...   bxc6

This is superior to 6...dxc6; for one thing, it is usually better strategy to capture toward the centre. In this case, it keeps a cluster of pawns in the centre and opens the b-file for the benefit of the a8-rook.

The continuation after 6...dxc6 might be 7 ♕xd8+ ♔xd8 8 ♗g5 ♗e7 9 0-0-0+ and Black is kept on the move.

7   e5

Not only does this evict the f6-knight from its fine post, but it also strengthens White's grip on the d6-square.

7 ...   ♘d5 (D)

Little thought would have been required to make this centralizing move. The only other spot available to the knight was g8, home base.

8 ♘e4

Exchanging knights would forfeit any advantage White enjoys. The move actually made intensifies the pressure on d6.

8 ... f5

No loitering on the premises! Either the knight leaves or it declares its intentions!

Black had another defence in 8...♕c7 9 f4 ♕b6, aiming to prevent White from castling kingside.

9 exf6

The knight must stay where it is for White to carry out his purpose, which is to take possession of the critical d6-square.

9 ... ♘xf6

Black does not take with the pawn, as that is answered by 10 ♕h5+. This would force his king to move and thereby deprive him of the privilege of castling.

10 ♘d6+

Compelling an exchange of pieces which leaves Black with a 'bad' bishop, one which is ineffective because of the pawns standing on squares of the same colour as the bishop. A bishop can accomplish

little if its pathway is cluttered up by pawns.

10 ... ♗xd6

The only other move, 10...♔e7, is not inviting.

11 ♕xd6 *(D)*

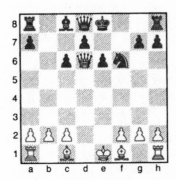

The recapture gives White a stranglehold on his opponent's position. Not only does White blockade the d-pawn, preventing the freeing ...d5 advance, but he also enables his king to flee to safety by castling. In addition, White exerts a great deal of pressure on the dark squares, a pressure that is accentuated by the fact that Black's king's bishop, operating on those squares, is off the board.

11 ... ♘e4

The queen must be driven off quickly, or Black will choke for lack of air.

There is no relief in 11...♕e7 12 ♗f4 ♕xd6 13 ♗xd6 ♘e4 14 ♗a3!, when White still bears down with a heavy hand.

12 ♕d4

In retreating, the queen manages to attack in two directions, threatening both the knight and the enemy g-pawn.

12 ...   ♘f6

The only move to parry both the threats.

13 ♕d6

White tries again, as he hates to relinquish this dominating position. Meanwhile, he hints that he can always draw if he wants to, by a repetition of moves.

13 ...   ♘e4 *(D)*

Black cannot let the queen stay at d6, and delay in evicting her might prove to be fatal.

That Black's difficulties are not insuperable was demonstrated by Alekhine, who suggested this continuation: 13...♕b6 (Black threatens 14...♕xf2+ 15 ♔xf2 ♘e4+) 14 ♗d3 c5 15 ♗f4 ♗b7 16 0-0 ♖c8.

14 ♕b4!

Very strong! If the queen cannot establish permanent residence at d6, this square is the next best thing. At b4 (odd place though it is) the queen attacks the knight, controls a diagonal which makes castling for Black impossible, and in a third direction prevents Black's a8-rook from seizing the open b-file.

14 ...   d5

Black protects his knight and prepares to challenge White's queen by 15...♕d6. Black's pawn-centre provides some compensation for his troubles.

15 ♗d3

An ideal move, as a piece develops with a threat – 16 ♗xe4 dxe4 17 ♕xe4 winning a pawn.

15 ...   ♕d6

Black offers to exchange, which will either rid the board of White's attacking queen or induce her to retreat from a dominating position.

16 ♕xd6

White is willing to simplify. He will still have advantages in his two powerful bishops and an enduring grip on the dark squares.

16 ...   ♘xd6 *(D)*

Black is content with his part of the bargain: both his rooks have open files on which to operate, and he has a group of pawns in the centre with which he expects to limit the scope of the bishops.

17 f4!

"An eye for the microscopic betokens the master," says the great Marco.

The e5-square is now controlled by White, while Black's e-pawn is restrained from advancing. One effect of this pawn's inability to move is that it fearfully circumscribes the mobility of Black's bishop.

17 ...   a5

Black must do something about getting the bishop into play. With this move he plans to develop it at a6 and exchange it for White's more powerful bishop.

18 ♗e3!

Excellent! This holds back Black's c-pawn, while two more dark squares, d4 and c5, come under White's domination.

18 ...   ♗a6

With this move Black hopes to clear the board of one of White's menacing bishops.

19 ♔d2!

The king is a strong piece and should be used aggressively in the ending. As the number of pieces on the board decreases, so is the danger of the king being exposed to a mating attack reduced, and its own power as a fighting piece magnified. In the ending, the king is unexcelled as a means of causing damage by getting in among the enemy's pawns.

That is why, in the present position, the king comes closer to the centre, where he is most useful, instead of castling and then working his way there.

19 ...   ♘c4+

Black's plan becomes manifest: he wants to force an exchange of knight for bishop. This would leave bishops commanding squares of different colours on the board, which

often exerts a drawish influence on the game.

Another alternative worth considering was 19...♘b7 in order to play 20...c5 and get his central pawn phalanx rolling.

20 ♗xc4

Practically forced, as Black was attacking both e3 and b2.

20 ...   ♗xc4 (D)

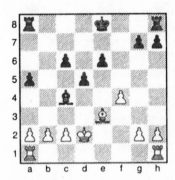

Let us size up the situation: the white bishop enjoys far more freedom than does Black's. The latter is greatly hampered in its movements by the many pawns standing on light squares, the colour of the squares on which the bishop operates.

White's king, being nearer the centre and the critical squares d4 and e5, is much better situated for the endgame than Black's.

Black's centre, the heart of his game, is held fast. The three pawns he has in that area are fixed and unable to move.

21 a4!

Blockade! The a5-pawn is stopped dead in its tracks; it is now a fixed target, always in danger of being attacked by ♗b6. In order to make sure it is not captured (for its removal gives White a passed a-pawn) Black must watch over it constantly with his a8-rook. Because of the need to guard this one pawn, Black is thereby deprived of the services of a rook.

21   ...   ♔d7

Black brings his king toward the centre for the endgame.

The rooks are now united, while the king himself heads for d6, where he hopes to support an advance by the e-pawn or the c-pawn.

22   b3

White attacks the bishop to force it to the side of the board. You will note that the bishop's scope is cut down as pawns *on both sides* are placed on light squares, the colour of the diagonals on which the bishop must travel.

22   ...   ♗a6

The only flight square open to the unhappy bishop!

23   ♗b6!

And now an attack on the pawn...

23   ...   ♗c8

...which can only be met by further retreat!

24   ♔e3

Continuing the trek to d4, e5, and, as we shall see, all points north! 24 ♗c5 was a bit more cruel, to prevent any demonstration by 24...♖f8.

24   ...   ♖a6 *(D)*

No better was 24...♔d6 to back up a pawn push, as the reply 25 ♔d4 nips that little idea in the bud.

Black's best chance was with 24...♖f8, to get some counterplay by getting his h8-rook into the game by way of the open file. The move he

does make attacks the bishop and succeeds in its object of driving it away from a good square – but only on to a better one!

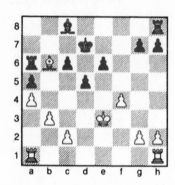

25   ♗c5!

White dominates every important square on the board! The bishop stops the h8-rook from getting to f8, the a6-rook from moving to b6, the king from d6, the d-pawn from advancing and the c-pawn from moving at all! Compare its control of eight squares with that of Black's bishop, whose influence is confined to one square! This difference in their potential accounts in great measure for the extent of White's attacking opportunities, and for the consequent difficulty Black will have in defending. Every gain or control of territory by White will result in more and more cramping of Black's position.

25   ...   ♔c7

Stepping aside, the king makes the d7-square accessible to the black bishop.

26   ♔d4!

Tightening the noose! This king also makes way – for the benefit of the h1-rook, who will turn the e-file to account.

26 ... ♗d7

Black will try to manoeuvre the bishop over to the kingside, for instance to g6.

His h8-rook seems to have a great deal of scope, but what does it avail him? If it moves to b8 (as good a file as there is) at what point can it penetrate? It cannot get to any useful square on that file.

27 ♖he1 *(D)*

Much stronger than the immediate occupation of e5 by the king. White intends to use this key square as a transfer point for his rook on its way to the g-file. After it gets there, White will settle his king at e5 and tighten his grip on the dark squares.

27 ... **h5**

Black prepares a pawn barricade against the rook's threatened attack on the kingside.

28 ♖e5

Second stop on the trip to g5.

28 ... **g6**

Battening down the hatches, Black gets ready for a hard winter.

29 ♖g5

White attacks the g-pawn and simultaneously makes room for his king.

29 ... ♖g8

The pawn must be protected, and this of course is more elastic than 29...♖h6, when the rook has no mobility to speak of.

30 ♔e5 *(D)*

Further penetration along the convenient dark squares. The threat is 31 ♔f6 ♗e8 32 ♖e1 (even stronger than 32 ♔xe6), followed by 33 ♖xe6.

30 ... ♗e8

Black abandons the e-pawn, as he cannot hope to save all his pawns. There is a slight chance, if White captures the pawn at once, 31 ♔xe6, of putting up some resistance by 31...♗d7+ 32 ♔f6 ♗f5.

Black's pitiable bishop is sadly hemmed in by the five pawns firmly fixed on squares of the same colour.

31 ♖e1

Before committing himself to decisive action, White applies more pressure. Notice how a master player puts every piece to work before he strikes a blow.

31 ...   **♖a8** *(D)*

To get back into the game, this rook has to return home!

There was no satisfactory defence in 31...♔d7 as the reply 32 ♔f6 uncovers the rook's attack on the e-pawn.

32 ♔f6!

White completes the plan of encirclement. Notice the effects of the arrangement of Black's pawns at e6, d5 and c6 – Black's own pieces are kept under restraint, while White's can utilize the weakened dark squares c5, d4, e5 and f6 to penetrate into the vitals of the enemy position. Notice also that these dark squares are 'holes', squares from which pieces cannot be dislodged by the opponent's pawns.

White does not resort to brutal attack or to intricate combination to accomplish his purpose but puts his trust in the dynamic power inherent in an overwhelming positional superiority.

32 ...   **♗d7**

Black reveals another reason for his previous move. In the continuation 33 ♖xg6 ♖xg6+ 34 ♔xg6 ♖g8+

35 ♔xh5 ♖xg2, Black suddenly turns on his foe.

33 g3

To guard against this possibility, and to lessen any chance of a breakthrough by one of Black's rooks, White fashions a chain of pawns on the kingside.

33 ...   **♖ae8**

Black can do nothing to improve his position, so this amounts to no more than a waiting move.

34 ♖ee5

White could play 34 ♖xg6 and have little trouble winning, but he makes doubly sure. He blockades the e-pawn first, to quell even a shadow of resistance!

34 ...   **♖h8**

"While there's life..."

35 ♖xg6 *(D)*

The first tangible gain. The rest is an interesting display of the art of winning a won game.

35 ...   **♖h7**

Fearing threats against his isolated h-pawn, Black prepares to double rooks on the h-file in an attempt to save it.

36 ♖g7

White keeps on gaining ground. Now he invades the seventh rank.

36 ... 罝eh8

Black holds on grimly.

37 罝xh7

Simplest, hence the scientific way to force the win. In endings where one side has a material advantage, the prescribed strategy is to exchange pieces, not pawns, and to bring it down to a pawn ending. *Endings with only pawns on the board are the easiest to win.*

37 ... 罝xh7

The recapture leaves Black only a pawn down – for the time being!

38 曑g6!

With every exchange, the king's power increases! Now the king threatens the rook and helps attack the h-pawn.

38 ... 罝h8 *(D)*

Strangely enough, the rook has only one move on the board!

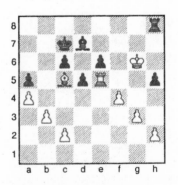

Does White now settle the issue by removing the h-pawn?

39 曑g7!

No, no, a thousand times no! If 39 罝xh5? then 39...兌e8+, when Black wins a whole rook and the game.

How easy it is to go wrong even in a simple ending!

White's actual move first banishes the rook from the premises.

39 ... 罝d8

The rook must leave the file, abandoning the pawn.

40 罝xh5

Now the capture is safe.

40 ... 兌e8

Hoping to bring the bishop over to the kingside and then attack White's queenside pawns.

41 罝h7 *(D)*

The rook hastens to the seventh rank, a rook's proper post in the ending.

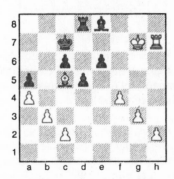

41 ... 罝d7+

Otherwise, White's procedure is 42 曑f6+ 兌d7 43 g4, and the pawn cannot be stopped.

42 曑h6

The king must stay within range of his rook.

42 ... 罝xh7+

The exchange of rooks cannot be avoided, so Black captures first to draw White's king away from h5. If the bishop can get there, it might still stir up some trouble.

43   ♔xh7

This meets with White's approval. His kingside pawns are mobile, while Black's pawns either cannot or dare not make a move.

43   ...   ♗h5

Now to get behind the queenside pawns!

44   h4 *(D)*

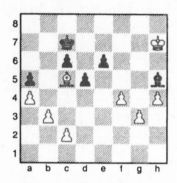

The queenside pawns cannot be rescued, so White starts his kingside pawns rolling.

44   ...   ♗d1

After so much inactivity, this bishop not only threatens the lives of all the pawns on light squares but restrains (for the time being) all the pawns on the kingside.

45   c3!

To save itself, this pawn flees to a dark square.

45   ...   ♗xb3

Black takes a pawn, more to distract White than anything else, since he has no real threats.

46   g4

Ready to refute 46...♗xa4 with 47 f5 ♔d7 (after 47...♗c2 48 ♔g6 the h-pawn walks up, or 47...e5 48 f6 ♔d7 49 f7, and White wins) 48 f6

♔e8, and 49 ♔g7 escorts the pawn through.

46   ...   ♔d7

The king rushes over to hold back the pawns.

47   g5

"The passed pawn's lust to expand", as Nimzowitsch puts it.

47   ...   e5 *(D)*

Desperation, but there is no promising defence. If 47...♔e8, then 48 g6 ♗c2 49 h5 ♗f5 50 ♔g7 wins for White.

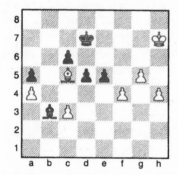

48   f5

The simplest. White's three connected passed pawns should be convincing enough.

48   ...   ♗xa4

After 48...♗c2, 49 ♔g6 is the clincher, protecting the f-pawn and making way for the h-pawn.

49   f6

Indicating that it's time to concede. The pawn cannot be stopped by 49...♔e8 as 50 ♔g7 sees it through.

1-0

A beautiful illustration of the technique of exploiting weaknesses on the dark squares.

Game 27
Chekhover – Rudakovsky
Moscow 1945
Queen's Gambit Declined

1　d4

This move, more than any other, offers chances of an opening advantage without taking risks.

Two pieces are released at once, and a pawn occupies a central square, as with 1 e4, but extra benefits accrue from 1 d4:
- The d-pawn is protected and safe from immediate attack.
- White is not exposed to the threats to his f2-pawn, which often arise in king's pawn openings. His control of c5 makes it impossible for Black to develop his dark-squared bishop at c5 to attack the vulnerable f2-pawn.

1　...　d5

The simplest way to prevent White from dominating the centre with 2 e4 next move.

2　c4

The characteristic move of the Queen's Gambit. The versatile c-pawn does many things. Three of these things are concerned with doing away with Black's centre:
- It offers itself in exchange, so that Black may be lured into accepting a side pawn in return for his centre pawn.
- It threatens, when the right moment comes, to destroy Black's centre by capturing the d-pawn.
- It exerts constant pressure on the d-pawn, so that Black is kept occupied with its protection.

Besides all this, the move of the c-pawn assures that the c-file is kept free and clear for the convenience of White's major pieces, while a pathway is opened for the queen, leading to the queenside.

2　...　e6

Black strengthens the position of his centre pawn. In the event that White plays 3 cxd5, he is ready to recapture with a pawn and thus maintain a pawn in the centre of the board. This is Black's safest defence, even though it does limit the scope of his c8-bishop.

3　♘f3

This is an excellent move, though not so sharp as 3 ♘c3, which adds pressure to the attack on Black's d-pawn. Either move complies with an injunction particularly applicable in queen's pawn openings:

Develop all the pieces as quickly as possible!

"The main principle in the openings," says Capablanca, "is *rapid and efficient development*." (The italics are his.)

3　...　♘f6

Black's knight moves in toward the centre, attacks the e4-square and adds its weight to the protection of d5.

It is good policy to mobilize the kingside pieces first, since only two of them need be developed to make castling possible.

4 ♗g5

A powerful move! The bishop is developed and a restraining hand is put on the enemy knight. There is no immediate threat in the move – White just 'threatens to threaten'.

4 ...   ♗e7

The proper way to unpin a knight. The inexperienced player often grows impatient and drives the bishop off by 4...h6 5 ♗h4 g5 6 ♗g3 only to find that he has ruined the pawn position on the kingside as a result of his violent action.

5 e3 *(D)*

White strengthens his pawn-centre and frees the light-squared bishop for action.

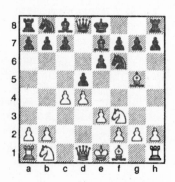

5 ...   0-0

Black gets his king into safety before revealing his plans for the development of the queenside pieces. His b8-knight may go to d7, or following an attack on White's centre, perhaps to c6.

6 ♘c3

White has no such problems. His queen's knight can move to c3, since it does not obstruct the c-pawn and the opening of the c-file. At c3 the knight takes an active part in the struggle for control of the centre.

6 ...   ♘bd7 *(D)*

This knight must never be developed at c6 before the c-pawn is moved. The pawn must be free, either to advance to c5 and fight for equal rights in the centre or to move one square to c6 where it bolsters Black's own centre. But the pawn must not be obstructed by ...♘c6!

The development by 6...♘bd7 is stronger than appears at first glance. Black's position is cramped for the moment, but the knight is ready to support a liberating movement and an attack on White's centre by ...c5 or ...e5.

7 ♕c2

A magnificent square for White's queen! From c2, the queen exerts her powerful influence in several directions: on the partly open c-file and on the centre, preventing Black from freeing himself by 7...♘e4. This attempt to force some exchanges and shake off the pressure is refuted by (after 7...♘e4) 8 ♗xe7 ♕xe7 9 cxd5 ♘xc3 (if 9...exd5, then 10 ♘xd5 wins on the spot) 10 ♕xc3 exd5 11

♕xc7 ♕b4+ 12 ♕c3, and White has won a pawn.

Another feature of 7 ♕c2 is that it vacates d1 for the queen's rook, whose presence on the same file as Black's queen will discourage the opponent from making a break in the centre. Exchanges of pawns in the centre would clear away some of the obstructions and intensify the rook's pressure on the file – a pressure which reaches all the way up the file to the queen.

      7 ...   **c6**

This move provides solid support to the centre pawn and gives the queen access to the queenside. It looks substantial enough, but the more aggressive 7...c5, disputing control of the centre by establishing a state of tension there, might be more to the point. The danger in delaying ...c5 is that Black may never again have a favourable opportunity to get in this thrust.

      8 ♗d3

White develops a fifth piece, pointing it at Black's kingside, and is ready to castle instantly on either wing.

      8 ...   **dxc4**

Black waited for White to move his f1-bishop before making this capture. Otherwise, the bishop recaptures and develops at the same time. Black's intention, in clearing d5, is to swing his knight over to that square, force some exchanges, and free his cramped position.

Nevertheless, Black has surrendered the pawn-centre, which he so carefully built up.

      9 ♗xc4 *(D)*

White is content with the result of the pawn exchange. Lines are opened which increase the mobility of his pieces.

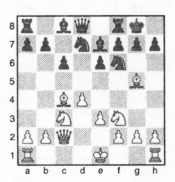

      9 ...   **♘d5**

Obviously to compel White to exchange bishops.

      10 ♗xe7

This is safer than 10 ♗f4 ♘xf4 11 exf4, when White is left with an isolated d-pawn. The pawn itself is in no great danger, but the d5-square, directly in front of it, is! It is in danger of being occupied indefinitely by one of Black's pieces. *A piece stationed on a square in front of an isolated pawn can never be driven off by enemy pawns.*

      10 ...   **♕xe7**

The proper recapture, letting the queen come into play; taking with the knight would be developing backwards.

      11 0-0

The king finds a safer shelter while the rooks get in touch with each other.

White's position is excellent, the result of simple straightforward development.

11 ...   b5

A shot at the bishop, to force its retreat. Meanwhile, Black gains time for the development of his own bishop.

12 ♗e2

The bishop withdraws – but not to d3, where an attack by 12...♘b4 enables Black to bring about an exchange of knight for bishop. White wants to preserve the bishop, which has excellent prospects for attack when it emerges later at d3 or f3.

[*Editor's Note:* 12 ♘xd5 exd5 13 ♗d3 wins an important pawn for nothing – brutal but effective.]

12 ...   a6 *(D)*

The usual manoeuvre of protecting the b-pawn, so that the c-pawn is free to attack White's centre. If Black can get in 13...c5 he will still have a respectable game.

13 ♘e4!

Uncovering an attack! The queen threatens the c-pawn, while the knight restrains it from advancing to c5. White's idea is to prevent the indispensable freeing move ...c5 forever and then barricade Black completely by planting a piece at c5.

13 ...   ♗b7

Black protects the pawn by developing another piece.

14 ♘e5! *(D)*

Very fine strategy! Before settling a piece on c5, White plays to get rid of one of the guardians of that square, Black's knight at d7. If he plays 14 ♘c5 at once, then 14...♘xc5 15 ♕xc5 ♕xc5 16 dxc5 leaves him with a pawn occupying c5. This does not have the same effect as a piece standing on that square. A pawn is immobile and does little to restrain the opponent, but a piece radiates power in all directions and has a terribly cramping effect on the enemy's movements in the whole surrounding area.

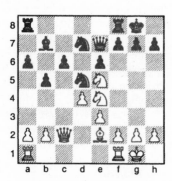

14 ...   ♖ac8

Developing another piece and defending the pawn which was attacked by two pieces.

Black did not care for the exchange 14...♘xe5 15 dxe5. White could then anchor his remaining knight at d6, follow up by planting his queen at c5, and throttle Black thoroughly.

15 ♘xd7

Removing one of the pieces guarding the vital c5-square...

15 ...   ♕xd7 *(D)*

...and luring the other one away!

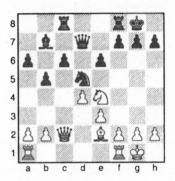

16 ♘c5!

With the domination of this square, White's advantage is decisive in the strategic sense. What remains is to exploit his superior position, to translate it into actual victory, and this process of consummating the win is one of the most fascinating parts of chess.

16 ...   ♕c7

Both queen and bishop were attacked, so the queen stays near the bishop.

17 ♖fd1

The practice of the masters has shown that rooks are most efficient when they control open files.

Suppose there are no open files? Then the rooks should be placed on partly open files, or on files likely to be opened.

Suppose none of those seem to exist? Then the rooks should be brought to the centre, to exert pressure on the centre files.

But the rooks must be developed!

17 ...   ♖cd8

There are various reasons for this move:

The rook has no future on the c-file while the pawn at c6 impedes its movements (and there is little prospect of the pawn coming to life).

The rook vacates c8 for the bishop. The bishop cannot stay indefinitely at b7, where it is hampered by the c-pawn, and where the queen is tied down to its defence.

18 ♖ac1

White's incidental threat of winning a pawn by 19 ♘xb7 ♕xb7 20 ♕xc6 is subordinate to the strategic concept of intensifying the pressure on the c-file.

18 ...   ♗c8 *(D)*

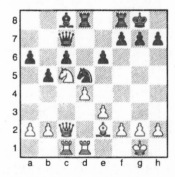

Black parries the threat of 19 ♘xb7 and frees his queen from the job of watching over the bishop. Now he can speculate on getting some counterplay by the break 19...e5.

19 ♕e4!

Magnificent centralization by the queen, who prevents 19...e5 (when that pawn would be simply snapped up) and prepares to switch over for a kingside attack.

19 ...   ♘f6

The knight, best defender of the castled position, returns to f6, incidentally with an attack on the queen.

Against other moves White could play 20 ♗d3, threatening 21 ♕xh7#. This would compel either a retreat by the knight or a weakening advance of one of Black's kingside pawns.

20 ♕h4 *(D)*

The queen evades the knight's threat and swings over to the kingside to get an attack rolling against the king.

20 ...   ♕a5

Black tries counterattack on the queenside – mostly to distract his opponent's attention. There is little he can do to strengthen the defence of his kingside. Any move of a pawn only loosens the position and reduces his chances of resistance. The break in the centre by 20...e5, which he contemplated making, is risky, to say the least, as 21 ♕g3 in reply, pinning the pawn, is troublesome.

21 a3

The simplest way to save the a-pawn and to keep the queen from moving to b4.

21 ...   b4

Hoping to disrupt White's queenside by continuing with 22...bxa3.

22 a4 *(D)*

White avoids any exchanges that might let the queen set foot in his territory.

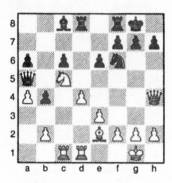

22 ...   ♘d7

Trying to shake off the grip of the knight, which is strangling his queenside to death. If he waits too long, White pursues his attack with 23 ♗d3, followed by 24 g4 (to dislodge the knight which guards against mate). After the compulsory reply 24...h6, White plays 25 g5, forcing an exchange of pawns which opens the g-file. White can then shift his king to h1 and swing a rook over to attack on the open file. Against this, Black could not hold out very long.

23 b3

Defending the a-pawn, and so relieving the knight of that task.

23 ...   ♘xc5

There is hardly anything better. The tempting 23...e5 succumbs to 24 ♘xd7 ♗xd7 25 ♖c5 ♕c7 26 ♖xe5, when White has won a pawn.

24 ♖xc5

The exchange of knights results in White's substituting another piece at c5, maintaining his grip on the position.

24 ...　　　　Wb6 *(D)*

Preferable to 24...Wc7, when the attack might proceed thus: 25 Qdc1 Bb7 (to protect both the c-pawn and the a-pawn) 26 a5 (to isolate the b-pawn by preventing 26...a5), and White follows up by 27 Q1c4 and 28 Qxb4.

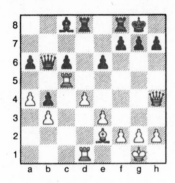

25 Qdc1

Doubling rooks on an open file more than doubles the pressure on the file (and on the opponent). White's immediate threat is 26 Qxc6.

25 ...　　　　Bb7

The bishop guards both light-squared pawns, but its mobility is almost nil.

The subject of mobility is interesting. While it is not always true that the player whose pieces have more room in which to manoeuvre enjoys an advantage, it applies often enough in practice for us to disregard the exceptional cases. It stands to reason that pieces that are free and untrammelled not only have more

striking power in the portion of the board they occupy, but they also control and limit the activities of the enemy. Add to this the ease with which they can reach other parts of the board, and you can see the advantages to be derived from the ability to move freely about.

Let us compare all the moves the pieces on each side can make. We are not evaluating their worth, whether good, bad or indifferent. What we want to see is the range of their action.

White		Black	
King	2	King	1
Queen	12	Queen	5
c1-Rook	8	f8-Rook	1
c5-Rook	11	d8-Rook	8
Bishop	9	Bishop	2
Total	42	*Total*	17

White's pieces are 250% as efficient as Black's! With so great a disparity in mobility (and consequently in attacking force) how long can Black continue the struggle?

26 a5

In order to isolate Black's b-pawn, and incidentally drive the queen back to the second rank.

26 ...　　　　Wa7 *(D)*

On the alternative 26...Wc7 White can either resume operations on the kingside or go after a pawn on the queenside by 27 Bf3 Qd6 28 Q1c4 followed by 29 Qxb4. Winning the pawn will not diminish the force of White's attack or loosen his grip on the position.

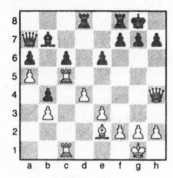

27 &d3!

Now that the queenside is fixed, White turns his attention to the kingside and threatens mate on the move. Black can easily dispose of this threat, *but only by moving one of the pawns near his king and thereby creating a weakness which is organic, permanent and irremediable!*

27 ...   g6

If 27...h6, then 28 ♕e4 forces 28...g6, when two pawns have been uprooted. White could then continue by 29 ♖h5 ♔g7 (if 29...gxh5, then 30 ♕h7#, or if 29...♔h7, then 30 ♕f4 wins) 30 ♕e5+ f6 (or 30...♔h7, when the neat double pin 31 ♕g5 wins) 31 ♕g3 g5 (if 31...f5, then 32 ♕e5+ ♔h7 33 ♕c7+ ♔g8 34 ♖xh6 wins) 32 ♖xh6! ♔xh6 33 ♕h3+ ♔g7 34 ♕h7#.

A simpler way, if White doesn't want to bother analysing combinations, is to maintain the pressure and then apply more! For instance, after 27...h6 28 ♕e4 g6, instead of playing 29 ♖h5 White could advance 29

h4, threatening to break up the pawns by 30 h5. If Black replies 29...h5 to stop the advance, White can either snap the h-pawn off with his rook or keep hammering away by 30 g4 hxg4 31 h5.

After the actual move, Black has weaknesses on the dark squares and holes in his position.

28 ♕f6! *(D)*

The queen plants herself securely in one of the holes created by Black's ...g6 advance. A hole is an unguarded square such as f6 or h6 brought into being by the advance of a nearby pawn. It is a weak square, because it is no longer under the surveillance of a pawn and is vulnerable to invasion by an enemy piece. Such a piece can settle itself comfortably in one of these holes, secure in the knowledge that no enemy pawn can disturb it.

White's plan, now that the queen has worked her way into a dominating position on the kingside, is classical in its simplicity: he will just advance the h-pawn to h4, h5 and h6, and then play ♕g7#. If, after the pawn reaches h5, it is captured *en route*, then mate by the rook is the instant punishment.

28 ...   ♜d6

Black vacates d8, so that his queen can return to that square and challenge White's. In chess language: if 29 h4 ♛a8 30 h5 ♛d8, White's queen must leave f6 and forego the threat of mate.

29 ♛e7 *(D)*

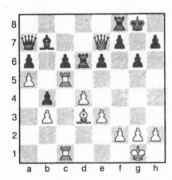

An attack on the exposed rook, so that Black will have his hands full warding off the accumulating threats. Black has three problems, each on a different part of the board:

1) on the kingside, he must guard against being mated;

2) on the queenside, he must release himself from White's stranglehold;

3) in the middle, he must rescue any pieces that are loose.

29 ...   ♜fd8

If instead 29...♛b8, 30 ♗e4 ♜c8 31 h4 ♛c7 32 ♛f6 ♛d8 33 ♛xd8+ followed by either 34 ♗xc6 or 34 ♜1c4, with an easy, routine win.

30 h4

White is still aiming for mate by h5, h6 and ♛f6.

30 ...   ♜8d7

The queen must be evicted. Black does not play 30...♜6d7 as he wants the first rank and the d8-square available to his own queen.

31 ♛f6

The danger of mate becomes more acute!

31 ...   ♛a8 *(D)*

Only by a retreat can Black's queen rush to the rescue!

If Black tries 31...♜d5 to stop 32 h5, White effects the advance by first dislodging the rook with 32 ♗e4.

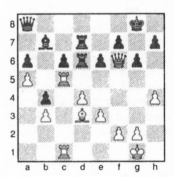

32 ♗e4!

Not at once 32 h5 because of 32...♛d8 in reply. After the textmove (which incidentally prevents 32...♜d5) White can meet 32...♛d8 by exchanging queens and taking the c-pawn, winning easily if prosaically.

32 ...   ♛e8

Hoping to lure White into the premature 33 ♗xc6, when 33...♗xc6 34 ♜xc6 ♜xc6 35 ♜xc6 ♜xd4 regains the pawn and gives him fighting chances.

33 h5!

Each step the pawn makes increases the danger to Black's king. The pawn is headed for h6, where it will settle itself firmly in the other hole in Black's position.

33 ...   Rd8 (D)

The rook withdraws, so that the c-pawn may have the added protection of the queen.

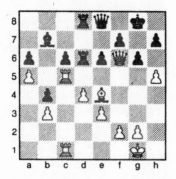

The fact that Black is kept busy warding off threats on both sides of the board is the clue to the next move, which presents Black with an insoluble problem (the hardest kind to face).

34 Bxc6!

Removing a pawn that is apparently adequately protected. As will be seen, though, one of its defenders is overworked. The queen not only has to guard this point (c6) and the rook at d8, but must also keep an eye out for mate threats on the king.

34 ...   Bxc6

Black must take the bishop or lose some material, since two pieces are attacked.

35 h6!

A *zwischenzug*, an in-between move, that threatens instant mate.

35 ...   Kf8

On the alternative defence by 35...Qf8 the win is forced with 36 Rxc6 (threatening 37 Rxd6 Rxd6 38 Rc8 Qxc8 39 Qg7#) 36...Qxh6 37 Rxd6 Rxd6 38 Rc8+ and Black must give up his queen.

36 Rxc6

White has regained his piece and now threatens 37 Rxd6 Rxd6 38 Rc8 Qxc8 39 Qh8+, winning the queen.

36 ...   Rxc6

There is not much choice: if Black plays 36...Qd7 (to meet 37 Rxd6 with 37...Qxd6), then 37 Rc7 Qe8 38 Qg7#.

37 Rxc6

White gets his rook back and prepares to seize the seventh rank by 38 Rc7. This would keep the king from escaping and again threaten him with mate by the queen.

37 ...   Rd7 (D)

There is no relief in 37...Qxc6, as White forces a winning ending by 38 Qxd8+ Qe8 39 Qd6+ Kg8 40 Qxa6 Qe7 (otherwise 41 Qb7 wins at once) 41 Qb6 and the passed pawn cannot be stopped.

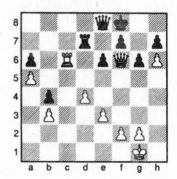

38 Rc8!

Attacking the queen with his unprotected rook. A pretty enough conclusion, but pedants may point out that White missed a brilliancy in 38 ♕g7+ ♔e7 39 ♖xe6+! ♔xe6 40 ♕e5#. Many a player has had quicker wins or more artistic ones than actually occurred pointed out to him by lesser lights, who revel in the fact that they found something the master overlooked. The reason the master didn't see the shorter line is that he was not looking for it in the first place! The move with which he wins is the one whose effects he foresaw earlier and analysed thoroughly *before* starting his final combination. Once the series of forcing moves clicks, there is no reason at all for him to waste time finding other moves that might win. It takes time to analyse combinations, and the shorter way, ventured on hurriedly, might turn out to have a hole in it. The moral is: *play the move that forces the win in the simplest way and leave the brilliancies to Alekhine and Keres.*

38 ... ♕xc8

Naturally, 38...♖d8 39 ♖xd8 does not help matters.

39 ♕h8+ 1-0

Winning the queen and the game.

Magnificent play by White, who never once relaxed his iron control of the game. A remarkable feature is the circumstance that none of Black's pieces or pawns, with the exception of the one brave little pawn at b4, ever crossed the fourth rank into White's side of the board!

Game 28
Tarrasch – Mieses
Gothenburg 1920
Scandinavian Defence

1 e4

In his delightful book *Chess for Winter Evenings*, written more than 140 years ago, H.R. Agnel proposed an interesting argument for the superiority of 1 e4 to 1 d4: "Moving the d-pawn two squares," he said, "gives the queen a range of two squares and the c1-bishop a range of five squares. But moving 1 e4 gives a range of four squares to the queen and five squares to the f1-bishop. You see therefore that e-pawn two squares is the most desirable move with which to open the game. There is another reason why this move is desirable – the pawn occupies a portion of the centre of the board. Two pawns abreast at your e4- and d4-squares, supported by pawns and pieces, must be considered as your best military position, and maintained with all the skill in your power."

1 ... d5

With his very first move, Black tries to uproot White's stake in the centre. Black is willing to take some risks for the sake of having the initiative. There is danger in the fact that his queen, in recapturing, will come into the game too soon and be chased around the board by White's minor pieces.

2 exd5 *(D)*

Simplest, and keeps Black on his toes. The alternatives 2 e5 and 2 ♘c3 are tame and cause Black no trouble at all.

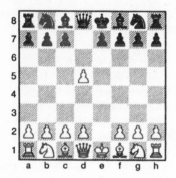

2 ...   ♕xd5

Black can play 2...♘f6 to avoid taking with the queen, but the continuation 3 d4 ♘xd5 4 c4 ♘f6 5 ♘f3 ♗g4 6 ♗e2 leaves White with both a fine pawn centre and the better prospects.

3 ♘c3

The knight develops and gains a tempo by attacking the queen.

One of the drawbacks of Black's system of defence is that it subjects his queen to harassment by the minor pieces without her being able to bother them in return. The queen, for example, cannot threaten to capture a knight that is protected as that amounts to giving up the queen for a knight. The knight, though, can attack and threaten to capture the queen, whether the queen is protected or not.

3 ...   ♕a5

This move, exerting pressure on the diagonal leading to White's king, is preferable to the shamefaced retreat by 3...♕d8. In either case, though, Black has had to make two moves with his queen, instead of developing another piece.

The beginner likes to give check whenever he can, and here it might lead to something like this: 3...♕e5+ 4 ♗e2 ♗g4 5 d4 ♕e6 6 ♗e3 ♗xe2 7 ♘gxe2, and White has three pieces in play to Black's one – and that one a badly placed queen.

4 d4 *(D)*

Once again seizing the centre. The pawn occupies d4, attacks the squares e5 and c5, and does further service in releasing the c1-bishop for action.

4 ...   e5

Black once again lashes out at White's centre!

5 ♘f3!

Far better than 5 dxe5, to which Black's reply is 5...♗b4. White combines a threat (6 ♘xe5) with the development of a piece.

5 ...   ♗b4

Black does not defend his pawn but intensifies the attack on White's pinned knight. He does not care for 5...exd4 6 ♕xd4, which only speeds White's development.

6 ♗d2

Chess can be so simple! White brings a third piece into play and at the same time eases the strain on his knight.

Meanwhile he threatens 7 ♘xe5, against which Black has no defence in 6...♘c6 as 7 a3 ♗xc3 8 ♗xc3 attacks the queen and wins the enemy pawn on e5. How does Black meet the threat?

6 ... ♗g4

Answer: by another pin! Apparently, Black is not interested in routine defence, or for that matter in normal development. He wants his pieces to rush out of their corners fighting. If this strategy is sound, what is to become of all the principles of development – the precepts which in the hand of a master are his greatest weapons?

So far, Black has violated the conventions governing proper development, by these acts:

1) he has brought the queen into play too early;

2) he has moved the same piece twice in the opening;

3) he has developed bishops before knights;

4) he has launched an attack before completing his development.

The question is: can he get away with all this?

7 ♗e2

White keeps on developing. He brings another piece out and unpins

his f3-knight. The threat of 8 ♘xe5 becomes more acute.

7 ... exd4

Black is practically forced to make this capture, even though it leads to a position in White's favour. But what else can he do? If he protects the e-pawn by 7...♘c6, then 8 a3 is again embarrassing, for example, after 8...♗d6 9 b4 ♕b6 10 ♘a4 his queen is lost, while 8...♗xc3 9 ♗xc3 ♕d5 10 dxe5 simply loses a pawn.

8 ♘xd4

The recapture discovers an attack on Black's g4-bishop.

8 ... ♕e5 (D)

Black's response pins the e2-bishop and attacks the unprotected d4-knight. Black rejects 8...♗xe2 as the recapture by 9 ♕xe2+ gains another tempo for White.

9 ♘cb5!

Suddenly White turns aggressor! He protects his exposed knight, attacks Black's b4-bishop and threatens by 10 ♘xc7+ ♕xc7 11 ♗xg4 to win a pawn. All this is directed toward bringing about further exchanges which will speed up his development and gain more and more tempi for him.

9 ...   ♗xe2

Black is forced into a series of exchanges which remove all the pieces he has developed from the board!

10 ♕xe2

The recapture pins Black's queen and forces the exchange of queens.

10 ...   ♗xd2+

The bishops too must come off, otherwise White wins a pawn after 10...♕xe2+ 11 ♔xe2 ♗d6 (to protect the c-pawn) 12 ♘xd6+ cxd6 13 ♘f5.

11 ♔xd2 *(D)*

The recapture benefits White in that it brings his king toward the centre for the endgame and clears away the last obstruction to the development of the rooks. They can now get to the important open files in the centre. As for the king, he is in no danger once the queens are off the board – and there is no way for Black to prevent them coming off!

11 ...   ♕xe2+

Delaying the exchange is dangerous as White threatens to win a rook by 12 ♘xc7+.

12 ♔xe2

Naturally, White takes with the king, as he does not want to displace the centralized knight.

Tarrasch himself considered the game to be won at this point: he is five tempi ahead – one move by the king and two by each of the knights.

12 ...   ♘a6

An awkward move, but it guards the c-pawn and facilitates queenside castling. On 12...♔d8 instead, Black's a8-rook will have trouble coming out.

13 ♖he1!

Very effective in that it prevents Black from developing his kingside. If he tries 13...♘e7, then 14 ♔f3 uncovers a pin on the knight and ties the king down to its protection, while 13...♘f6 is refuted by 14 ♔f3+ ♔f8, and Black's h8-rook is shut in indefinitely.

13 ...   0-0-0 *(D)*

The king flees (meanwhile mobilizing a rook) rather than stay in the centre and be harassed by White's rooks. Has Black wriggled out of the coils?

14 ♘xa7+!

A startling combination, but combinations always appear for the player who has established a superior position. They do not emerge by chance but are the logical outcome of orderly, methodical play.

At first glance, White's capture looks unsound, as both his knights will soon be *en prise*, and one of them apparently is doomed.

14 ...   &b8

The king attacks one knight, the rook the other. How do the knights escape? If 15 ♘ab5, then 15...c6 wins a piece, while 15 ♘db5 c6 is similar. *Two knights dependent on each other for protection are helpless against a pawn attack on either of them.*

15 ♘ac6+!

The point! White will get a rook and two pawns for his knights. This exchange favours White in material terms and he gains other advantages, as we shall see.

15 ...   bxc6

Black has no choice, as 15...&c8 instead loses rook and pawn for the knight.

16 ♘xc6+

White continues with the combination.

16 ...   &c8

Necessary in order to capture the knight.

17 ♘xd8

Removing Black's most dangerous piece. After his knight is taken, White will be left with two pieces against three, but these two are dynamic rooks with a whole chessboard to roam around in, while of Black's pieces, two are stuck away

in a corner and one stands awkwardly on the sidelines.

17 ...   &xd8 (D)

Black still has the job of mobilizing his kingside pieces while staving off threats on the queenside. On that wing, White has three pawns to one, and this, after an exchange of pawns, can become two pawns to none.

Black may have to face an advance of two connected passed pawns on the queenside.

18 ♖ad1+

More gain of time! The rook grabs the open file with check, and Black must lose a move getting his king out of the line of fire.

18 ...   &e8

After 18...&c8 19 &f3 (threatening 20 ♖e8+ &b7 21 ♖dd8 winning a piece) 19...♘f6 20 ♖e7 ♖f8 White can either attack on the kingside by 21 g4 or start his pawn phalanx on the queenside rolling by 21 a3 followed by 22 b4.

19 &d3+

The king moves toward Black's disorganized queenside, where defence will be difficult.

19 ...   ♘e7

Reluctantly, it would seem, Black finally develops his king's knight, but then again anything else loses! If 19...♚f8, then 20 ♚c4 (threatening instant mate) 20...g6 21 ♖d8+ ♚g7 22 ♚b5 and White wins the a6-knight, or if 19...♚d8, then 20 ♚c4+ ♚c8 21 ♖e8+ ♚b7 22 ♖dd8, and the g8-knight falls.

20 ♚c4

The king gets out of the path of the rook and prepares to assist his queenside pawns.

20 ... h5

A peculiar way to develop the rook, but how else can it come out of the corner?

Black is ready to repel the invasion 21 ♚b5 by 21...♖h6 followed by 22...♖b6+.

21 ♖d3 *(D)*

So White abandons this tack and indicates that he intends to double rooks on the e-file and win the pinned knight.

21 ... ♘b8

The knight retreats in order to reach c6 and the aid of his companion.

22 ♖de3

Doubles the pressure and threatens to capture the knight.

22 ... ♘c6

The only possible way to save the pinned knight.

23 b4

Preparing to stab at the defending knight, drive it off, and win the other one.

23 ... f6

Providing a new spot for the c6-knight. In reply to 24 b5 he can now play 24...♘e5+, intercepting the attack of the rooks. If later on the knight is evicted from e5, it can retreat to g6, where it again protects the e7-knight.

24 f4!

This stops the knight reaching e5 and renews the threat of 25 b5.

The position seems lost for Black, but Mieses not only ingeniously slips out of the pin and its terrors but also manages to set a subtle trap into which anyone might plunge!

24 ... ♚f7! *(D)*

If White now tries to win a piece, this is what he might fall into: 25 b5 ♘a5+ 26 ♚b4 ♘d5+ 27 ♚xa5 ♖a8#!

25 a4

White avoids the pitfall and proceeds with the simple strategy governing all endgames: he pushes the passed pawn!

25 ... ♖b8

Temporarily halting the march of the two pawns. White cannot play 26 a5 as 26...♖xb4+ wins a couple of pawns, while after 26 b5 ♘a5+ 27 ♔c5 (not 27 ♔b4 ♘d5+, and White's in the mating trap) 27...♘b7+ 28 ♔c4 (moving to b4 or d4 allows a check by the other knight winning the exchange) 28...♘a5+ the king is making no progress – he must either retreat or submit to a perpetual check.

26 c3

Simple and strong! White guards the b-pawn and prepares to advance the a-pawn.

26 ... ♖d8

There is no way to stop 27 a5 so Black tries to get counterplay on the open file.

27 ♖d3! *(D)*

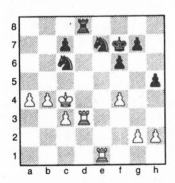

Brutal but necessary. *White must oppose rooks on the file.* Black will either have to exchange rooks or move his rook away, leaving White in full possession of the file.

One of the points a beginner learns painfully is that he must fight for control of every bit of territory, whether it is a file, a diagonal or a square. It is often necessary to offer an exchange of pieces to secure possession of an important point or area. Such offers must not be avoided for fear of their leading to a dull game, or that such strategy is unsportsmanlike. The player with a material advantage who temporizes because he wants to win brilliantly, and avoids exchanges because they are dull and unsportsmanlike, is only torturing his opponent. *A win must be completed in the quickest, most efficient way possible.*

27 ... ♖xd3

Relinquishing the file offers the black rook no future on any other file – so he exchanges.

28 ♔xd3

White is left with one piece to two, but his lone rook with its enormous mobility is more than a match for Black's knights, who must keep in constant touch with each other to assure their mutual safety.

28 ... ♔e8

The king rushes to the queenside to head off the passed pawn.

29 a5

Every move of this pawn increases Black's danger. Keeping it under restraint will tie up his pieces so that he will have no time to think of counterattack.

29 ... ♔d7

Black moves closer to the a-pawn, meanwhile unpinning his knight.

30 a6

Putting a stop to the king's little trip, as 30...♔c8 is punished by 31 b5, when Black must give up one of his knights. Note again that having the two knights lean on each other for support is not an ideal arrangement.

30 ... ♘d5 (D)

The knight is on its way to the queenside. Meanwhile it attacks the loose f-pawn.

31 ♖a1!

One way to dispose of a threat is to disregard it and counter with a more urgent one! White's threat is 32 a7, which would force Black to sacrifice his knight for the pawn.

31 ... ♘a7

The pawn must be blockaded! On 31...♘xf4+ 32 ♔e4 ♘xg2 33 a7 ♘xa7 34 ♖xa7 the win is elementary.

32 g3

White stabilizes the kingside pawn position before proceeding with affairs on the queenside.

32 ... c6

With the double object of making it more difficult for White's b-pawn

to advance, and to vacate c7 for his king.

33 ♖a4!

"Every one of White's moves in this ending deserves an exclamation mark!" enthusiastically cries Mieses, who played the black pieces in this game.

White's idea is to protect the b-pawn so that he can then oust the black knight from its strong post in the centre by 34 c4.

33 ... ♘b6

The knight does not wait but turns on the rook.

34 ♖a5 (D)

The rook leaves but loses no time, as it threatens to capture Black's h-pawn.

34 ... g6

The only way to save the pawn. Black can try interposing the knight at d5 instead, but after 35 ♔c4 and 36 ♔b3 (to protect the b-pawn) White evicts the knight by 37 c4 and wins the unguarded h-pawn.

35 c4

Keeping the knight away from d5 forever!

35 ... ♘bc8 (D)

Black is running out of good moves: he cannot play 35...♔d6 on account of 36 c5+ nor can he solidify the kingside position by 35...f5 without letting White's king break in later by way of e5.

36 ♖a1

Rather surprising! White delays any further manoeuvres with the queenside pawns and proposes to bring his king and rook to more aggressive positions. The king will move to d4 and then c5 and the rook to the open e-file, eventually to penetrate to the sixth or seventh rank. Black will then have to fight off the rook's threats against the kingside pawns as well as to hold back the dangerous pawns advancing on the queenside.

36 ... ♘d6

Black can do nothing but defend patiently.

37 ♔d4

Meanwhile White proceeds to bring his king to c5.

37 ... ♘dc8

If Black plays 37...♔c7, ready to reply to 38 ♔c5 with 38...♘e4+, White forces an entrance by 38 ♖e1

(threatening a deadly check at e7) 38...♔d7 39 ♔c5 ♘dc8 40 b5.

38 ♔c5

The king is now ideally placed, and White is set for a quick finish by 39 b5 and 40 b6.

38 ... ♔c7

Certainly not 38...♘d6, when 39 ♖d1 pins the knight. A pretty continuation could then be 39...♘c8 40 ♖xd6+! ♘xd6 41 a7, when the pawn cannot be stopped.

39 ♖e1

Poised for invasion at e6 or e8 and a raid on the kingside pawns.

39 ... ♘b6

If 39...♔d7 (to keep the rook from moving to e6 or e8), then 40 b5 cxb5 41 cxb5 ♔c7 42 ♖e6 and White wins as he pleases.

40 ♖e7+

The rook finally breaks into the enemy camp!

40 ... ♘d7+ *(D)*

Not, of course, 40...♔b8, when White's reply 41 ♖b7+ wins a knight or two.

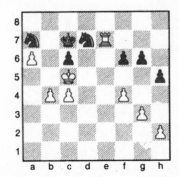

Black's interposition with check looks as though it might still give White some trouble. For instance, after 41 ♔d4 c5+ 42 bxc5 ♘c6+ Black wins a whole rook.

41 ♖xd7+!   1-0

A brilliant finish! After 41...♔xd7, 42 b5 cxb5 43 cxb5 ♘c8 (or 43...♔c7 44 b6+) 44 b6 followed by 45 a7 resolves any lingering doubts.

An impressive display in the art of utilizing the advantages accruing from gain of time in the opening.

Game 29
Marshall – Tarrasch
Nuremberg match (1) 1905
Queen's Gambit Declined

1   d4

Although queen's pawn openings are played with the idea of obtaining an early positional advantage, Marshall considered the best way to start an attack was to begin the game with 1 d4. One reason for his view might have been that the e-pawn openings no longer could be depended on to lead to wide-open games with opportunities for combinative play. In the old days when White began with 1 e4, the reply almost automatically was 1...e5. White could then offer a pawn by 2 f4, rely on its being accepted, and joyfully swing into the excitement of a King's Gambit. In taking the pawn and grimly holding on to it, Black gained material, but the loss of time involved threw him on the defensive. Gradually, after sustaining many defeats, the players of Black tired of being the victims of brilliancies. They took a more rational attitude, and grew cautious. They resorted to 1...e6, 1...c5 or 1...c6, steering the game into channels of their own choosing. The result was that an aggressive player, starting the game with 1 e4, found himself facing 'irregular' defences, which

forced the game into unfamiliar channels. He found himself involved in tightly knit positions requiring systematic planning, when he was itching to get an attack rolling. He was supposed to have the initiative, but here it was wrested away from him! How could he play a gambit (even at best a risky matter) if his opponent did not oblige him with a forthright 1...e5 in answer to his own enterprising 1 e4?

In beginning the game with 1 d4, White gets an advantage, slight though it may be, against any system of defence – and with it he retains excellent attacking chances as well!

1   ...   d5

Undoubtedly one of the strongest replies. Black stabilizes the pressure in the centre, prevents White from strengthening his hold there by 2 e4, and himself opens lines for two of his pieces to get into the game.

2   c4

An offer of a pawn (with strings attached) to induce Black to surrender the centre.

2   ...   e6

Taking the pawn is perfectly sound, but why give up the centre to win a pawn which it turns out you cannot keep? Playing 2...dxc4 is equivalent to exchanging a centre pawn for a side pawn, in itself an unprofitable transaction. However, many leading players are happy to play this opening, so there must be some counterbalancing plus points. The main advantage is that Black no longer has the responsibility of supporting the d5-pawn, and this makes it easier for him to organize the crucial thrust ...c5, exchanging his own c-pawn for White's d-pawn. Thus, although White has a temporary superiority in the centre, it is often not long before Black can restore a symmetrical central situation.

After Black's actual move, his d-pawn is firmly supported. If now 3 cxd5, *Black recaptures with a pawn*, maintaining a pawn in the centre.

It is true that Black's c8-bishop is shut in by the e-pawn, making its development difficult, and this is a drawback to the defence. But if Black's first two moves are good, and they probably form the best reply to the Queen's Gambit, then one can appreciate the terrific strength of this opening, and why so many players adopt 1 d4 unhesitatingly whenever they have White.

3 ♘c3

This is somewhat sharper than developing the other knight first, as additional pressure is immediately put on the central point d5.

3 ... ♘f6 (D)

Tarrasch did not approve of this knight move, which most of us would make instinctively. It is true that f6 is the most useful square for the king's

knight 99.44% of the time, since from there it influences affairs in the centre strongly, enjoys great freedom of movement, and is magnificently placed for attack and defence. However, Tarrasch feared the strength of the pin that White can clamp on the knight next move. Instead of 3...♘f6, he therefore recommended that Black challenge White's centre at once by 3...c5 (the advance ...c5 is almost a must at some stage in queen's pawn games), meanwhile opening up the c-file for the use of his own heavy pieces.

Why then, you may ask, did Tarrasch play a move that he himself disparaged? His explanation is that this was the first game of a match against one of the world's leading masters (Marshall had recently won the Cambridge Springs tournament without losing a game, ahead of Lasker, Schlechter, Pillsbury and Janowsky) and he did not wish to stray so soon from orthodox paths.

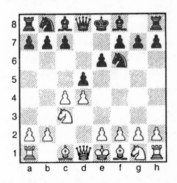

4 ♗g5!

Naturally! Not only because the bishop exerts uncomfortable pressure on the knight, but also because it is good policy to play moves that the opponent finds disturbing. If Tarrasch thinks that pinning the knight is troublesome – pin the knight and make him uneasy!

4 ...   ♘bd7

This looks clumsy, with the knight blocking what little view the c8-bishop had, but pieces can easily step out of each other's way. The knight belongs on d7 and not on c6, where it obstructs the c-pawn. This pawn must not be hindered from advancing sooner or later to c5. Little as the pawn is, it represents a major force in disputing possession of the centre!

With 4...♘bd7 Black sets a little trap for the unwary, invented by Tarrasch. If White, relying on the impotent state of Black's pinned knight, tries to pick up a pawn by 5 cxd5 exd5 6 ♘xd5, Black gives up his queen with 6...♘xd5 (breaking the pin by force) 7 ♗xd8, only to regain it with another piece thrown in by 7...♗b4+ 8 ♕d2 ♗xd2+ 9 ♔xd2 ♔xd8.

The moral is: don't go pawn-hunting in the opening!

5 e3

This sort of pawn move is not a waste of time. Without a liberating pawn move the bishops can never get off the ground, so this is part of the process of bringing the pieces into play.

With the text-move, White opens two diagonals at once, one for his f1-bishop and another one for the queen. The e-pawn contributes an additional service in bracing up the pawn-centre.

5 ...   c6

Black too reinforces his pawn-centre and gives his queen an outlet on the queenside.

6 ♕c2 (D)

It is customary to develop the minor pieces first, roughly in this order:

First the knights, generally to c3 and f3, but toward the centre in any event; then the bishops (after the necessary pawn moves), either to control vital diagonals or to pin enemy knights; following this, it is time for the queen to make her entrance. If the queen comes into the game too early, she incurs the danger of being harassed – perhaps even surrounded and captured – by enemy minor pieces.

Last come the rooks, which after castling are brought to e1, d1 or c1, to head files in the centre which are partly open. These files are likely to become completely open after pawn exchanges in the centre.

This method of development is not by any means to be considered a fixed course to pursue. Nothing in chess – no convention, principle or recommended procedure – is to be practised rigidly. The value of any single move or combination of moves can only be measured with respect to the particular position on the board. It must fit in with the scheme of the game you are playing and be tempered by the demands of the opponent. A great deal depends on what he does, or lets you do. This is why you may find it expedient to develop the queen at the sixth move or to castle at the sixtieth move.

In this position Black has indicated that he might counterattack by 6...♕a5 and 7...♗b4, pinning the c3-knight and then increasing the pressure on it. It might have been more to the point for White instead to mobilize another minor piece by 6 ♘f3 (like putting money in the bank), with an eye to speedy castling or perhaps to neutralizing the anticipated pressure on the c3-knight by swinging the f3-knight over to d2.

6 ...   ♕a5

A many-sided move: the queen not only unpins the f6-knight but starts a counteraction by pinning the white knight; Black threatens to intensify the pressure by bringing the f8-bishop to b4. As an extra, added attraction, Black sets a little trap to catch the careless – and this might even include expert players who at times treat the opening in a perfunctory way. The trap might snap shut on a player who innocently develops his bishop at d3 only to find that 7...dxc4 threatens both his bishops at one blow. White cannot escape from the trap by 8 ♗xf6 as 8...cxd3 attacks his queen and wins a bishop.

It might be as well to state at this point that Tarrasch did not expect to catch Marshall with such a primitive trap. Master players do not set traps if it involves injuring their own position. A trap which arises in the natural course of development is one thing, but to play for them deliberately at the risk of wasting valuable time is unforgivable.

7 cxd5

White neutralizes the queen's indirect attack on his bishop and clears away the c-file for the benefit of his major pieces.

7 ...   ♘xd5 *(D)*

Tarrasch had planned to recapture by 7...exd5 in order to maintain a pawn in the centre. Now he realizes that danger may be involved in delaying the development of the queenside pieces any longer.

His c8-bishop is locked in on one side by the d7-knight, and this knight must stay where it is, as it supports the other knight on f6. If he tries to develop the bishop on the queenside, then after ...b6 he cuts off the queen's retreat. But the strategy of a master player must be flexible: it must be consistent with the requirements of the particular position at hand. Tarrasch would very much like to have a strong pawn-centre but dares not neglect the exigencies of development. So he heeds Nimzowitsch, who once said, "Giving up the centre must not here be regarded as illogical; was happiness no happiness because it endured for but a short time? One cannot always be happy."

Meanwhile the knight does add to the pressure on White's pinned knight and renews the threat of winning the exposed bishop by 8...♘xc3 9 bxc3 ♕xg5.

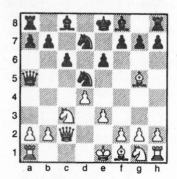

8 ♘f3 (D)

"In his anxiety," says Tarrasch, "to guard the threatened bishop, White makes a decisive mistake."

This is an interesting example of the value of accurate timing in chess. The fact that a normal developing move has intrinsic strength is secondary to the question of its usefulness *in the one position in front of you*, not in vaguely similar positions.

Despite the fact that the knight occupies a most useful post at f3, and at the same time protects the bishop, its development is either too soon or too late. White is doing nothing about the problem of his pinned knight. This is where pressure is exerted; this is where danger is threatened.

More to the point is 8 e4 instead, evicting Black's knight and forcing it to declare its intentions. If then 8...♘xc3 9 ♗d2 ♕a4 10 ♕xc3, White has resolved an uncomfortable situation.

8 ... ♗b4

Tripling the attack on the knight. Black threatens to win at once by 9...♘xc3 10 bxc3 ♗xc3+ followed by 11...♗xa1.

How shall White meet the threat? If he plays the natural 9 ♖c1, the knight is adequately guarded since it is attacked three times and defended three times. However, Black then capitalizes on a curious fact about the power of a pinned piece: not only is it helpless to make a move but it has also lost its ability to defend! Translated into chess language, this means that 9 ♖c1 can be met by 9...♕xa2, a capture startling at first glance but an obvious one if we realize that the knight's defensive power is illusory! I stress this circumstance because it is important. Knowing it, recognizing it and applying it has caused (chess) kingdoms to topple.

All this fuss about winning a miserable a-pawn! Let's see what would happen thereafter:

After 9 ♖c1 ♕xa2, Black's method is classical in its simplicity. He follows up by ...♗xc3+ and after the recapture by the pawn exchanges queens. He has an extra pawn, but this is not enough advantage to bring about checkmate. He must increase his material superiority sufficiently to justify him in going after the king, and this can only be done by turning one of his pawns into a queen. So he selects the most likely candidate, in this case the passed a-pawn, and pushes it step by step up the board. The pawn's advance faces the opponent with a problem that becomes more acute with every step taken by the pawn. He must head off the pawn or blockade it completely, in either case tying up one or more of his pieces to do so. The defence is under the strain of keeping the pawn under constant surveillance, while at the same time having to guard against a sudden switching of the attack toward his king. What often happens is that he either has to give up a piece for the pawn or allow further exchanges of pieces, a procedure which leads to inevitable loss.

Such long-range plans are not based on exact calculation; they represent a general idea of the method for winning in positions of this nature.

9 ♔d2

Not an appetizing move, as the king loses the privilege of castling, but it's the only way to guard against losing some material.

9 ... c5!

"Hits the nail on the head," says Tarrasch. With the subsequent exchange of pawns, the c-file will be prised open, further endangering the unfortunate knight.

10 a3 *(D)*

White is anxious to bring matters to a head. The alternative 10 e4 yields to 10...cxd4 11 exd5 (or 11 ♘xd4 ♘xc3 12 bxc3 ♕xg5+ and Black wins a piece – the exposed bishop that seemed doomed from the start) 11...dxc3+ 12 bxc3 ♕xd5+ and Black is a pawn up with a winning position.

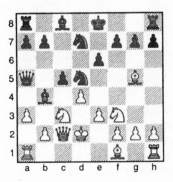

10 ... ♗xc3+

Tarrasch simplifies and avoids the difficulties attendant on winning the exchange, such as: 10...cxd4 11 axb4 dxc3+ 12 ♕xc3 ♕xa1 13 ♕xg7 ♖f8 14 e4 ♘xb4 15 ♗b5 ♕xh1 16 ♕f6 and White forces mate. It is true that Black could win the game at his fifteenth move by playing 15...♕a5, but why risk all these complications when the advantage can be maintained by less hazardous means?

11 bxc3

The only way White may recapture.

11 ... cxd4

Continuing the good work of opening up the c-file.

12 exd4

Again, White has no choice of recapture: the c-pawn is pinned, and

12 ♘xd4 is refuted by 12...♘xc3 13 ♕xc3 ♕xg5, when Black has won a pawn.

    12 ...   ♘7b6 (D)

White's pinned knight is gone, but it has been replaced by a pawn – and this pawn is also pinned! It makes a fine target, so Black directs his fire on it. He threatens to strike at it again by 13...♘a4 or by 13...♗d7 followed by 14...♖c8.

    13 ♗d3

Finally, another kingside piece sees daylight!

    13 ...   ♗d7

Black can pounce on the pawn with 13...♘a4, but he prefers to complete his development first and then bring all his pieces to bear on it. "Besides," as he says, anticipating Nimzowitsch, "the pawn does not run away."

    14 ♖hc1

White must develop and defend at the same time. If he gets a moment's respite, he will free the pinned pawn by 15 ♔e2, 16 ♗d2 and 17 c4.

    14 ...   ♖c8

But Black doesn't let up even for a moment! The rook seizes control of the beautiful open file and immediately adds its weight to the pressure on the immobilized c-pawn.

    15 ♕b3

Trying to lure Black into 15...♘a4 16 ♕xb7 ♖xc3 17 ♖xc3 ♕xc3+ 18 ♔e2, when he has counterplay.

    15 ...   0-0

"First," thinks Tarrasch, "let's get the king away from the fighting and bring the other rook closer."

    16 ♔e2 (D)

Clearly the c-pawn must be lost, as Black can attack it with more pieces than White can summon up for defence, so White saves time by abandoning the pawn and fleeing with his king.

    16 ...   ♖xc3

The first material gain, and with it entry to the enemy position.

    17 ♖xc3

Avoiding the exchange of rooks by 17 ♕b2 lets Black retain his grip on the open file.

    17 ...   ♕xc3

Much better than taking with the knight. Black's idea is to occupy a strategically strong outpost on the only open file or force an exchange of queens. The removal of the queens would simplify matters to his advantage, as he is a pawn ahead.

18 ♕b1

Forced into retreat, White manages to incorporate the threat of 19 ♗xh7+, regaining his pawn.

18 ... h6

The simplest way of saving the pawn, this also provides the king with a useful escape square against a surprise check on the last rank.

19 ♗d2

Driven back, this piece too retires with a threat.

19 ... ♕c7

The queen reluctantly leaves the beautiful outpost at c3 but stays on the all-important c-file. Note the reason the queen selects the c7-square: at c6 the action of the bishop is interfered with, at c8 that of the rook.

Black threatens 20...♘f4+, forcing an exchange of the knight for one of White's bishops.

20 ♔f1 *(D)*

Everybody going home?

20 ... ♘c4

Begins a new phase in which Black drives pieces into the enemy's territory. These will control key squares and cramp White's movements by limiting the mobility of his pieces.

21 ♗c1

Just about the only place left, if White wants to keep both his bishops.

21 ... ♗a4

And this cuts down the activities of White's queen.

22 ♕a2

Double attack on the knight! This is less a threat than a convenient means of gaining time to switch the queen over to the kingside. White's only chance, of course, is to dream up some sort of counterattack. Passive play will only lead to his being gradually crushed to death.

22 ... ♖c8

Black protects the knight and simultaneously takes undisputed possession of the c-file.

23 ♕e2

White intends to stir up trouble by playing 24 ♕e4 (threatening 25 ♕h7+ ♔f8 26 ♕h8+ ♔e7 27 ♕xg7). Then if 24...♘f6, the reply 25 ♕h4, threatening 26 ♗xh6, might whip up some sort of attack on the kingside.

23 ... ♘c3!

Not only does this move put a stop to any notions White might have had of starting a counteroffensive, but it also restricts his queen, which is attacked, to one solitary move! Such is the extent of Black's domination of the board!

24 ♕e1

The only refuge left from the terrible knights who cover seven of the queen's flight squares!

24   ...   ♞a5 (D)

With the obvious plan of penetrating deeper into White's position by 25...♞b3. This would result, as a start, in winning the exchange.

25   ♗xh6

Lashing out with the wildness born of despair!

The game could not have been saved by 25 ♗d2 as after 25...♞b3 (the knights now circumscribe the rook's activities as they did the queen's) 26 ♗xc3 ♛xc3 27 ♖d1 (or 27 ♛xc3 ♖xc3 28 ♖d1 ♞c1, when Black wins the exchange or a piece) 27...♞c1, when the attack on White's rook and bishop will win some material.

25   ...   ♞b3

Taking the bishop might lead to a win, but why expose the king needlessly? Black's actual move is simpler and more in keeping with his queenside manoeuvres up to this point.

26   ♗d2

White could not rescue the helpless rook, so must content himself with the fact that he has regained the pawn he lost.

26   ...   ♞xa1

Winning the exchange is the culmination of some clever horseplay by the knights.

27   ♛xa1 (D)

White must capture this way, and not 27 ♗xc3, which loses a whole rook after 27...♛xc3.

27   ...   ♗b5!

The fine art of simplification! Black exchanges pieces to cut down resistance. With fewer pieces on the board, fewer complications can be introduced by White, while Black's material advantage becomes proportionally greater. Notice how Black engineers these exchanges without weakening his grip on the position.

28   ♗xb5

As good as there is: after 28 ♗xc3 ♗xd3+ followed by 29...♛xc3 Black wins a piece, while 28 ♛xc3 ♛xc3 29 ♗xc3 ♗xd3+ and 30...♖xc3 does likewise.

28   ...   ♞xb5

Now Black threatens 29...♛c4+ 30 ♔e1 ♞c3, and the threat of mate at e2 forces 31 ♗xc3, whereupon 31...♛xc3+ 32 ♛xc3 ♖xc3 leaves an elementary winning position.

29 g3 *(D)*

White hopes to find shelter for the king at g2, where it is less exposed, and also sets up a pawn support for the bishop, which might get a new start at f4.

29 ... ♕c6!

The queen pounces on the light squares that have been weakened by White's last move. The attack on the knight gains a tempo for the queen's further penetration into White's territory.

30 ♔g2

An advance by the knight, e.g. 30 ♘e5, loses the queen after 30...♕h1+, while protecting the knight with 30 ♔e2 runs into 30...♕e4+ 31 ♗e3 ♖c2+ 32 ♘d2 (or 32 ♔d1 ♘c3+ winning) 32...♖a2! when 33 ♕xa2 ♘c3+ costs White his queen, while otherwise the d4-pawn falls with check.

30 ... ♖d8

Now onto this file, where the isolated pawn makes a fine target.

31 ♗e3

Guarding the d-pawn, since the pinned knight is no protection.

31 ... ♕e4

The queen works her way deeper into the heart of the position.

32 ♕b2

White tries to get some play for his queen, while the other pieces huddle around each other for mutual protection.

The queen does not rush to seize the open file, as after 32 ♕c1 ♘xd4 33 ♗xd4 ♖xd4 the threat of 34...♖d3 is more than White can stand.

32 ... ♖d5! *(D)*

A diabolical move! Not only does Black guard his own knight, but he also threatens to win White's by 33...♖f5 34 ♕e2 ♘xd4!, an attack on the queen and a triple attack on the knight. There is no answer to this as White is pinned all over the place!

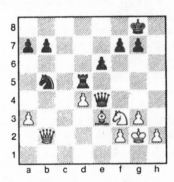

33 a4

Driving the knight off so that it no longer attacks the d-pawn.

33 ... ♘d6

The knight leaves, taking care to protect the b-pawn.

34 ♗f4

Otherwise, Black plays 34...g5, threatening 35...g4 or 35...♖f5, or both!

34 ... ♘f5

Once more striking at the d-pawn.

35 ♗e3 (D)

White cannot afford 35 ♕xb7 as after 35...♘xd4 36 ♕c8+ ♔h7 37 ♕c3 g5 he loses more material.

35 ...   ♘xe3+

Simpler than combinations beginning with 35...e5. After the textmove, two more pieces come off the board, and another pawn will fall.

36 fxe3

White must recapture.

36 ...   ♕xe3

This unpins the knight, but the knight must stay where it is to protect the d-pawn.

37 g4

White must not play 37 ♕xb7 as the reply 37...♕e2+ forces the king away from the knight and costs a piece. His actual move stops Black from increasing the pressure by 37...♖f5.

37 ...   f5

Black can afford this opening up of the position. His king suffers less from exposure than does White's. The threat of course is 38...fxg4, winning at once.

38 g5

After 38 h3 fxg4 39 hxg4 ♕f4 40 g5 ♕g4+ 41 ♔f2 ♖f5 the threats of 42...♕xf3+ and 42...♕xg5 cannot both be met.

38 ...   ♕e4

Once more clamping a pin on the knight!

39 ♕c3

Carefully avoiding 39 ♕xb7, when 39...f4 faces him with loss of the knight by 40...♕e2+ or loss of the g-pawn by 40...♖xg5+.

39 ...   f4

Not at once 39...e5 because 40 g6 leaves White threatening sudden mate!

40 ♕c8+

If White had tried 40 g6 then 40...♖g5+ would end the g-pawn's career.

40 ...   ♔h7

To escape any more checks by the queen.

41 ♕c3 (D)

Back to the defence of the knight and the d-pawn.

41 ...   e5!

This signals the beginning of the last phase: the break-up of White's centre.

This is stronger than 41...♖xg5+ 42 ♔f2 ♖h5 43 h4, when White threatens 44 ♘g5+.

The idea of the text-move is to continue with 42...♖xd4, with which Black accomplishes these things:

• He has demolished White's centre.
• He threatens an immediate win by 43...♖d3.
• He is assured (if the foregoing is not convincing enough) of remaining with two connected passed pawns in the centre.

42 h4

Marshall sees that 42 dxe5 loses a piece after 42...♖d3 but he still has a few tricks up his sleeve.

42 ... ♖xd4

Intending to attack queen and knight by 43...♖d3, incidentally cutting off the queen from the knight's defence.

43 g6+

This is one of the traps: if Black plays 43...♔xg6, White replies 44 ♕b3 (apparently trying to get a perpetual check) 44...♖d3, and now instead of 45 ♕e6+ White plays 45 ♕xd3 ♕xd3 46 ♘xe5+ followed by 47 ♘xd3 regaining the queen and winning a rook.

43 ... ♔h6

Black side-steps this one.

44 ♔h2

So White sets up another trap: if 44...♖d3 45 ♕xe5 ♕xf3, then 46 ♕g5#!

44 ... ♕e2+

0-1

To this there is no reply: 45 ♔g1 ♖d1+ 46 ♘e1 ♖xe1+ wins, or 45 ♔h3 ♖d3, pinning the poor knight for the last time, puts out the last flickers of resistance.

Game 30

Capablanca – Villegas
Buenos Aires 1914
Queen's Gambit Declined

1 d4

In this game, the art of chess is reduced to a simple formula: *get a passed pawn, move it up the board, and win!*

White begins by getting a foothold in the centre, while releasing two of his pieces.

1 ... d5

This is probably Black's strongest reply. It equalizes the pressure and prevents White from monopolizing the centre with 2 e4.

2 ♘f3

The knight leaps in toward the centre, intensifying the pawn's pressure on e5. The knight does its best work at f3, covering eight squares in the circle of its attack.

2 ... ♘f6

Black applies the same formula, developing his g8-knight to its most effective post. Aside from its admirable potential for attack, the knight also serves while it stands and waits. In the service of the king, especially after castling, the knight defends as no other piece can.

3 e3

Not the most energetic procedure, but White need not be aggressive from the start. The opening itself is so strong that White can build up a promising position merely by developing his pieces so that they occupy the most suitable squares immediately. The method is simplicity itself:

Put every single piece to work, and move no piece twice until development is complete.

The fact that 3 e3 releases one bishop but shuts in another is of little moment, as the c1-bishop can get into the game by way of b2. White does not indicate his specific intentions: he might play the Colle Attack or perhaps simply develop the bishop at d3 with a view to early kingside castling.

3 ...   c6

Black supports his d-pawn, anticipating an attack on it by 4 c4. He prefers this to the alternative pawn support by 3...e6, which confines his queen's bishop.

However, if Black wants to free his bishop, why not move it at once to f5? There it would stand ready to oppose White's bishop when it moves to d3. The almost inevitable bishop exchange then removes White's attacking bishop from the board and takes the sting out of the Colle system of attack.

Another possibility was pushing on to c5 at once with his pawn, striking at White's centre, and opening the c-file for the use of his own heavy pieces. But why play 3...c6, moving a pawn unnecessarily in the opening? Why waste time defending when nothing is threatened?

4 ♗d3

Quiet, forceful development: the bishop surveys two fine diagonals and is ready for action in either direction. Meanwhile the kingside is cleared for castling.

4 ...   ♗g4

As good as there is for this bishop. The best square the bishop could occupy is f5, but White's last move made this square unavailable.

5 c4! *(D)*

Alert play! White strikes at the enemy centre and prepares to open the c-file for the convenience of his major pieces. The diagonal created for his queen also holds out prospects of a raid by 6 ♕b3 on Black's queenside, weakened by the absence of his bishop.

5 ...   e6

Black's f8-bishop is provided with an outlet, while the central d-pawn is given further support.

6 ♘bd2

White defends the f3-knight with a minor piece, relieving the queen of a duty. This method of developing the knight is preferable to placing it at c3, where it might interfere with the future operations of the queen or the rook on the c-file.

The sortie 6 ♕b3 yields no immediate advantage, since Black's reply 6...♕b6 leads either to an exchange of queens or a retreat by White's queen.

6 ... ♘bd7

For Black's knight, too, this is model development. At d7 it cooperates with the f6-knight and supports an eventual attack on White's centre by ...c5 or ...e5. Either of these freeing moves is an objective Black must strive to attain in this opening.

7 0-0

The king rushes off to safer quarters while the rook comes out of hiding.

7 ... ♗e7 (D)

This develops a piece and enables Black to castle but is rather unenterprising. A more spirited course was 7...e5 attempting to have something to say about affairs in the centre.

8 ♕c2!

So White puts a stop to any such ideas! An advance by 8...e5 now costs a pawn, as White's knight, no longer pinned, is free to pick off the pawn.

The queen's development at c2 is modest, but in the early stages of the game, the queen should rarely venture beyond the third or fourth rank. What *is* important, though, is to move the queen off the back rank and into active play.

8 ... ♗h5

Black prepares to swing the light-squared bishop around to g6 to exchange it for White's aggressive d3-bishop. Had he castled instead, then 9 ♘e5 ♗h5 (9...♘xe5 10 dxe5 ♘d7 11 ♗xh7+ wins a pawn for White) 10 f4 gives White a powerfully centralized knight and excellent attacking prospects.

9 b3

A pawn move that provides an outlet for a piece is always justified. This one makes room for the c1-bishop's development.

9 ... ♗g6

Black continues with the business of forcing an exchange of light-squared bishops.

10 ♗b2 (D)

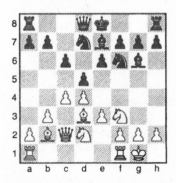

From a distance, the dark-squared bishop intensifies White's pressure on the important central square e5. With this square under control, it will be difficult for Black to get in the freeing move ...e5.

10 ...   ♗xd3

There was no hurry about this exchange. Why not calmly keep on with the job of developing pieces, as White does?

11   ♕xd3 *(D)*

After this recapture, White has all the play. He can choose from various plans:

1) a break-up by e4, to open lines of attack for his pieces;

2) the establishment of an outpost at e5 by the knight;

3) a hemming-in process, beginning with c5.

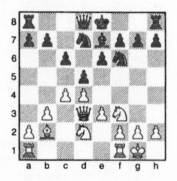

11 ...   0-0

There is no way for Black to meet all these continuations, so he transfers his king to a safe shelter.

12   ♖ae1

Before committing himself, White brings another piece into play. The rook's presence on the e-file will add power to the e-pawn's advance.

White does not take action until his development is complete.

12   ...   ♕c7 *(D)*

Black mobilizes another piece, hoping for some counterplay by 13...c5. The development of the queen also enables the rooks to establish communication with each other.

13   e4!

Opening up lines of attack, which, says theory, will favour the player whose development is superior.

White rejects 13 c5, the reply to which would be 13...e5 14 dxe5 ♘xc5. 13 ♘e5 is no more promising, since 13...♘xe5 14 dxe5 ♘d7 15 f4 f6 lets Black off too easily.

13   ...   dxe4

Otherwise Black must live in constant dread of e5 or exd5, either of which White can play at his own convenience.

14   ♘xe4

The recapture leaves White with a formidable centre.

14   ...   ♘xe4

Black exchanges pieces to help free his crowded position.

15   ♖xe4!

Anticipating the natural defensive response 15...♘f6, to which White would reply 16 ♖h4. The plan is then to dislodge Black's knight, which guards against mate. This might be accomplished by 17 d5 followed by 18 ♗xf6 or by 17 ♘e5 followed by 18 ♘g4. To prevent capture or uprooting of his knight and the consequent ♕xh7#, Black would have to play ...g6 or ...h6, in either case loosening the pawn structure and thereby weakening the king's defences.

15 ... ♗f6 (D)

This prevents 16 ♖h4, gives the bishop more scope and puts pressure on White's centre. It also incorporates a pretty threat in 16...♘c5 17 dxc5 ♗xb2, simplifying to Black's advantage.

16 ♕e3

White puts an end to that little scheme!

16 ... c5

This certainly looks attractive! Black plans 17...cxd4, a capture that White cannot avoid, his d-pawn being pinned. With the disappearance of White's troublesome central pawn, the squares e5 and c5 then become

available to Black's knight, and the c-file opens up for counterplay by his queen and rook.

17 ♘e5

The knight establishes an outpost. It seems harmless enough: it threatens nothing and does not interfere with whatever ideas Black has in mind.

17 ... cxd4 (D)

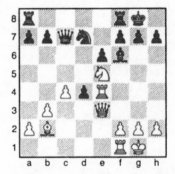

Counting on the continuation 18 ♗xd4 ♗xe5 19 ♗xe5 ♘xe5 20 ♖xe5 ♖fd8, when Black's control of the open d-file greatly increases his chances.

18 ♘xd7!

A remarkable concept! Not because White plays a combination which involves a queen sacrifice, but that the offer of the queen is only a detail! It is subordinate to the overall strategy of the game, which is being conducted on positional lines and will be won that way. Any combinations that arise will be incidental to the general plan, which is to create a passed pawn, move it up at every opportunity and promote it to a queen.

18 ... ♕xd7

If he accepts the offer and plays 18...dxe3 White reveals this combination: 19 ♘xf6+ ♔h8 (or 19...gxf6 20 ♖g4+ ♔h8 21 ♗xf6#) 20 ♖h4 (threatening 21 ♖xh7#) 20...h6 21 ♖xh6+! gxh6 22 ♘d5+ ♔g8 23 ♘xc7 and White, with two pieces for a rook, wins easily.

19 ♗xd4

White regains the pawn, and his bishop now attacks in two directions. On the one hand, it threatens to take the a-pawn, on the other it aims at checkmate by 20 ♗xf6 gxf6 21 ♖g4+ ♔h8 22 ♕h6 ♖g8 23 ♕xf6+ and mate next move.

19 ...   ♗xd4

The bishop must be done away with!

20 ♖xd4

White recaptures and gains a tempo by attacking the queen.

20 ...   ♕c7

The best square. From here the queen's mobility is at its maximum.

21 ♖fd1

Now we can appreciate the significance of White's offer of the queen. It was not an attempt to win the game by surprise tactics; it was the employment of a combination as a device to gain ground positionally! White's doubling of the rooks on the d-file gives him full control of that file, and his pawn majority of three to two on the queenside offers the possibility of creating a passed pawn on the c-file.

21 ...   ♖fd8 *(D)*

Black must oppose rooks before White either establishes a rook on the seventh rank or triples pieces on the file.

22 b4!

This starts the queenside pawns rolling! Capablanca does not even cast a glance at such a transparent trap as 22 ♖xd8+ ♖xd8 23 ♖xd8+ ♕xd8 24 ♕xa7 ♕d1#.

22 ...   ♖xd4

The exchange is almost forced. Otherwise, the need to protect the rook ties down Black's queen and his other rook.

23 ♕xd4

Naturally, White takes with the queen to keep two major pieces on the open file.

23 ...   b6

Black must play this or 23...a6 in order to make use of his rook. Note that he cannot dispute the open file by 23...♖d8, as White snaps off the rook and mates next move.

24 g3

A safety measure to give the king a flight square from surprise checks on the first rank; such checks very often turn out to be fatal.

24 ...   ♖c8

Doubling the attack on the c-pawn.

25 ♖c1

In order to save the pawn, White must shift his rook from the d-file, but now the rook is behind the c-pawn (the candidate for promotion) and is in position to keep it under protection, no matter how far the pawn moves up the file.

25 ...   ♖d8

Black's object is to drive the queen off and command the d-file himself with his rook.

26 ♕e3

A shrewd move: the queen keeps in touch with the rook, prevents Black's rook from coming in at d1, and keeps a weather eye on the strategically important c5-square, the c-pawn's next stop.

26 ...   ♔f8

The king approaches the field of action. In the event of a general exchange of pieces, he is prepared to head off the c-pawn.

27 c5

White's pawn advances at every available opportunity.

27 ...   bxc5 *(D)*

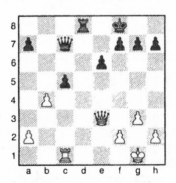

Expecting White to recapture by 28 bxc5, whereupon he blockades the pawn effectively by 28...♕c6.

28 ♕e4!

Very clever! White need not recapture immediately, as Black's pawn is pinned and cannot escape capture. Meanwhile, the queen move stops the intended blockade by 28...♕c6 and prepares 29 bxc5 followed by 30 c6.

28 ...   ♖d5

The rook rushes to help the c-pawn.

There is a temptation for White to go pawn-hunting now by 29 ♕xh7 followed by 30 ♕h8+ and 31 ♕xg7, picking up a couple of pawns and creating for himself a passed h-pawn. But this sort of random play would not be consistent with White's orderly, economical conduct of the game, and entirely out of character for a Capablanca!

29 bxc5 *(D)*

A passed pawn at last!

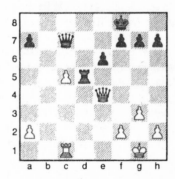

29 ...   g6

It would not do to recapture by 29...♖xc5 as White punishes the offending rook by 30 ♕b4 pinning and then winning it.

30 c6

Passed pawns must be pushed! With each step forward, the scope of

White's rook increases, while the freedom of Black's pieces becomes more limited.

30 ... &g7 *(D)*

Black realizes that bringing the king to the centre might be suicidal, viz.: 30...&e7 31 ♕h4+ &d6 32 ♕b4+ &e5 33 ♕f4#!

31 a4!

A beautiful preparatory move! If White were to play 31 ♕b4 at once, aiming for 32 ♕b7 (in order to dislodge the blockader) Black could exchange queens and then stop the pawn by 33...♖b5, coming behind it. However, with White's a-pawn at a4, Black could not bring his rook to b5!

31 ... ♖d6

Putting the pawn under lock and key. It cannot advance, and White's intended stratagem of manoeuvring his queen over to b7 is not feasible, Black's reply to 32 ♕b4 being simply 32...♖xc6. But the very fact that one pawn can keep Black's queen and rook occupied is a tribute to the power of a passed pawn.

32 ♕e5+!

In spite of the heavy guard surrounding the pawn, White with one stroke will lift the blockade!

32 ... f6

No matter how Black gets out of check, he cannot stop the coming combination.

33 ♕xd6!

Destroying one of the guards!

33 ... ♕xd6

And the recapture lures the other one away!

34 c7 1-0

The pawn becomes a queen next move, leaving White a whole rook ahead.

Game 31
Havasi – Capablanca
Budapest 1929
Nimzo-Indian Defence

1 d4

One way of getting a good share of the centre is to take it!

White does so here by planting one of his pawns right in the middle of the board. It occupies d4, one square, and secures a grip on two others, e5 and c5.

1 ... ♘f6

More elastic than 1...d5. Black develops a piece and bears down on the centre instead of occupying it with a pawn. His knight attacks d5 and e4, and prevents White gaining more ground with 2 e4.

2 c4

This advance is a valuable freeing move in queen's pawn openings. It attacks the central square d5, makes the c-file a favourable one for the rook (because of the likelihood of the file being later opened up) and offers the queen access to the queenside.

2 ... e6

Not at once 2...d5 as 3 cxd5 ♕xd5 (or 3...♘xd5 4 e4 ♘f6 5 ♘c3, when White has more of the centre than he is entitled to) 4 ♘c3 gains time for White by the attack on the queen.

With 2...e6, Black prepares a pawn support for a later occupation of the centre by ...d5. Meanwhile, he releases his f8-bishop.

3 ♘c3

This is sharper than developing the g1-knight. It backs up a threat of 4 e4, presenting a formidable array of pawns in the centre.

3 ... ♗b4

The bishop clamps down on the knight and, by its pin, deprives it of the power to attack or defend. Thus, if White carelessly played 4 e4, Black could snap up the pawn at once.

4 ♕c2

With a number of objects in view:

1) the square c2 is generally the queen's most useful post in this opening;

2) the queen guards the knight: in the event of Black playing 4...♗xc3+, the queen may recapture and leave White's pawn structure undisturbed;

3) the queen exerts pressure on the c-file, the advantage of which

becomes manifest with the opening of the file;

4) the queen, by controlling e4, renews White's threat of advancing the e-pawn two squares.

4 ... d5

Wresting control of e4 from White and restraining his ambitious e-pawn from taking too long a first step.

5 ♘f3 (D)

Quiet, perhaps too quiet. It gets the king's knight off the ground, but the lull gives Black an opportunity to seize the initiative.

5 ... c5!

"Black equalizes in any queen's pawn opening," says Reuben Fine, "where he can play both ...d5 and ...c5 with impunity."

With 5...c5 Black aims to destroy White's pawn-centre, or at the very least to maintain a state of tension in that important area. As a fringe benefit, his queenside pieces have a bit more elbow-room.

6 cxd5

White's idea is to clarify the position in the centre. The disappearance of his c4-pawn also helps to increase the pressure of the queen on the c-file.

6 ...   Wxd5

Preferable to 6...exd5 which allows 7 ♗g5, an annoying pin of the knight. The queen is strongly centralized at d5, and in no danger of being annoyed by White's minor pieces.

7 a3

White has had enough of this tiresome bishop!

7 ...   ♗xc3+

Black must exchange. If instead 7...♗a5, then 8 b4 (threatening 9 ♘xd5) 8...cxb4 9 ♘xd5 b3+ 10 ♗d2 bxc2 11 ♘xf6+ gxf6 12 ♗xa5 and White has won a piece.

8 bxc3 *(D)*

Capturing with the queen instead lets Black gain a tempo by 8...♘e4 attacking the queen, whereupon the prospect of White's playing e4 seems further away than ever.

In compensation for White's theoretical advantage of the two bishops against knight and bishop, Black's pawn position on the queenside is distinctly superior.

8 ...   ♘c6

The knight develops with a threat. There is now a triple attack on White's d-pawn, and this limits his choice of reply.

9 e3

The least of the evils, though it does shut in the c1-bishop. The alternative 9 dxc5 Wxc5 saddles White with two weak, isolated pawns, while after 9 c4 ♘xd4 10 Wa4+ (or 10 cxd5 ♘xc2+ and Black wins a rook) 10...Wd7 Black is a pawn up.

9 ...   0-0 *(D)*

The king finds a safer shelter, while the h8-rook makes its appearance.

10 ♗e2

The bishop develops gingerly. A more energetic procedure was 10 c4 to dislodge the queen from the centre, followed by 11 ♗b2, with fair chances.

10 ...   cxd4

This clever pawn exchange keeps the position fluid and gives Black a slight advantage after any recapture.

11 cxd4 *(D)*

Understandably, White rejects 11 ♘xd4 as 11...Wxg2 12 ♗f3 ♘xd4 in reply is ruinous. With his actual move, White adheres to the principle of capturing toward the centre and increases the queen's sphere of action by opening the c-file. Nevertheless, it might have been better policy to play 11 exd4, activating his dark-squared bishop.

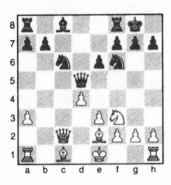

11 ... b6

Preparing to develop the bishop at b7, where it will command one of the longest diagonals on the board.

Black's advantage consists mainly in his two pawns to one on the queen-side, and this, after an exchange of pawns, can turn into one pawn against none. As for the c-file, it can be seized by the a8-rook. The rook will drive White's queen off and remain in control of the file.

12 ♘d2

White wants the long diagonal for himself, so he vacates f3 for the bishop. He hardly hopes to lure Capablanca into a cheap trap by 12...♕xg2, when 13 ♗f3 wins a piece. This sort of thing does not happen in real life.

12 ... ♗b7

The bishop stands beautifully here, despite the fact that two pieces

obstruct its path. Meanwhile, the c8-square is ready for occupancy by another tenant, the a8-rook.

13 ♗f3

The bishop is well posted here, but at what a cost in time! The knight has had to retreat, and the development of White's queenside pieces has been neglected.

13 ... ♕d7

The queen keeps in touch with the knight, which is under attack by two pieces.

14 0-0

Trying to get in the advance of the e-pawn is premature as 14 e4 ♘xd4 costs a pawn, while 14 ♗xc6 ♗xc6 15 e4 ♕xd4 16 ♕xc6 ♕xa1 loses the exchange.

14 ... ♖ac8 *(D)*

Black threatens 15...♘xd4, and thereby suggests that White's queen leave the c-file.

15 ♕b1

The aggressive 15 ♕a4 is risky as 15...♘e5 16 ♕xd7 (16 ♕xa7 ♘xf3+ 17 ♘xf3 ♕c6 followed by 18...♖a8 puts the queen in trouble) 16...♘xf3+ 17 ♘xf3 ♘xd7 is strong for Black.

15 ... ♘a5! *(D)*

Offering an exchange of bishops. Refusing it leaves Black in full possession of the long diagonal.

16   ♗xb7

It might have been safer to concede the diagonal by 16 ♗e2 and keep more pieces on the board. Exchanging simplifies the position and accentuates Black's superiority.

16   ...   ♕xb7

Black is now ready to exploit the circumstance that his opponent's light squares are vulnerable to invasion. These squares have been weakened by the disappearance of the light-squared bishop. This advantage, together with that of Black's pawn majority on the queenside (a circumstance which generally results in the creation of a passed pawn) should be enough to forecast a win for him.

From this point on, we will see a demonstration of the technique of winning a won game.

17   ♗b2 *(D)*

Finally, White gets his queenside rolling. Laudable as this object is, it was essential to anticipate Black's next move and play 17 ♕d3. This would strengthen White's weak squares and hold off for a time the threatened invasion.

17   ...   ♕a6!

A very fine manoeuvre! The queen takes leave of the long diagonal to exert great pressure on a more important one.

The queen threatens to come in strongly at e2 and make coordination by White's pieces difficult.

18   ♖e1

Parrying the threat. On 18 ♖c1 instead (to put up a fight for the c-file), Black plays 18...♕e2 19 ♘f3 (or 19 ♖a2 ♘g4 20 ♖xc8 ♕xf2+ and Black wins) 19...♘b3 20 ♖xc8 ♖xc8 21 ♖a2 ♖c1+!, and White must give up his queen or be mated.

18   ...   ♘d5

Admirable centralization – but it's only temporary. The knight is on its way to the queenside, the theatre of action.

19   ♖a2

Intending either to oppose rooks by 20 ♗a1 followed by 21 ♖c2 or to continue with 20 ♕a1 preventing 20...♘c3.

19   ...   ♖c6

Clearly in order to double rooks on the c-file. Black is in no hurry to move his knight to c3; first he wants to induce White to dislodge the knight from the centre.

20 e4 (D)

A deceptive move. It looks strong, but the central pawns are exposed and can easily become targets of an attack.

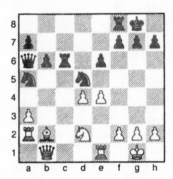

20 ... ♘c3!

It may seem strange that Black gives up a healthy knight for a sickly bishop, but this precaution is necessary before the rooks venture into enemy territory. With less material on the board, the rooks will be less exposed to the stings of the minor pieces.

21 ♗xc3

The knight had to be removed, as it was attacking queen and rook.

21 ... ♖xc3

The recapture enables the rook to penetrate deeper into White's position.

22 ♘f3

White makes an effort to regroup his pieces. If he tries to dispute the c-file by 22 ♖c1 then 22...♖xc1+ 23

♕xc1 ♕d3 24 ♕b2 ♖d8 wins a central pawn.

22 ... ♖fc8

The doubled rooks now dominate the open file.

Theoretically, Black has a won game. His positional superiority is undeniable, and winning, in a favourite phrase of the masters, 'is simply a matter of technique'. A pleasant state of affairs, but one which involves a psychological danger. There is a tendency to relax and let up on the attack. It is easy to be lulled into a false sense of security, a circumstance which prompted Marshall's observation, "The hardest thing is to win a won game".

23 h3

White gives his king an escape square – in lieu of anything better to do.

Black's rooks cannot be driven off (if 23 ♖e3, then 23...♖c1+ wins the queen) so White temporizes and awaits the turn of events.

23 ... ♘c4

The first in a series of skilfully blended moves which speed up the tempo. To begin with, there is a triple attack on the a-pawn.

24 a4

No other move saves the pawn.

24 ... ♘a3

Very neat! The knight attacks the queen and simultaneously cuts off the a-pawn's protection by the rook.

25 ♕b2

Voluntarily giving up a pawn which he cannot keep. If he tries to hold on to the pawn by 25 ♕d1, then 25...♕c4 26 ♖b2 (the rook was attacked) 26...♘c2 (now the other one is threatened) 27 ♖e2 ♕xa4 28 ♘e1 (striking at the pinned black knight) 28...♕xd4! wins for Black.

25   ...   ♕xa4 *(D)*

The first tangible gain. Now watch the greatest genius the game of chess ever produced demonstrate the art of transforming a passed pawn into a queen. Notice how any combinations that do not relate to that objective, no matter how attractive, are carefully avoided. Such intensity of purpose is frightening (especially to one who has to face it!).

26   ♖e2

White is running out of good moves. He rejects 26 ♕e2 as the reply 26...♖c2 leads to further exchanges. An attack on the pinned knight by 26 ♖ea1 is cleverly met by 26...♕b5, nimbly extricating the knight from danger.

26   ...   b5

Passed pawns must be pushed! Everything else – combinations to win pieces, gathering up stray pawns, even attacks on the king – must be relegated to the background as incidental to the main theme of queening the advanced pawn.

27   d5

White opens lines for some sort of counterattack, trying to create a diversion.

27   ...   exd5

The simplest response, as the recapture will give White an isolated pawn in the middle of the board.

28   exd5 *(D)*

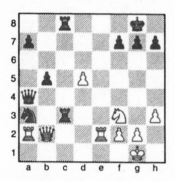

In return for this, White's e2-rook looks out on a completely open file. In fact, White threatens 29 ♕xc3 ♖xc3 30 ♖e8#.

28   ...   b4!

An obvious move, but brilliant nevertheless in the number of things it accomplishes:

1) it nullifies White's threat, the e8-square now being covered by the queen;

2) it defends the knight, freeing the queen from that duty;

3) it advances the pawn one step nearer its ultimate goal, the eighth rank.

29   ♕d2

Not only to support his own passed pawn but to bring the queen into active play.

29   ...   b3

Complying with the Manhattan Chess Club epigram, "Black passed pawns travel faster than White".

30 ♖b2

This holds out longer than 30 ♖a1 ♖c2 31 ♕e3 b2, when Black wins more quickly.

30 ... ♖c2 (*D*)

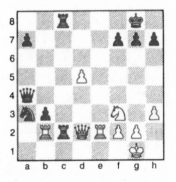

Black's play is crystal clear: the passed pawn must be pushed and its path is blocked by a rook. Therefore the blockader must be removed!

31 ♕e3

White hopes to complicate matters, as 31 ♖xc2 is not attractive.

31 ... ♖xb2

The proper rook to capture, this begins a series of pretty moves that decides the game.

32 ♖xb2

White must recapture.

32 ... ♘c4!

An attack on queen and rook which threatens to win the exchange.

33 ♕c1

White rescues the rook by pinning the knight. It would not do to play 33 ♕xb3 instead as Black simply takes the rook, and his knight now protects the queen.

33 ... ♕a3!

The pin of the knight is met by a counter-pin of the rook, which Black now threatens to take with his queen.

34 ♖b1

But the rook wriggles out of the pin. Has Black let the win slip?

34 ... ♕xc1+!

Not at all! This compels capitulation since after 35 ♖xc1 b2 (the pawn must move on) 36 ♖b1 ♖b8 37 ♔f1 ♘a3 (driving off the last blockader) 38 ♖d1 b1♕ the passed pawn wins the game for Black.

0-1

Game 32
Canal – Capablanca
Budapest 1929
Queen's Indian Defence

1 d4

A favourite of modern players, this is one of the best possible ways to begin the struggle for mastery of the centre – by occupying it with a pawn and permitting two pieces to come quickly into play.

1 ... ♘f6

Unlike 1...d5 this does not meet the opponent head-on, but it does prevent him from continuing with 2 e4 and has the added merit of developing a piece at once to its proper square in the opening.

2 c4

There are many good points about this move:

1) It restrains Black from an immediate 2...d5, as the reply 3 cxd5 *forces a recapture with a piece* and destroys his short-lived pawn-centre.

2) It opens the c-file for the use of White's major pieces.

3) It makes a diagonal available to the queen.

4) It enables the two pawns standing side by side to get a grip on four squares on the fifth rank.

2 ... e6 (D)

Black's f8-bishop is to be developed aggressively, to influence affairs in the centre. If White replies 3 ♘c3, for example, in order to follow up with 4 e4, Black pins the knight and makes 4 e4 impossible.

3 ♘f3

White cannot enforce the advance of the e-pawn, so he makes a normal developing move and awaits events.

3 ... b6

Further restraint on the project! Black intends to place his bishop at b7, where it attacks from a distance. The bishop will add its strength to that of the knight in the control of the critical e4-square.

4 g3 (D)

White's best course is to oppose bishops on the long diagonal as one does with rooks on an open file. In setting up an equal opposing force, he takes the sting out of the enemy bishop's attack.

4 ... ♗b7

Strictly a modern concept! In olden times they filled up the centre with pawns and then fianchettoed the bishop, with the result that the bishop was deprived of any usefulness. Nowadays the bishop is free to strike all along the diagonal, unhampered by fixed pawns cluttering up his path.

5 ♗g2

With the completion of the fianchetto, White's kingside is cleared, and he is ready to castle.

5 ... ♗b4+

Before attempting to undermine the centre by ...c5, Black develops a piece. Not only does the bishop's move expedite castling, but it also brings about a favourable exchange of bishops.

6 &d2

This is preferable to 6 ♘bd2, a passive interposition which gives Black time to castle and then attack the centre by 7...d5.

6 ... &xd2+

Black proceeds with the exchange as the best means of freeing his somewhat cramped position. Instead, withdrawing the bishop to e7 throws him on the defensive and lets White retain the initiative.

7 ♘bxd2 *(D)*

Theorists and critics of master chess recommend that White capture with the queen instead. Despite their shrieks that the knight belongs at c3 in order to help attack the d5-square, the players themselves persist in recapturing with the knight. They advance as argument that in doing so another minor piece is developed, but the real reason might be sheer stubbornness – rebellion against authority. In any case, if it is less effective than 7 ♕xd2, it is not to be so roundly condemned.

7 ... 0-0

Before taking any decisive action in the centre, Black sees to the welfare of his king and removes him to a safer part of the board.

A strong alternative is 7...c5 challenging White's pawn-centre. To this, White cannot reply 8 d5 as it loses a pawn.

8 0-0 *(D)*

White makes his king's position more secure and presses the h1-rook into service.

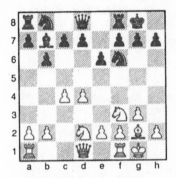

8 ... c5!

A strong move, whose object is to undermine White's centre.

9 dxc5

White has little choice. Moving the pawn to d5 loses a pawn, supporting it with 9 e3 (in order to recapture with a pawn and maintain a pawn in the centre), ties down the e-pawn to the job of defence. The chances then of the e-pawn's ever reaching e4 are rather dubious.

9 ... bxc5

Black has gained three advantages by a simple exchange of pawns:

1) He has exchanged a centre pawn for a less central pawn.

2) His c-pawn controls d4, making it impossible for White to settle a piece on that square.

3) His queen and a1-rook will be able to operate with good effect on the newly opened b-file.

10   ♕c2

In most cases the function of the queen in the opening is not so much to be moving around as it is to get off the back rank and out of the way, so that the rooks can get together and work on the centre files.

With the departure of the queen, the f1-rook can occupy d1, exert pressure on the d-file, and make life uncomfortable for Black's forces on that file.

10   ...   ♘c6 *(D)*

The knight develops toward the centre and intensifies the pawn's grip on d4.

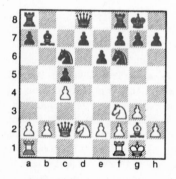

11   ♖fd1

The tempting 11 e4 meets its refutation in 11...e5 (strengthening the pressure on d4) followed by 12...♕e7 and 13...♘d4. White would then face a problem: the pressure of the knight at d4 is almost intolerable, but removing it lets Black recapture by 14...cxd4, leaving him with a passed pawn on the d-file.

11   ...   ♕b6!

Now there are three pieces bearing down on d4, while the queen herself gets a purchase on the open b-file.

12   a3 *(D)*

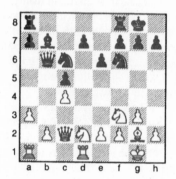

White has no wild dream of starting a counterattack with 13 b4; mainly he wants to rule out ...♘b4 at some later stage.

12   ...   ♖ab8

Fine positional play! One is apt to forget that a rook's first duty is to seize upon any file that is open, not only since the rook's attack extends the whole length of the file but because the rook has a convenient avenue for its progress to other points.

13   ♖ab1

White's rook also goes to b1, but what a world of difference there is in the two moves! White's rook has no open file; it has little prospect of increasing its mobility, and its function is purely defensive. In protecting the b-pawn, though, it relieves the queen of a responsibility.

13   ...   ♖fc8

The rook was doing nothing at f8, so it is transferred to a file where it is likely to become useful.

There was no hurry about playing 13...a5 since White is in no position to try for the break by 14 b4.

14 e4

White's move has a superficial appearance of strength. In reality, the pawn occupies a square that should be kept clear. White's pieces lose a great deal of mobility in not being able to make use of e4 as a jumping-off point to their various destinations.

14 ... e5

Stifling 15 e5, White's e-pawn's lust to expand.

Notice how Black has reinforced his hold on d4. This point now has the power of the queen, a knight and a couple of pawns trained on it.

15 ♕d3

White hopes for some counter-play along the d-file, either by 16 ♕d6 or in manoeuvring his knight by way of f1 and e3 to d5. In the meantime, he prevents Black from playing 15...♘d4, the response to which is 16 ♘xe5.

15 ... d6

A witty, almost impudent, reply. Black guards the e-pawn (so that he can play 16...♘d4) with a pawn which itself is unprotected!

White, of course, must not take the d-pawn, the penalty for 16 ♕xd6 being 16...♖d8, winning the queen.

16 ♘f1

Indicating that he wants to deploy the knight to e3 and then d5. Excellent strategy, if White can carry it out.

16 ... ♘d4! *(D)*

However, Black gets there first! Not only does he establish an out-post at d4, but he also hinders White from continuing his manoeuvre. If White tries 17 ♘e3, then 17...♗xe4 18 ♘d5 ♗xd3 19 ♘xb6 ♘xf3+ 20 ♗xf3 ♖xb6 21 ♖xd3 e4 wins a piece neatly.

17 ♘xd4

The advanced knight cramps his style, so White gets rid of it.

17 ... exd4

Black is happy to exchange: he has a passed pawn on the d-file, which in the course of time might become a queen. More than that, the pawn guards the exits. It hinders White's knight from coming out at e3 and puts an end to its ambition to reach d5.

The passed pawn at d4 is apparently the logical candidate for promotion to queen, but there are surprises to come – many of them!

18 b4

Suddenly White bursts forth! His chief threat is 19 bxc5 ♕xc5 (Black must recapture with the queen, as she is doubly attacked) 20 ♖xb7 ♖xb7 21 e5, and the discovered attack will net White two pieces for a rook.

How does Black meet this threat? Obviously not with 18...cxb4, as 19 ♖xb4 gives White the better of it. Also not by 18...♕c7, when after 19 bxc5 dxc5 (to protect the passed pawn) 20 f4 threatening 21 e5 follows, and White's pieces spring to life.

Capablanca's actual reply initiates a remarkable combination. He lets White obtain an advantage in material in return for a position which looks far from promising – except to a Capablanca!

18   ...   ♕c6! *(D)*

Triple attack on the e-pawn! This forces White either to defend the pawn tamely, or else to go ahead boldly with the combination he planned.

19   bxc5

White plays to win! He takes a pawn off, opens a file for his rook, and threatens to remove the passed d-pawn.

19   ...   dxc5

Black must recapture with the pawn to preserve the precious passed pawn.

20   ♖xb7

This tempting combination wins two pieces for a rook.

Has Capablanca been caught off-guard, or does he see much further into the resources of the position than his opponent?

20   ...   ♕xb7

Black captures with the queen to maintain control of the valuable open file.

21   e5 *(D)*

Discovered attack on the queen, and direct attack on the knight.

21   ...   ♕b3!

A remarkable offer to exchange queens! Usually, the side that is ahead in material tries to clear the board and simplify to an ending.

22   exf6

White rejects 22 ♕xb3 as it leads to 22...♖xb3 23 exf6 ♖xa3, when Black is left with two passed pawns.

22   ...   ♕xd3

The idea of this is to force the white rook off the last rank. The rank then becomes available to Black's rook as a point of entry, enabling it to get behind White's pawns.

23   ♖xd3

White has no choice.

23 ...   Rb1!

The knight is pinned as a start, and White has to scramble frantically to break the pin.

Against passive play, Black continues with 24...Re8 followed by 25...Ree1 and 26...Rec1. This wins the c-pawn since White cannot protect it by 27 ♗d5 without abandoning the knight. After capturing the pawn, Black would have two dangerous connected pawns rushing to become queens.

24 ♗d5

White's plan is clear: he protects the precious c-pawn and vacates a square for his king. Following 25 ♔g2, the knight, no longer pinned, can come into the game.

24 ...   Rcb8

The doubled rooks give Black undisputed possession of the all-important b-file.

White is now faced with two threats:

1) 25...Rc1 intending 26...Rbb1. The attack on the knight would compel the bishop to return to g2, whereupon Black picks up the c-pawn.

2) 25...R8b3, forcing an exchange of rooks, after which one of White's queenside pawns must fall.

25 ♔g2

White unpins the knight, which has been a spectator for the last ten moves.

25 ...   R8b3!

A daring concept! Black offers to exchange rooks and let White remain with two pieces to his one!

26 Rxb3

White is happy to oblige!

26 ...   Rxb3 *(D)*

Now the a-pawn is in peril.

27 ♘d2

White could not save the a-pawn (if 27 a4, then 27...Rb4 28 a5 Ra4), so the knight counterattacks by going after a pawn.

27 ...   Rxa3

Winning a pawn and simultaneously creating a passed pawn on the a-file. Will this be the one to become a queen?

28 ♘e4

Now White's pieces spring into action! The threat is 29 ♘xc5, knocking the support out from under the d-pawn and giving himself a passed c-pawn.

28 ...   a5!

Much better than 28...Ra5 which ties the rook down to defending a pawn and makes his role in the ending a subordinate one.

29 ♘xc5

After this capture, White's own passed pawn begins to look menacing.

29 ...   gxf6

Not so much to gain a pawn as to give the king more freedom. If at once 29...♔f8, then 30 ♘d7+ drives the king back to g8, as 30...♔e8 allows 31 fxg7 winning for White.

29...d3 allows 30 ♔f3 followed by 31 ♔e3, when White wins the d-pawn.

30 ♔f1

The king turns back to head off the passed pawns.

30 ... a4

Black does not fear a double attack on this pawn by 31 ♗c6. He would refute this by 31...♖a1+ followed by 32...a3, and the pawn has moved another step forward.

31 ♔e2 (D)

The king comes closer, definitely putting an end to any danger from the d-pawn.

How does Black proceed?

31 ... ♖a1!

By scaring White with the threat of queening the a-pawn! Black intends 32...a3, followed by 33...a2, 34...♖e1+ (to make way for the pawn without loss of time) and 35...a1♕.

32 ♘d3

White blockades the d-pawn and prepares to advance his own passed pawn.

32 ... a3

Back at the seventeenth move it seemed that the d-pawn would reach the eighth rank and become a queen. The d-pawn is blockaded, and it now appears that the a-pawn is the one that will be promoted.

But will it be the a-pawn?

33 c5

White's pawn can cause trouble, too!

33 ... a2

Threatening to win on the spot by 34...♖e1+ 35 ♘xe1 a1♕.

34 ♔f3

The king steps aside to evade the check.

34 ... ♖d1

This move, which attacks the knight as well as threatening to queen the pawn, adds to White's difficulties.

35 ♗xa2

White must destroy this dangerous creature at all costs!

35 ... ♖xd3+

With this capture Black nets a piece for his a-pawn.

36 ♔e4

White does not fall into the trap 36 ♔e2 losing his passed pawn after 36...♖c3.

36 ... ♖d2

The text-move attacks the bishop and the f-pawn. Moreover, it revives the d-pawn's prospects.

Is this pawn to be the candidate after all?

37 ♗c4!

An admirable spot for the bishop.

Black can now easily go wrong by 37...♖xf2 38 c6 ♖b2 (if 38...♖c2, then 39 ♔d5 wins for White) 39 c7, and White's pawn crashes through!

37 ... ♔f8! *(D)*

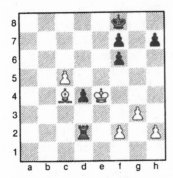

The king takes over the job of re-straining the dangerous pawn.

38 f3

Advancing the c-pawn is useless: 38 c6 ♔e7 and the pawn can go no further. With the text-move, White offers his h-pawn in return for Black's d-pawn.

38 ... ♖xh2

Black falls in with the suggestion. Instead of grimly holding on to the passed pawn, he is willing to sim-plify, confident that his superiority is enough to secure the win. This re-quires a belief in justice on the chessboard, and confidence in one's ability to mete it out properly.

39 ♔xd4

With this capture, White's pros-pects look brighter. His king and bishop are in close attendance on the passed pawn and will bend all their efforts to escort it to the far side of the board.

39 ... ♔e7

Ready to blockade the pawn.

40 ♗d3

Apparently with the idea of switch-ing the bishop to e4. From there it guards his f-pawn, prevents Black's doubled pawns from advancing, and is prepared to protect his c-pawn when it reaches c6.

40 ... h5 *(D)*

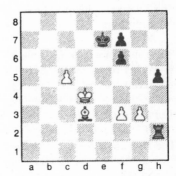

Threatening 41...♖g2 42 g4 h4, when Black wins.

Is the h-pawn to be the passed pawn that becomes a queen?

41 ♔e3

The king comes closer to rescue the g-pawn.

41 ... ♖g2

In forcing the king to defend the g-pawn, Black draws him farther away from his own passed pawn.

42 ♔f4

The only move. Against 42 g4 the win is easy: 42...h4 43 ♗f1 ♖c2 44 ♔d4 ♖f2 45 ♗h3 ♖xf3 46 ♗g2 ♖g3 47 ♗f1 h3, etc.

42 ... ♖g1

Now to get behind the passed pawn! In the ending, the rook does its best work behind the enemy's pawns. Its power to strike extends all along the line, so that *no matter how far the pawn advances on the file, it can never escape from the rook's at-tack.*

43 ♗e4

Preparing to protect the pawn when it reaches c6. If at once 43 c6, then 43...♖c1 44 ♗e4 (but not 44 ♗b5 ♖c5 45 ♗a4 ♖c4+ winning the bishop), and we have the position reached a little later in the game by a transposition of moves.

43 ...   ♖c1

To the uninitiated, this appears strange! Why help the pawn move farther up the board?

Black's idea is to compel the pawn to move to a light square. This will tie the bishop down to its defence and considerably limit the bishop's sphere of activity.

44 c6 *(D)*

The pawn moves up to come under the bishop's protection.

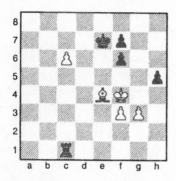

44 ...   ♖c3!

A tremendously effective move! It reduces White to a state of *zugzwang* – compulsion to move. What this means is that White might hold the game, except that he must make a move, and any move he makes is fatal because it disturbs the position unfavourably!

45 c7

Voluntarily giving up the pawn he cannot save! The alternatives are extremely interesting:

1) 45 ♔f5 ♖c5+ (to drive the king back) 46 ♔f4 ♔e6 47 ♔e3 (a bishop move loses the pawn at once, while 47 g4 allows 47...h4 giving Black a passed pawn) 47...f5 48 ♗d3 ♖xc6 and Black wins.

2) 45 ♗d5 ♖c5 46 ♔e4 (46 ♗e4 ♔e6 leads to play as in line '1') 46...f5+ 47 ♔d4 ♖xd5+! 48 ♔xd5 f4! 49 ♔c5 (or 49 gxf4 h4 50 ♔c5 ♔d8 51 ♔b6 ♔c8 wins) 49...fxg3 50 ♔b6 g2 51 c7 g1♕+ 52 ♔b7 ♕b1+ 53 ♔c8 ♕b6 54 f4 ♕a7 55 f5 ♕a8#.

45 ...   ♖xc7

Removing a potential danger. The ending still requires winning, and the manner of achieving the win is an illustration of smooth, flawless technique. The demonstration is as lucid and accurate as though it were the solution of a composed endgame study.

46 ♗d5

To keep Black from moving his king to the fine square e6.

46 ...   ♖c5

The rook intends to pursue the bishop until it leaves the diagonal overlooking the e6-square.

47 ♗a2

Understandably, the bishop tries to stay on the diagonal as long as possible. If instead 47 ♗b3, then 47...♖b5 forces 48 ♗a2 (48 ♗c4 ♖b4 pins the bishop, while 48 ♗a4 ♖b4+ also wins the bishop) 48...♖b2 49 ♗d5 ♖b4+! 50 ♔f5 (50 ♗e4 ♔e6 51 ♔e3 f5 wins, or if 50 ♔e3 then 50...f5 followed by 51...♔f6 and Black wins) 50...♖b5 51 ♔e4 f5+ 52

♔d4 ♖xd5+! 53 ♔xd5 f4 54 gxf4 h4, when the pawn cannot be stopped!

47 ... ♖b5! *(D)*

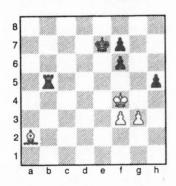

Complete domination! The bishop has no moves!

48 ♔e3

Or 48 ♔e4 f5+ 49 ♔f4 ♔f6 50 ♔e3 (the bishop cannot move, and 50 g4 loses to 50...hxg4 51 fxg4 ♖b4+ 52 ♔f3 fxg4+) 50...♖b4 51 ♗d5 f4+ 52 gxf4 h4 53 ♔f2 ♖b2+ 54 ♔g1 ♔f5 55 ♗xf7 ♔xf4 56 ♗d5 ♔g3 57 ♗e4 ♖a2 58 ♔f1 h3 and Black wins.

48 ... ♖a5

Allowing the bishop one square on the a2-g8 diagonal.

49 ♗c4

The bishop could not go to b3 on account of the ensuing pin, and 49 ♗b1 is answered by 49...♔e6 50 ♔f4 ♖a4+ 51 ♔e3 (51 ♗e4 f5 wins the bishop) 51...f5 52 ♗c2 f4+ 53 gxf4 (or 53 ♔d2 fxg3) 53...♖a3+ 54 ♔d2 ♖a2 55 ♔c1 ♖xc2+ and Black wins.

49 ... ♖c5

Dislodging the bishop from the diagonal leading to e6.

50 ♗a6

50 ♔d4 ♖g5 wins a pawn at once, while 50 ♗a2 is refuted by 50...f5, clearing f6 for Black's king.

50 ... ♔e6

Another step nearer the centre and White's remaining pawns.

51 ♔f4 *(D)*

White puts up a hard fight! He is ready to pounce on 51...f5 with 52 ♔g5.

51 ... ♖c3!

Again restricting White to a move by the bishop. Playing 52 ♔e4 succumbs to 52...f5+ 53 ♔f4 ♔f6, etc.

52 ♗f1

White must keep watch over c4, otherwise (if he plays 52 ♗b7, for example) 52...♖c4+ forces his king to retreat while Black's can advance.

52 ... f5

Finally! This pawn moves up a square and vacates f6 for the king.

53 ♗a6

The number of moves White has left is dwindling! 53 g4 fxg4 54 fxg4 h4 55 g5 h3 56 ♔g4 h2 57 ♗g2 ♖c1 wins for Black, while after 53 ♔g5 ♖xf3 54 ♗c4+ ♔e5 55 ♔h4 f4 Black again wins easily.

53 ... ♔f6

Stalemating White's king. What remains now is to force him back to the third rank while Black's king moves up to the fourth.

54 ♗b7

If the bishop stays on the longer diagonal, for instance by 54 ♗e2, Black plays 54...♖b3 and then drives the king back by 55...♖b4+.

54 ... ♖c4+

Compelling the king to retreat.

55 ♔e3

The only move.

55 ... ♔g5

With the pretty threat 56...f4+ 57 ♔d3 (57 gxf4+ ♖xf4 gives Black a passed pawn, while 57 ♔f2 ♖c2+ 58 ♔g1 fxg3 gives him two) 57...fxg3 58 ♔xc4 ♔f4!, and Black wins neatly.

56 ♔f2 *(D)*

A thrust at the rook by 56 ♗d5 allows this finish: 56...f4+ 57 ♔e2 ♖c2+ 58 ♔d3 ♖c7 (simple but brutal), and Black wins.

With the text-move, White retreats in order to head off the potential passed pawn, whichever one that may be!

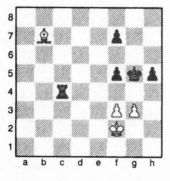

56 ... f4!

This is the key move in all cases! Black threatens to win at once by 57...♖c2+ 58 ♔g1 fxg3.

57 ♔g2

Ready to reply to the check with 58 ♔h3 saving the pawn.

57 ... f5! *(D)*

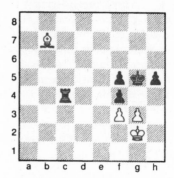

Passed pawns must be pushed. This pawn, which stood patiently at f7 for 56 moves, is, believe it or not, the one that was destined to become the passed pawn that wins the game!

0-1

White does not wait for the proof: After 58 ♔h3 fxg3 59 ♔xg3 h4+ (a likely-looking candidate, but not the final choice) 60 ♔h3 ♖c3 61 ♗d5 ♔f4 62 ♔xh4 ♖xf3 63 ♗xf3 ♔xf3 64 ♔h3 f4 65 ♔h2 ♔e2 the pawn marches straight through to be queened.

The whole game is beautiful, and the ending so fascinating that I could not resist a detailed analysis of its many fine points. A study of it is far more rewarding in entertainment and instruction than the playing over of a host of 'brilliancies' that feature a flinging about of pieces in wanton display.

Game 33
Rubinstein – Maroczy
Gothenburg 1920
Queen's Gambit Declined

1　d4

This opening move, seizing the centre with a pawn and making room for two pieces to come out, is efficient. White intends to develop all his pieces as quickly as possible, posting each of them in one move on its most suitable square. He will make only those pawn moves that speed his development (by releasing pieces or attacking the centre) or hinder that of his opponent.

1　...　♘f6

Model development in every respect: the knight leaps in toward the centre where it has the greatest potential for attack, exerts immediate pressure on the important squares d5 and e4, and prevents White from establishing a strong pawn formation by 2 e4.

2　♘f3

White develops the kingside pieces first, to enable early castling on that side. At f3, the knight stands on its most useful square in the opening. It is beautifully placed for attack – notice how it supplements the pawn's grip on e5 – and is a peerless defender of the kingside after White castles.

2　...　d5

Black cannot wrest the initiative by brute force. He may get it if White plays carelessly (wasting time in the opening or chasing after pawns) but against normal development Black

must content himself with achieving equality.

Black's second move neutralizes White's central pressure and opens lines for two of his own pieces.

3　c4 *(D)*

One of the rare occasions when a pawn move which does not aid development is opportune. This one attacks and threatens to eliminate, by 4 cxd5, Black's centre. It does additional service in increasing the mobility (actual and potential) of White's pieces. It clears a diagonal for the queen and assures the opening of the c-file for the later use of the queen or a1-rook.

3　...　e6

Black supports the d-pawn with another pawn. If White tries breaking up the centre by 4 cxd5, Black is prepared to recapture with a pawn, to keep the centre intact by maintaining a pawn at d5.

Although 3...e6 has the drawback of shutting in the c8-bishop, it is still Black's best move. The difficulty in developing the bishop effectively may not seem alarming, but if it is not overcome, it will amount to Black playing a piece short. For the present, in partial compensation, the f8-bishop has lots of elbow-room.

4 ♗g5 *(D)*

This move has a terribly cramping effect on Black's game. It clamps a pin on the knight and thereby exerts pressure on any pieces behind it. Black cannot move freely about while his kingside is gripped by the bishop.

In the 19th century, White would more often have developed the dark-squared bishop at f4, where it commands a useful diagonal. Nowadays we look for sharper, more vigorous moves. If we can mobilize our forces and at the same time restrain the enemy's development, we accomplish more than with routine, often innocuous, measures. The pin of the knight paralyses Black's only developed piece.

4 ...   ♗e7

Why all the fuss when the pin is so easily lifted? For one thing, in unpinning the knight, the bishop is restricted to a defensive, passive role. Its development has been dictated by the fact that White put pressure on the knight.

Black's play, incidentally, is in no way to be deprecated. The bishop's move, modest as it is, is a step forward in the process of development. The bishop has left the last rank, taken up a strong defensive post, and cleared the kingside, enabling Black to castle.

5 e3

Pawns should be moved sparingly in the opening, but since *some* pawns must be moved to get the bishops into play, this must be regarded as a developing move.

5 ...   ♘bd7

In the Queen's Gambit Declined, the ideal square for the development of the b8-knight is not c6 but d7. From d7, the knight supports an eventual thrust at White's centre by the e-pawn or the c-pawn.

The knight must not develop at c6, where it blocks the c-pawn. *This pawn must not be prevented from advancing to c5, where it can dispute control of the centre.*

6 ♘c3

The white queen's knight, contrariwise, is posted excellently at c3. It does not block the c-pawn and bears down on d5 and e4, two of the four important squares in the centre.

6 ...   0-0 *(D)*

Black transfers his king to a more secure location and brings his h8-rook closer to the centre files.

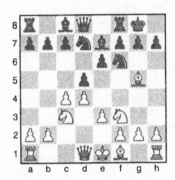

7 ℤc1

The rook develops where it has the most attractive prospects for attack. At c1 it controls and will exert pressure all along the open c-file. The file is obstructed now by White's own knight and pawn, but the pawn can be disposed of by an exchange and the knight can move and clear the file. Strictly speaking, the file is only partly open, but open or not, the rook goes to c1 because:

Control of the c-file is absolutely vital in the Queen's Gambit.

7 ...   ℤe8

Black's rook moves to a centre file, where it may play a useful part in any action that takes place in the centre. The rook's presence on the file is of little consequence now, but with every clearance on the file, its influence grows stronger and stronger.

Black's game is cramped, but alternatives aimed at freeing it immediately are not convincing:

1) 7...dxc4 8 ♗xc4 and White gains a tempo with this bishop, since it recaptures and develops at the same time.

2) 7...a6 (in order to continue with 8...dxc4 9 ♗xc4 b5 10 ♗d3 ♗b7) 8 c5 can be very constraining.

3) 7...c5 8 dxc5 ♘xc5 9 cxd5 exd5 (not 9...♘xd5 10 ♘xd5 exd5 11 ℤxc5! ♗xg5 12 ℤxd5, when White wins the bishop) and Black's d5-pawn is weak, while White has the fine d4-square as a central point for manoeuvring his pieces to any part of the board.

8 ♕c2

The best place on the board for the queen! From c2 the queen increases the pressure on the c-file and seizes control of the centre, making the problem of freeing himself troublesome for Black.

8 ...   dxc4

Black gets impatient and tries to break loose. It would have been better to delay this capture, though, and wait for White to move his f1-bishop. Then the recapture costs the bishop an extra move. Black might have played instead 8...c6, strengthening the position of the d5-pawn and offering the queen an outlet to the queenside.

9 ♗xc4

Obviously a gain of time for White, whose light-squared bishop recaptures a pawn and develops to a good square simultaneously.

9 ...   c5

Black must counterattack or be crushed to death. This offers the most practical chances in that he establishes tension in the centre and disputes control in that area. Furthermore, he prepares to oppose rooks on the c-file and fight for equal rights on the file.

10   0-0

The simplest way to keep up the pressure is to continue developing. At one stroke White removes his king to a safer part of the board and brings the h1-rook out of the corner and toward the centre.

10   ...   cxd4 *(D)*

Black's intention is to force White to a decision regarding the centre. If White recaptures with a pawn, it saddles him with an isolated pawn in the middle of the board; if with a piece, then his pawn-centre is no better than Black's.

11   ♘xd4

Rubinstein prefers this to 11 exd4, which maintains a pawn, but one that is isolated, in the centre.

The weakness of a pawn separated from its fellows lies not so much in the fact that the pawn can only be defended by pieces, but in the peculiar circumstance that enemy pieces can settle themselves on the square directly in front of the pawn (in this case d5) and stay there indefinitely, secure in the knowledge that no enemy pawns can drive them away.

The strength of an isolated pawn in the centre (for instance at d4, if White recaptured by 11 exd4) consists of its control of the strategically important e5- and c5-squares, its ability to spearhead an attack to break up a position, and its value as a support for an outpost – in this case a knight at e5.

11   ...   a6

Mainly to secure the b5-square from invasion by one of White's minor pieces. The objection to this move is that pawn moves that do not contribute to development are a waste of valuable time in the opening. More to the point is 11...♘e5 12 ♗b3 ♗d7 13 ♖fd1 ♕b6, with a view to getting some action out of his pieces.

Notice that White has made only those pawn moves which were necessary to release pieces, or which added to the mobility of pieces already developed. Every single move, of piece or pawn, furthered the development of White's position and increased its potential energy.

12   ♖fd1

Now the rook swings over to the centre, placing itself at the head of a file facing the queen. The queen is sure to feel uncomfortable, no matter how many pieces separate the two, as threats are constantly in the air. For instance, if Black should play the plausible 12...♘b6, attacking the bishop, the reply 13 ♘xe6 wins the queen by a discovered (and double) attack.

Yates and Winter comment admiringly at this point, "A classical example of correct development.

White has brought his queen, rooks, bishops and one knight to almost ideal squares in one move each."

12 ... ♕a5

The queen flees the line of fire, gaining a little time by attacking a bishop.

13 ♗h4

The bishop retreats but maintains pressure on the knight.

13 ... ♘e5 (D)

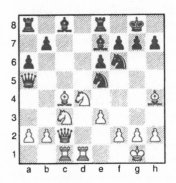

Now the other bishop is threatened, apparently with more gain of time for Black.

14 ♗e2

Both bishops have been driven back, but, despite this, their latent power is enormous. The potential of two bishops working in harmony is not be to given up lightly, so White does not consider a move such as 14 ♗d3 which lets Black play 14...♘xd3 and exchange a short-stepping knight for a long-range bishop. Condensed, it comes down to this:

It is an advantage to keep both bishops.

14 ... ♘g6

Swinging over to the kingside, the knight attacks the dark-squared bishop and forces it still further back. Meanwhile, more and more barriers are being put up about Black's king, who now seems firmly entrenched in a bomb-proof shelter.

Despite all the time Black seems to have gained in his attacks on the white bishops, he should have done something to get his queenside pieces off the ground, for instance by 14...♗d7 instead. Then the continuation 15 ♘b3 ♕c7 16 ♕b1 ♗c6 gives him reasonable fighting chances.

15 ♗g3

The bishop must step back a square and relax its pressure on the knight, but now it commands a magnificent diagonal.

Black cannot continue chasing the bishops in an effort to get rid of one of them since after 15...♘h5 16 ♘b3 ♕g5 (the queen must protect the knight) 17 ♘e4 ♕h6 18 ♗c7 White dominates the board.

15 ... e5

An extremely attractive move! These are all the things the pawn does:

1) It occupies a square in the centre.

2) It opens a path for the c8-bishop.

3) It cuts down the scope of White's g3-bishop.

4) It will drive off White's knight from its centralized position.

Against this, Black's move offers one objection, seemingly a slight one. The d5-square, no longer under the pawn's control, has been weakened. It offers White the prospect of utilizing this central point for the easy manoeuvring of his pieces to any part of the board.

Will this one liability outweigh all the assets? It is this judgement of imponderables, where exact calculation is not possible, that makes chess a fascinating blend of art and science.

16 ♘b3

The knight must leave but retaliates by getting in a thrust at the queen.

16 ...   ♕c7 (D)

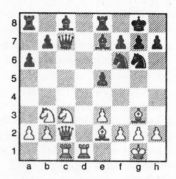

The queen evades the attack, and Black prepares to regroup his pieces, perhaps by 17...♗d7, 18...♗c6 and 19...♖ad8.

17 ♕b1!

This is White's fifth retreating move in succession, but with every step backward his position improves! Though driven back to the first three ranks, his pieces will gain in dynamic energy. Gradually they will take up stronger positions, dominate the board, and put the enemy to flight.

Black has no time now to develop his c8-bishop as after 17...♗d7 18 ♘d5 ♕d8 (if 18...♘xd5, then 19 ♖xc7 ♘xc7 20 ♖xd7 wins) 19 ♘c7 White wins the exchange.

17 ...   ♕b8

Black's queen was forced to retreat (by the threat of a discovered attack) while White's queen moved to b1 voluntarily.

The difference in the positions is apparent:

1) White's queen does not obstruct the rooks, which together control the two open files; Black's queen and bishop separate his rooks, one of which is completely shut in, while the other's action is severely limited.

2) White has two agile, long-range bishops; Black has one, with the other undeveloped and still at home.

3) White's queen can leap into the fray quickly; Black's must skulk on the fringes of the board.

18 ♗f3

The bishop seizes the long diagonal and prevents Black from playing 18...b5 (the punishment being 19 ♗xa8) and then fianchettoing his bishop.

18 ...   ♕a7

Black's manoeuvring is tortuous, but evidently he wants to bring his rook to b8, then play ...b5, and finally develop his queen's bishop at b7.

19 ♘a5!

A fine preventive move! It stops 19...♖b8 followed by 20...b5 as then 21 ♘c6 wins the exchange, while the direct 19...♗d7 or 19...♗e6 costs Black his b-pawn.

Notice how White not only sees to the development of his own pieces but hinders that of his opponent.

19 ...   ♝b4

Black tries to chase off the knight, which is hampering the free movement of his queenside pieces.

20   ♞c4

The knight must leave, but in compensation it enjoys the advantage of being nearer the centre.

20 ...   ♝d7 (D)

The bishop moves to the only square available for its development! If Black tries instead 20...♝e6, then 21 ♞xe5 wins a pawn, while on 20...♝g4 21 ♝xg4 ♞xg4 22 ♞d5 the threats of 23 ♞xb4 (winning a piece) and 23 ♞c7 (winning the exchange) cannot both be met.

21   ♞d5!

The knight leaps to d5 and attacks pieces all over the place! It threatens one bishop directly (by 22 ♞xb4) and the other indirectly, by 22 ♞xf6+ gxf6 23 ♖xd7. In addition to this, it threatens 22 ♞c7, attacking both rooks and thereby winning the exchange.

21 ...   ♞xd5

Obviously, such a dangerous beast must be removed!

22   ♝xd5

White recaptures with the threat of 23 ♝xf7+ ♔xf7 24 ♖xd7+, winning a pawn. He gains a tempo with this, as Black must drop whatever he is doing to parry the threat.

22 ...   ♝e6

Black must rid the board of the terrible bishop which attacks his kingside and restrains his queenside. It would not do to play 22...♝c6 as 23 ♝xc6 bxc6 24 ♕e4 wins the c-pawn or the e-pawn.

23   ♕e4!

A master move in every respect, and a one-move lesson in positional play! Where most of us think of an exchange in terms of what happens after 23 ♝xe6, the great master visualizes an exchange as an opportunity to substitute another piece for one that must come off the board. White is willing to exchange, but only if he can be assured of keeping control of d5 by replacing the bishop with another piece.

Let me reword this, so that the message is unmistakable:

Supporting a piece under attack (here the bishop at d5) puts more pressure on Black, where a direct exchange or a retreat might relieve it.

Note incidentally the full effect of the queen's magnificent centralization, and her radiation of power in so many directions:

1) The queen supports the bishop at d5.

2) The queen adds to the bishop's attack on the b-pawn.

3) The queen helps in the attack on the e-pawn.

4) The queen threatens (indirectly) Black's b4-bishop.

23 ...   ♗xd5

Practically forced in view of the many threats. An attempt to drive the queen off by 23...f5 is brusquely refuted by 24 ♕xf5 and Black (whose bishop is pinned) is unable to take the queen.

24 ♖xd5

Black rids himself of one troublesome piece only to have another one take its place! For the third time, White anchors a piece at d5, each time intensifying his grip on the position. Now there is a fourfold attack on the e-pawn, by rook, knight, bishop and queen. While this pawn is being rescued, White will gain the time needed to double his rooks on the d-file, guaranteeing him permanent possession of this vital highway. The effect on Black will be to cut communication between his forces, making an organized resistance difficult.

24 ...   ♖ac8 *(D)*

Protecting the pawn indirectly by pinning one of its attackers.

White cannot take the pawn with the knight on pain of mate, nor with the rook or the queen, as that results in loss of material to White. This leaves 25 ♗xe5, and Black is ready to punish that with 25...f6 26 ♗d4 ♖xe4 27 ♗xa7 ♖exc4, when he has gained a piece.

25 ♖cd1

Doubling the rooks on an open file, an act that more than doubles the strength of the rooks. White's knight is now unpinned, and the attack on the e-pawn renewed, with incidentally a threat of discovered attack on the bishop.

White has a won game theoretically, and Rubinstein wins it in a way that is both efficient and artistic.

25 ...   ♗f8

Black transfers the exposed bishop to the defence.

Against the immediate counterattack by 25...f5, White has a winning continuation in 26 ♕xf5 ♖xc4 27 ♖d8! ♖xd8 28 ♖xd8+ ♘f8 29 ♕e6+ ♔h8 30 ♕xc4, when he is the exchange ahead.

After Black's actual move, he can answer 26 ♘xe5 with 26...f6, winning the unfortunate knight. In addition, he contemplates the thrust 26...f5, which after 27 ♕d3 (to protect the knight) 27...f4 occasions some trouble for the bishop.

26 b3

Frees the queen from the duty of guarding the knight and stops any such move as 26...f5, when the pawn would simply be snapped up.

Against passive play, White will continue by 27 ♖d7, invading the seventh rank.

26 ...   b5 *(D)*

The object of this is not so much to dislodge the knight as it is to open a line for the queen, enabling her to return to the kingside and the defence of the king.

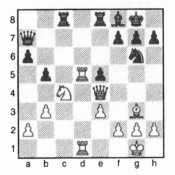

27 ♘d6!

A knight fork which will force an exchange – a simplification to White's advantage. He will maintain the pressure inherent in a superior position without running the risk of being involved in unnecessary complications.

A premature attack, in fact, might even result in a loss for White! Consider this pretty possibility (instead of the actual move): 27 ♘xe5 f6 28 ♖d7 (apparently a saving move, as White attacks the queen and threatens to follow with 29 ♕d5+ unpinning his knight) 28...♕xd7! and Black wins! The recapture by the rook allows Black to mate, while 29 ♘xd7 ♖xe4 leaves Black a rook ahead.

27 ... ♗xd6

Black had no choice, as the knight attacked both his rooks.

28 ♖xd6

The recapture vacates the d5-square for occupation by the queen; the tripling of heavy pieces on the d-file would increase the advantage

that White already has. However, an even more potent threat is the possibility of establishing a beachhead on the seventh rank by 29 ♖d7.

The posting of a rook on the seventh rank, in the middlegame or the ending, is a tremendous positional advantage.

28 ... ♖c7 (D)

Black does what he can to keep the enemy rook out and seals up all the entrances.

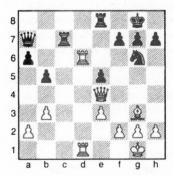

White has the superior position, but how does he break through?

Let us listen in on what Rubinstein might say to himself in reasoning out a course of action:

My rooks are as well placed as they can be and doing a good job in controlling the open d-file. My queen is strongly centralized and exerts pressure in every direction. My bishop bears down on his e-pawn and keeps a rook and knight chained to its defence. My pieces are all usefully occupied and must stay where they are.

How about my opponent? His defence just about holds together, but his pieces must stay where they are to guard his weak points. If I leave him alone, he might consolidate his forces, and even counterattack.

If I leave him alone...

Say, isn't that the key to the position?

I must not leave him alone! I must interfere with the arrangement of his pieces. I must drive them off from their present positions. In fact, I might ruin his game by driving off even one defender!

Since my pieces are all useful where they are, I must not disturb them but look to my pawns to break up the defence. Which pawn shall I use, and which of his pieces shall I try to dislodge?

The first thing to do is to find a target. His queen and rooks are too far away and too agile to be bothered by pawns. Any of them can move off to a different square on a file or a rank and still control it. I must aim at a fixed target – some piece that is needed at the spot where it is stationed and loses its effectiveness as soon as it is displaced. How about the knight? Suppose I played 29 h4 and gave it a nudge by 30 h5? It would have to leave its fine defensive position immediately. Where could it go? If to e7, it blocks the action of the e8-rook, and if it retreats to the back rank, it is out of play for a time. Besides, I get another benefit in moving the h-pawn. It gives my king a flight square, so that he doesn't fall into a surprise mate on the first rank.

29   h4!

This is the key to the decisive attack! The obvious threat is 30 h5, dislodging the knight, and then capturing the e-pawn. The ulterior purpose is to compel Black to protect the endangered pawn by 29...f6, weakening the cordon of pawns near his king. Further weaknesses may then be induced by h5 and h6, attacking the g-pawn.

29   ...   f6 *(D)*

Clearly, to give the e-pawn the solid support only another pawn affords.

The alternative 29...♖ce7 succumbs to 30 ♕c6 followed by 31 ♖d8, with an easy win, while 29...h5 (to prevent 30 h5) allows 30 ♕f5, winning the h-pawn.

30   ♕d5+

Simple and strong! The queen makes a powerful entrance at d5, seizing control of a diagonal leading to the king and at the same time tripling heavy pieces on the open central file. Notice the admirable use of d5 as a pivot for the manoeuvring of the various pieces. It has been occupied in turn by knight, bishop, rook and queen – aptly enough, in order of strength!

30   ...   ♔h8

Hoping for safety in the corner. If instead 30...♖f7, then 31 h5 ♘h8 32 h6 decisively breaks up Black's defensive pawn wall, or if 30...♚f8, then 31 h5 ♘h8 32 ♖d8 ♘f7 33 ♖xe8+ ♚xe8 34 ♕e6+ ♚f8 35 h6 ♖e7 (nothing else saves the game, as 35...♘xh6 allows mate on the move, and 35...gxh6 36 ♕xf6 leads to ruin for Black) 36 ♕c8+ ♖e8 37 hxg7+, and White wins a rook.

31 h5 *(D)*

This move not only evicts the knight from its strong defensive post but also drives a wedge into Black's position.

31 ...   ♘f8

Against the only other possibility, 31...♘e7, White wins easily by 32 ♕f7 with a million threats. Let's take a look at some interesting possibilities then:

1) 32...♖g8 33 h6 (threatening 34 ♖d8 followed by mate at g7) 33...♘f5 34 hxg7+ ♘xg7 35 ♕xf6 and Black both loses a pawn and falls into a deadly pin.

2) 32...♕b8 33 h6 gxh6 34 ♕xf6+ ♚g8 35 ♗xe5 ♘g6 36 ♖d7 with a quick mate.

3) 32...♖cc8 33 h6 gxh6 34 ♗h4, threatening 35 ♗xf6#. Black cannot guard against that mate by a knight move as it leaves his queen *en prise*.

How many of these variations did White foresee? And how many did Black know he was avoiding when he moved his knight to f8 instead of to e7?

The answer is – probably none! A good player can, almost at a glance, sense the effect of a move that is obviously decisive. He saves himself a great deal of valuable time when he does not even bother about analysing the resources of such a defence as 31...♘e7. The fact that it permits such a paralysing entrance into the vitals as 32 ♕f7 practically rules it out from more than fleeting consideration.

32 h6

White drives the wedge in still further. White's object is to break up the pawn position around Black's king. If Black's g-pawn can be uprooted, it will make the f-pawn, the keystone of his game, vulnerable to attack. And if that falls, Black's whole position falls with it.

White's immediate threat is 33 hxg7+ ♚xg7 34 ♗h4 ♖f7 35 ♕c6, with an attack on the e8-rook and a triple attack on the f-pawn.

32 ...   ♘g6 *(D)*

Black gets his knight back into active play and prevents White from striking again at the f-pawn by 33 ♗h4. He side-steps the pretty loss 32...gxh6 33 ♖xf6 ♖d7 34 ♗xe5! ♖xd5 (if 34...♖xe5, 35 ♖xf8+ and mate next move) 35 ♖xf8# – double check and mate!

33 ♕e6!

A spectacular move! White is not playing to the gallery in offering a queen sacrifice. All that he wants is to penetrate still deeper into the heart of Black's position, and this is the simplest way to do so. The move is brilliant nevertheless, and making a move of this sort (even vicariously) gives one a thrill.

I must warn the player who likes the excitement of springing a surprise move on his opponent that it is a waste of time to look for brilliant moves in the course of a game unless the position warrants it. You must first get an advantage, however slight. Work on increasing the advantage until you have built up a position that is definitely superior. Once you have established your right to look for combinations, the brilliant moves will come of themselves.

White of course does not expect Black to take his queen and allow 34 ♖d8+ and a quick mate. What he has

in mind primarily is to secure complete control of d7, an important square for his rooks to exploit.

One of the most interesting things to me in the position is that White threatens his opponent with disaster on three ranks:

1) On the eighth rank by 34 ♕xe8+ followed by mate.

2) On the seventh rank by 34 ♖d7 followed by 35 hxg7#.

3) On the sixth rank by 34 hxg7+ ♔xg7 35 ♕xf6+, winning easily.

33 ...   ♖f8

There isn't too much choice, in view of all the threats. Black's move gives the f-pawn added protection.

34 ♖d7

Threatening 35 hxg7# – mate on the move!

34 ...   gxh6

34...♖xd7 is no better since the recapture 35 ♖xd7 threatens mate on one side, and the queen on the other. White also forces mate after 34...♖g8 35 hxg7+ ♖xg7 36 ♖d8+.

35 ♗h4!

The bishop, which has stood in one spot for twenty-five moves, applies the finishing touch! The threat is 36 ♗xf6+ ♖xf6 37 ♕xf6+ ♔g8 38 ♕g7#.

1-0

If 35...♘xh4, then 36 ♕e7 threatens 37 ♕xf8#, 37 ♕g7# or 37 ♕xh7#, and no one can survive such a display of feminine power!

An impressive, deeply satisfying game, one of the finest in the literature of chess.

Index of Players

Numbers refer to pages.
A number in bold indicates that the first-named player was White.

CK

Index of Openings